Together Always

A JOURNEY OF ADOPTION AND BEYOND

> Lois Redeker-Mencher Palms #202
> I hope you enjoy my mother's story.
> Blessings,
> Caryn, your talented friend

CARYN MEARS

outskirts press

Together Always
A Journey of Adoption and Beyond
All Rights Reserved.
Copyright © 2020 Caryn Mears
v1.0

The opinions expressed in this manuscript are solely the opinions of the author and do not represent the opinions or thoughts of the publisher. The author has represented and warranted full ownership and/or legal right to publish all the materials in this book.

This book may not be reproduced, transmitted, or stored in whole or in part by any means, including graphic, electronic, or mechanical without the express written consent of the publisher except in the case of brief quotations embodied in critical articles and reviews.

Outskirts Press, Inc.
http://www.outskirtspress.com

ISBN: 978-1-9772-2682-2

Cover Photo © 2020 shutterstock.com. All rights reserved - used with permission.

Outskirts Press and the "OP" logo are trademarks belonging to Outskirts Press, Inc.

PRINTED IN THE UNITED STATES OF AMERICA

DEDICATION

Dedicated to my Grandfather,
Alfred Emery Bates,
who made my mother the woman she became.

TABLE OF CONTENTS

Prologue i
1. Dancing Brown Eyes 1
2. Who's Your Daddy? 9
3. A Swedish Upbringing 15
4. The Path of Destruction 21
5. She'll Make Some Family Happy 26
6. How Many Foster Homes Can One Girl Have? 30
7. Not Your Typical Teenager 38
8. A Little Sister 43
9. The Chosen One 48
10. Life on the Farm 55
11. Matching Red Dresses 66
12. A One Room Country School 74
13. Life Goes On 81
14. Life at the Grangers 85
15. The Bull and the Barn 90
16. Stories with Dad 100
17. The Wicked Witch of the West 105
18. A Tornado Visits Wells 118
19. An Unexpected Birthday Present 124
20. Shattered Dreams 129
21. One – A Mother Without a Mother 136
22. A New Community 144
23. More Children 151

24. Mrs. Minnesota and Beyond! 158
25. War on the Homefront.. 174
26. Where to Go from Here.. 187
27. Off to Las Vegas 194
28. Daddy's Gone... 216
29. Who Do I Look Like?... 226
30. Who's Looking for Whom? 236
31. Ode to a Brother.. 244
32. Searching for Viola 253
33. How Can I Go On?... 258
34. A Break in the Search 265
Epilogue 274

PROLOGUE

RISING BEFORE DAWN as I'd always done, I was eager to share a sunrise with my soul. This was the only peaceful lull before my busy day. Shivering, I clutched my faded blue robe around my small frame and thought, "It's going to be a late spring again." The early morning chill hung within the four walls of my comfortable home. I gently closed the bedroom door, smiling at Bill and his contented sleep. My heart tugged as I remembered the gentle tenderness of last night.

Tiptoeing to the kitchen, I quickly made my usual pot of coffee. Oh, how I loved that first cup with its fresh aroma as I thought about my morning routine. Pouring the delicious brew into my favorite mug, I cupped my hands around it to feel the warmth. Hurriedly, I opened the drapes to capture the first warm rays of sun as it peeked over the crest of Sunrise Mountain. The burst of spring warmth flowed into the cozy room, as a ray of sunlight on the table caught the glistening brass around the room, seemingly dancing and laughing in the early morning seduction.

I was preoccupied with thoughts and didn't recognize the natural beauty that caressed the room. Words were leaping inside my head and phrases were getting jumbled in my mind from the arousal caused by the first sip of coffee. It was time for a plan and time to get motivated. "Write a book?" seemed to be jumping into my brain. "Talk, talk, talk; that's all you've ever done," I said to myself. "It's time for action!" To leave a legacy of love has always been one of my fondest dreams, and journalism seemed to flow through my veins.

Vivid imaginations had captured precious thoughts and moments in my poetry for years. "Should I? Could I?" I knew I had put it off too long! That urgency to attempt an even greater challenge was now. The words were there, but could they really be ready to transfer the feelings I'd hope to convey? "Where would my outline begin?" I wondered. My eyes filled with tears as incidents began to flash too quickly. "Damn," I thought, even the first word wouldn't come. Looking around the fun filled room, I wondered, "Why did I always feel my father's presence when I was trying to make explicit decisions?"

"You can do it, baby!" he'd always said.

"I know I can!" I thought. All the anxieties that had been kept silent for so long were now spilling over and out of my heart as I painfully remember minute details, each one making me so aware of life. Experiences were about to surface that I had always kept so deep within and had never explained to anyone. A strong feeling had worried me through these last few years. "Was someone else speaking to me, or was I at last realizing the joys and sorrows throughout the years that were now my fulfillment of totally being a woman that loved and had been loved?" These thoughts were powerful, and I knew now that I could accept this challenge and pursue sharing the true meaning of my message.

As I looked wistfully into the sunlight, I realized that my story was mine and only mine to tell. "I'll tell it just as it happened, fact for fact, including all the details." I said to myself, knowing I had to share my overwrought heart with the ones I truly loved. My family, I wondered, would the most treasured people in my life fully see me and truly understand the how's and whys for my reactions and choices throughout the years? Sharing myself had always been my choice. Past experiences, throughout my lifetime had made me what I'd become. Yet, I felt that all my motives had not been sincere. I felt an urgent need, more so now than ever before, to finally share my story.

My surroundings were peaceful. A part of my life I have always treasured was about to unfold. I know now, why I'd waited so long. A warm mellowness filled my aging body, truly giving me the attitude, I needed to share this incredible story. Racing thoughts exploded within my busy head as I attacked the keys of the trusty old typewriter. With jaw firmly set I had a look of concentration that gave me a "Do not interrupt me" type of attitude. Today I had reached a final decision. Sharing moments of my life had to be captured and that moment was now! I seemed almost vehement in my mechanical attack. The inner struggle gave me the ability to challenge myself and the timing was perfect!

Love,
Connie

LOVE

Is expressed

with a glowing smile,

A tender caress,

Meaningful wink,

And truthfulness.

Sharing of feeling

Meeting a demanding schedule,

Expressing a firm opinion

And not having to be careful.

Words, grimaces and shrugs

Have a meaning for each other,

While all others are totally unaware

That true love is really there.

We sometimes become too busy

To acknowledge the simple fact,

"I LOVE YOU" - three little words

To seal a simple pact.

rebellious was an understatement. The state suggested a foster home, and when that didn't work, they suggested she go to a reform school. Considered a juvenile delinquent by the courts, Viola was then sent to the Minnesota Home School for Girls in Sauk Center, Minnesota. She had been under the care of the Juvenile court system throughout her teen years as she jumped from one bad situation to another, and this was the final attempt at getting her to reform. The state hoped she would meet new role models there and become a more compliant citizen.

When Viola had fulfilled her term at the Home School for girls, she was again living with her father. At seventeen, Viola was starting her senior year of high school and was totally ready to be independent. "Only one more year and I'll be free!' she mused, but this evening she had one focus. She was ready to be out from under anyone telling her what to do!

"Tonight", she thought to herself, "I'm going to do what I want to do, and no one can stop me! I'm going to Becker Hall with my friends, and I'm going to dance!" Dancing was Viola's favorite thing to do and knowing her favorite band was playing was all the enticement Viola needed. When she was dancing, it seemed as though she could truly throw her cares to the wind! "Tonight's going to be special!" she grinned to herself, for she was looking for one special fellow at the dance.

Standing an average five feet, four inches tall, and weighing one hundred and forty pounds, Viola appeared to be your average teenager. However, sporting the latest shortly coiffed hairdo, her auburn hair fell softly around her face, and made a beautiful frame around her clear complexion. No pimples dotted this teenager's face. Her complexion was flawless! Her resemblance to the character Snow White was incredible, with her soft milky skin and her roaring 20's haircut, she could have easily played the part. With an infectious smile, she revealed beautifully straight white teeth, and her laugh seemed to entice others to join her. Her deep brown eyes tossed out a spark of mischievousness and made everyone wonder what she was thinking.

No! Average or ordinary was not the way one would describe Viola. Everything about the young girl seemed to make her stand out, from her beautiful smile to her seductive brown eyes, even Viola's vivacious personality stood out.

As she zipped up her red dress, she looked at herself in the mirror and thought, "This red dress will make people notice me!" Always wearing a red dress when she went dancing, Viola felt more sophisticated. She didn't want to look like the other teenagers who wore their white blouses and dark skirts! She wanted to look more mature than her seventeen years. She carefully added a long strand of iridescent beads around her neck and as she swung them around in a circle to her imaginary beat, she thought, "These beads make dancing even more fun." Buckling her plain brown heels, she stood up and again looked at herself in the mirror one last time. "Perfect," she said to herself and headed downstairs!

Walking as quickly as she could, Viola reached the front door and quietly peeked out the window just in time to see the black Model A Ford pull up to her father's house. Waving at her friends from the window she thought, "Perfect timing!" She quickly grabbed her heavy brown coat to face the blustery winter wind, and simultaneously opened the front door. Racing hurriedly down the front steps of the porch, before they could honk the horn, she quickly ran to the car with nary a word to those left inside the house. She braced herself against the cold Minnesota winter and stepped up onto the running board to squeeze into the old car with her friends.

"Squish in by me, Viola!" said her first friend, Mary.

"Do you have your red dress on?" facetiously asked another one of the girls, knowing full well Viola always wore a red dress when she went out dancing.

"You look gorgeous tonight, Viola!" said Catherine from the front seat.

"I'm so lucky I was ready before you arrived, I didn't have to say goodbye to anyone." laughed Viola. She hated answering questions about where she would be and who she would be with. It was her life, and she wasn't about to answer to anyone. She was happy to catch a ride out to Becker Hall with her friends.

Going to any dance created a feeling of excitement for Viola, and she couldn't wait to be dancing! The other girls carried on with their conversation, and Viola fell deep into thought, thinking about the dance and who she would meet. Settling in for the ride, her friends giggled and chatted about who would be at the dance, but Viola was thinking about only one person. As the row of trees lining the road seemed to whiz by the car, and she didn't even realize where she was! She was thinking about Howard.

Howard Oberg was the dance band leader, and her reason for following this dance band. He had the most beautiful brown eyes. They reminded her of a puppy dog; deep, soft, and brown. His eyes seemed so loving and kind. They were eyes that sparkled and danced with the music and they seemed to follow her around the dance floor. As the car reached Becker Community Hall near Lake Sallee, Viola was so deep in thought, she hadn't even realized the car had stopped. The others excitedly scrambled out of the car and raced toward the building. Luckily, someone yelled, "Come on, Viola!" and she was jolted back to reality. Sliding across the seat, she thought, "Boy, it's cold out tonight!" Still thinking about Howard's beautiful brown eyes and how they followed her around the dance floor, she quickly jumped out of the car and ran to catch up to the others. "I sure hope he'll feel the same way about me as I feel about him," she thought to herself, not wanting to say anything out loud. And then, suddenly, as if whipped by a fierce wind, Viola burst into Becker Hall.

Tonight, would be the fourth time she had seen her favorite dance band. She had been following Howard Oberg and his orchestra for a few weeks now and she loved their music. Having lived through the roaring 20's, Viola had listened to the latest music on the family Victrola. She loved to dance the jitterbug and the foxtrot, and she loved music, like "Ain't Misbehavin'" and "Puttin' on the Ritz". Oh, how Viola loved to dance, and it didn't really matter who she danced with. She would dance with anyone who asked her, if she could get out on the dance floor, she was happy! Everyone knew Viola loved to dance, but what they didn't know was that Viola had her eye on one specific musician. She was interested in the leader, Howard Oberg, himself, who also played the big standup bass.

Howard was twenty-five years old, almost eight years Viola's senior. He was short in stature, standing only two inches taller than Viola's five-foot, four-inch frame. When he saw Viola enter the Hall, he let out a small gasp! He couldn't get over how beautiful she looked. Her red dress attracted him immediately, only to be captured by her snow-white complexion, auburn hair and her infectious smile. "Mesmerizing", he said to himself. "That's the word to describe her, she's truly mesmerizing. Her beautiful white skin, contagious smile and perky manner were truly enchanting. And then her dark brown eyes seemed to stare right into his soul. Making eyes at him all evening piqued his interest, as she coyly looked towards him, and then would look away, flirting with him even while she danced with other men.

"Why does she want *me*?" Howard wondered. "Why, out of all the other younger, taller, more handsome men? Why does she want *me*?" Howard was baffled, but he enjoyed the attention Viola seemed to be throwing his way. "I know she's danced with every guy in this place over the past four weeks!" he said to one of his friends in the band.

"Who? Viola? Why, she's danced with all of us!" answered one of the guys in the band. "She seems to love to dance, and it doesn't seem to matter who she dances with! It's like the song, 'I've Got Rhythm' was written for her!"

"Maybe 'Ain't Misbehavin' or 'Puttin on the Ritz' are tunes for her also!" joked one of the band members.

Over the past few weeks, Howard could tell she was flirting with him, and he mused out loud, "I can't believe my good luck!" He had seen her at his other dances for the past few weeks, constantly following him with her mesmerizingly beautiful eyes. "Oh, that smile," Howard remarked.

"Viola? Yeah, she's one of our most devoted followers, and she certainly can dance!" They both laughed as they watched her circling around the dance floor. And dance! Oh my, this young girl could dance! Howard found himself staring back at Viola! She was captivating! He loved watching her snow-white complexion, auburn hair and enticing smile as she twirled around the room. Howard was totally enamored with this young beauty!

When the band took a break, he set his big string bass violin on its stand, and carefully stepped away from the microphone. Heading down the steps of the stage, he went straight to Viola's table and introduced himself. "Hello there! It's good to see you again!" he said. Viola wasn't the least bit shy.

"I love your band and your music!" she blurted out, "That's why I'm here! I love to dance to your music!" Her heart was racing so fast she could barely breathe. She truly put her heart and soul into the music but looking at Howard's dark brown eyes also made her heart skip a beat! She loved looking at Howard and those dark brown eyes.

"I see!" said Howard. "Would you like a drink?"

"Yes! Please!" Viola replied without hesitation. Although underage, no one would notice her drinking some clear pop. Howard ordered a vodka and seven, and as she sipped some of the cool clear liquid, she batted her flirtatious eyes at Howard. She loved the attention from this older man, and he seemed to linger on her every word. And as they chatted, Howard felt this young girl was truly someone he wanted to get to know better. There was something intriguing about her, and he was totally smitten. As he mustered his band members back onto the stage to continue playing, he thought, "This young girl is more than charming. She's captivating!" He wanted to learn more about her.

Viola didn't mind dancing the night away! She continued to keep eye contact with Howard even when she was dancing with someone else. She loved his brown eyes and they seemed to follow her around the dance floor to every tempo he played. And then, much to Viola's surprise, Howard gave his bass violin to another band member and came down to ask her for a dance. Viola's heart was all a flutter as their bodies touched. When his hand slipped around her waist and he swung her close, Viola felt safe and secure. She had hoped to dance with Howard, but never dreamed it would happen. And now, here she was dancing with him! She felt butterflies in her stomach, and it was a glorious feeling. She never wanted it to end. It made her feel warm all over, as if her body was melting into his. This hadn't happened with any of the other men she had danced with, and she had danced with just about every available man in the dance hall. This was a new feeling and Viola loved it!

When the band played their last song, her friends started pushing her to leave, "Come on Viola, Frank's leaving." But instead of going home with her friends, as she had usually done, Viola said, "I'll catch a ride with someone else!"

"Suit yourself!" they yelled and waved goodbye to Viola as they raced into the cold evening.

CHAPTER **2**

WHO'S YOUR DADDY?

HOWARD M. OBERG had been raised on a farm near St. Paul, Minnesota. He had acquired the Minnesota work ethic, helping with the harvest, working the fields and taking care of the livestock. His two younger sisters, Blanche and Pearl, had learned to help on the farm as well. It was the midwestern work ethic that motivated this Swedish farm family. They worked hard, but they also learned to play hard. Each of the children learned to play the piano and the violin at an early age. Evenings found the three children practicing their instruments and learning to play duets and trios together with their mother at the piano. Music was often coming from the Oberg house! In high school, when the music teacher had needed someone to play the big string bass, Howard volunteered. Here he was, playing an instrument which stood several inches above his head, but he loved playing that big ole string bass violin, and he became very adept at performing with it. He loved keeping the beat and doing fancy bass runs for the new songs of the era!

Finishing high school in St. Paul, Minnesota, Howard knew there had to be more to life than just farming. Farming was hard backbreaking work. And working out in the cold Minnesota winters and the hot humid summers made Howard laugh to himself, "Ah, yes! Minnesota the land of two seasons; shovel and swat! If I'm not shoveling snow and milking cows, I'm swatting mosquitoes and baling hay." He hated milking cows in the morning, especially after playing a late-night gig. It was difficult to drag himself out of bed in the dark cold weather. And he hated baling hay with a passion. He was not a big strong man by any means, so lifting those bales onto the wagon was even more difficult for him. There really wasn't much Howard liked about the farm, but he truly loved music! "Music," he thought, "Music could be my ticket away from farming!"

So, as a young man, Howard gathered his musician friends. All he needed was a drummer to keep the rhythm going and an accordion player to do the melodies. They practiced and practiced using Howard's house as a studio, and his new dance band took off. Later they added saxophones for a more "Big band" feel. "We're pretty good!" Howard thought, "even if I do say so myself!" And before long, Howard and his orchestra became quite notorious as the dance band to dance to in Thief River Falls and the surrounding areas.

Howard knew he needed a job, as the pay from a dance band was not a lucrative income. So, he started taking pre-med courses at a nearby college and found a job working in a local doctor's office as a nurse's assistant by day, helping his father on the weekends and playing gigs around the area by night.

At the time Howard met Viola near Thief River Falls, he was married. But life wasn't going well for this young couple. Anna, his wife, was a jealous young woman, and she hated the fact that Howard was always gone. If he wasn't working or going to school, he was out at night playing with his dance band. She'd initially met him while he was playing a gig one night, but she'd grown bored sitting in the dance halls every night listening to the same old songs, so she started staying home alone. She was feeling more and more lonely, and more and more neglected. She and Howard had tried to have children, but to no avail. And with no children, she was totally feeling the need to be with Howard, but Howard was always busy trying to earn money. Anna and Howard began arguing. Little things became big things, and then it seemed that Howard could do nothing right. The few moments he was home were just opportunities for Anna to nag at him. His life had become one constant argument with incessant fighting and bickering. Friends say they had been having trouble for quite some time, and their marriage was not in a good situation when he met Viola. In Howard's mind, he was through with this marriage, and it was time to move on and find someone else. When Viola showed up on the scene, it seemed like she was perfect! Here was a girl who loved his music and loved to be at his dances. He loved being with Viola and seeing her on the dance floor made his heart skip a beat. The sparkle in her eyes and the laughter in her voice were like enticing sirens of the sea! She was so beautiful, and in his mind, it was perfectly fine to be with her. After all, he and Anna were heading for a divorce.

When Howard found out Viola was pregnant, he had been working in a doctor's office by day and playing in the dance band orchestra by night. He explained to Viola, "I'm madly in love with you and I want to do the right thing and marry you!" Viola was thrilled! She knew she was totally in love with Howard. The butterflies she'd felt when she was with him were all the proof, she needed to know she was in love with Howard. His brown eyes were captivating to her, and she loved the fact that she could go along with him to his dance gigs. Howard admitted he was the father of her baby, but what he didn't tell Viola was that he was a married man!

As time went on, Viola continued to see Howard. He finally had to come clean and confess to her he was already married to Anna. At first, she was excited when he asked for her hand in marriage, "Yes! Yes! Yes!" she cried. "I can't wait to be your wife!"

"Well, there's something I have to tell you!" Howard sheepishly admitted. "I'm already married but I'm in the process of getting a divorce."

"Oh, no!" Viola started to cry. "How long will it take to get a divorce?" she whimpered through sniffles. "When can we be together?" Howard reached into his pocket for a handkerchief and explained he was working on it!

Unfortunately, Howard knew his answer was inadequate. Things weren't working out the way he had planned. Anna became a very vindictive wife and wasn't ready to grant Howard a divorce!

"This is going to take some time," Howard thought sadly. "How am I ever going to be with Viola when Anna won't let me go?" Then he explained to Viola, "We'll have to wait and see how the courts handle it. Have you talked to your father yet?" he asked.

Viola looked up at Howard and regretfully admitted, "No, I haven't told him! Who knows what he'll say!

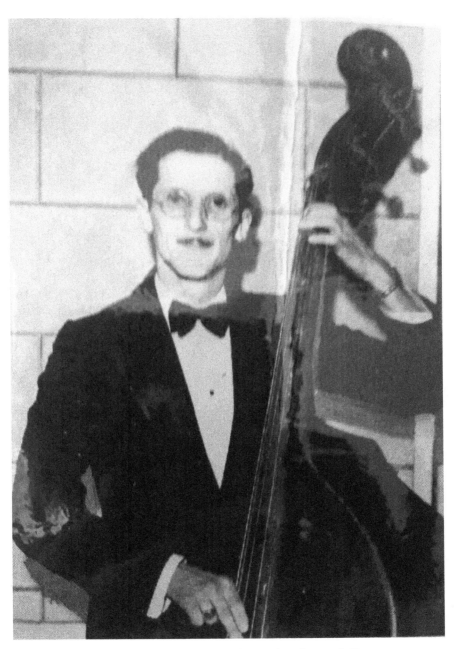

Howard Oberg playing his string bass violin.

TOGETHER ALWAYS

WHY DON'T WE- - -

Show more love with hugs and kisses.
    Smile, for all to see, forget the "Hits and Misses."

Laugh and dance, with real funnin'.
    "Smell the roses," and Stop forever runnin'.

Tell only the best, of what we really like.
    Select redeeming features. Take time to "Fly a kite".

Show our generosity with eager giving,
    Stop fussing'. Really enjoy a fuller livin'.

Read more good books - Take restful trips
    Sit still for a minute - Shut our lips.

Use our mouths for only cheery sounds.
    Heap praises where needed - Forget work "mounds".

Enjoy surroundings - seek God with a daily prayer,
    Acknowledge the Provider - Not worry about "our share".

We're always too busy - Not realizing His presence is Ominous.
    Learn to Listen, Love, take time for others, forget "Us".

Express true feelings - Omit the harsh word.
    Forget about yesterday - Forever look forward.

CHAPTER **3**

A SWEDISH UPBRINGING

PHILLIP LUNDBERG, VIOLA'S father, was a staunch Swede who attended the local Lutheran church in Thief River Falls. His parents had immigrated from Sweden in 1865, to Wisconsin, when Phillip was just a year old. The family grew by leaps and bounds, adding a sibling every two years, until the Lundberg family had ten children! As the oldest of those ten children, Phillip learned to be a responsible, hard worker. Having gained an eighth-grade education, Philip began working with the railroad as a car maintenance man. He was a big man, standing well over six foot three inches tall, and his strawberry blonde hair let everyone know he was probably of Swedish descent!

Phillip demanded a lot from his young wife, Clara, as well as his own children. As many say, he ran a very strict ship. Lloyd was his first-born son, and Phillip expected him to work hard. Two years later, Viola came a long and she quickly learned to obey her father at an early age. The third child to arrive was Clifford, but sadly, "Cleve", as he was called by the family, only lived for three days. He had developed bronchial pneumonia at birth and was quickly consumed by this disease as an infant. The entire family was devastated with the loss of Cleve, but Phillip was especially saddened by the loss of a son, and he seemed to become even more strict. Some say he ruled his family with a heavy hand. A few years later, the birth of Ella seemed to cheer everyone up. She was the light of everyone's eye, especially

TOGETHER ALWAYS

Viola. With seven years between the two sisters, Viola adored the new baby, and loved taking care of "her baby sister". She would wrap Ella up in a blanket and carry her around, chatting with her as if Ella truly understood what her big sister was saying. She loved helping her learn to crawl and eventually toddle around the house. The two sisters were inseparable, and a strong bond was created between the two of them, especially when Clara, their mother, was working.

Clara Louise Jensen, Viola's mother, was a strong, hard working woman, even though she stood an entire foot shorter than Phillip. Clara, too, was the oldest of ten children, although two of those children did not survive. Like her Norwegian mother, Clara learned strong work ethics. She married Philip Lundberg when she was just eighteen years of age and got pregnant on their wedding night. Philip, six years her senior, was pleased to see Clara obtain a domestic job working at a boarding house down the street to help contribute to the family income. At the boarding house, Clara would cook, clean, and do the laundry for a wealthier family in Becker. Eventually, with the addition of children, their financial struggles led Clara to obtain a better position with the railroad cafe in Thief River Falls. Every morning at 4:00AM, Clara would rise, get herself ready for the day, prepare food for her own family, and then walk to the railroad cafe where she would start baking bread, pies, and cakes for the restaurant. She spent her entire day working as a cook and waitress, only to have a babysitter eventually taking care of her own children, Lloyd, Viola and little Ella.

Mae Wynkoop was the young woman hired to work as a domestic caring for Clara's own children while she was earning a higher wage for the family at the railroad station restaurant. After several years, Mae was quite comfortable working in the Lundberg home, and eventually she seemed as if she were a part of the family. Not having any children of her own, Mae was especially good with the Lundberg children.

Clara would return from work at mid-afternoon when Lloyd and Viola were getting home from school. "It's so nice to come home and

A SWEDISH UPBRINGING

have the evening meal prepared," thought Clara as she entered her home. "The laundry is done, and the house is clean. I couldn't ask for a better situation." Mae never seemed to have any problem with the children and Clara knew her children were well cared for. It was almost as if Mae were bringing up the Lundberg children as her own! In fact, many believed that little Ella might have belonged to Mae because they were so close. Ella had not spent much time with Clara, her own mother, as Mae had been there every day since her birth!

When little Ella was in school full time, things seemed to change around the house. One day, Clara returned home from work earlier than usual! She looked in the kitchen, thinking Mae would be there fixing the evening meal. When she didn't find Mae in the kitchen, or in the parlor, she walked into the bedroom. There, to her horror, she found young Mae and her husband, Phillip, in bed together! Clara screamed, "Oh my God!" and immediately turned on her heels and ran out of the house! There was no turning back or reconciliation for Clara. She'd been betrayed by Phillip and Mae, and she knew what she had to do. With a broken heart, she knew her son, Lloyd, who was fourteen, Viola, who was twelve, and little Ella who was only five would have good care with Phillip and Mae, so she promptly filed for a divorce as fast as possible. This was 1927 and she was determined to get away from Phillip's adulterous ways. Being accused of running off and leaving her children, Clara told her children, "I'm not leaving you. I know you are well cared for. I'm leaving my cheating husband, Phillip, and his mistress. There is no place in my heart for this man."

After the divorce was final, Phillip and Mae later married, making Mae a stepmother to Lloyd, Viola and little Ella. Lloyd didn't seem to be bothered one way or another. Although he loved his mother, he was very independent, and his thoughts were about school, and work and he didn't feel he needed a mother or a stepmother. Little Ella grew to love Mae as if she were her very own mother, having spent almost every day of her life with Mae in the mother role. Ella loved working around the house with Mae, but Viola was a different story. She was a very strong-willed twelve-year-old and would have nothing to do with Mae. She felt Mae had broken up her mother and father's marriage. Heading into puberty, Viola would shout at Mae, "You can't tell me what to do, you're not my mother!" Poor Mae, who was only fourteen years Viola's senior, had no recourse other than to go to her new husband, Phillip. When Phillip approached Viola, she and her father would have words. All the adults in Viola's life were trying to guide her down the right path, but Viola was not about to listen to any of them. She wasn't going to listen to Mae, her father, or her mother.

Viola, 15, Phillip Lundberg and Ella, 7

HAPPINESS MEANS...

"LOVE!"

"WARMTH!"

"GROWTH!"

and "QUIET"!

"LAUGHING!"

"SCRATCHING!"

and a needed "DIET!"

"NAPS!"

"RIDES"

And dinner with "FRIENDS!"

I love "LIVING"

and then the "CHALLENGES of each day,

Make me reach and aspire, with "HOPES" that it never ends!

CHAPTER 4

THE PATH OF DESTRUCTION

VIOLA WAS ON the path to destruction from that moment on. No one could control her. She spent time with her father and Mae, but Viola was talking back to Mae, and consequently, she was sent to live with her mother. But not wanting to follow her mother's rules either, Viola was eventually sent back to her father's house, and eventually her parents contacted the Juvenile system. The courts labeled her "immature, unstable and promiscuous with men". They tried having her live with a foster family, but even that didn't work out. In those days, it was not uncommon for parents to think reform school was the place for an unmanageable child, so Phillip, under duress, felt he had no choice and Viola was taken to the Minnesota Home School for Girls, a reformatory school in Sauk Centre, Minnesota.

The Minnesota Plan for these "unmanageable girls" was a progressive piece of legislature implemented for social welfare of wayward girls. Instead of allowing young girls to live with their families, this plan placed girls in a home where they could be mentored to avoid pregnancy, as many of the girls had promiscuous tendencies. Hoping Viola would adapt to more appropriate choices, she was placed at the reform school around the age of fourteen. Throughout her teenage years, Viola was in and out of the juvenile system, bouncing from her mother's home to her father's home and even a foster home, as well as her stint in the Minnesota Home School for girls. While Lloyd and Ella seemed to thrive with their new stepmother, Viola was rebelling with all her might.

At her mother's home, Viola was learning to deal with her new stepfather, Joe Henry. He was also a big man, mostly known as a gentle giant. Viola wasn't exactly sure how to deal with this new stepfather. Using her flirtatious manner, Viola was able to be very manipulative. "Hi Joe," she would say as she entered her mother's house, batting her eyes at the tall man. "How are you doing?" Joe Henry looked at Viola and thought, "Man, she is such a cute little version of her mother! Someday, someone's going to take advantage of her!"

As her teenage years went by, Viola was in and out of her mother's house. She had a difficult time staying out of trouble. She was constantly breaking her curfew and drinking underage. Approaching her senior year in high school, Viola's mother and Joe Henry were fit to be tied. They basically threw their arms up and let Viola do what Viola wanted. They had their own baby arriving and were preoccupied with their own new challenges. It was February 1932, when Viola, who was sixteen years old, became a big stepsister to her mother's new baby named JoAnn Henry. Later that year, Viola would turn seventeen and go out dancing with Howard at Lake Sallee. It was the same year she became pregnant!

In those days, when an underaged daughter wanted to marry, the father had to sign papers, allowing his daughter to wed. Viola's father, Philip, being the stalwart master of his family, refused to allow his seventeen-year-old daughter, Viola, to marry Howard Oberg. And he had a good reason. "He's not even divorced from his first wife, and now he wants a second wife!" Phillip yelled. He had done his research and found out that Howard was still legally married to Anna. "I forbid you to be with Howard Oberg!" he raged!

Viola was hurt beyond measure. She thought Howard was in the process of getting a divorce. She just knew she and Howard were truly in love, and she went to Howard in tears. "My father says I can't be with you because you are still married. He is refusing to sign the paperwork allowing me to marry you! When will your divorce be final?" she sobbed, tears running down her cheeks.

Howard took her into his arms. "I love you, Viola, and I am truly in the process of getting a divorce. I don't love Anna. She and I haven't gotten along for months," he softly told her, wiping her tears and tucking a curl behind her ear. "I love you very much and want to be with you," he explained.

Viola sniffed and whipped her nose, "Once you get a divorce, and I turn eighteen, we won't need my father to sign any ole papers," she said. "Then we can get married and be on our own. We'll show them!"

But it didn't take long for Phillip to learn that Viola and Howard were secretly seeing each other. He discovered that Viola had been sneaking out to the dance hall and when he found out she was pregnant with Howard's baby, he put his foot down, "Get out of my house," he yelled, "you are no longer welcome here! No daughter of mine tramps around like this! Get out of my house!"

This seemed like a double standard to Viola! "How could he cheat on his own wife, and then think that my pregnancy is worse?" she wondered to herself. Both were sins in her mind, but certainly two vastly different sins in Phillip's mind. Having an unwed mother was a terrible disgrace for Phillip, the staunch religious man that he was! Viola had already been such a strong-willed child and had been in and out of juvenile services when the adults around her couldn't control her. The courts had even deemed her a "difficult child to manage", so Phillip contacted her social worker and made arrangements for Viola to again be taken to the Minnesota Home School for Girls, a home for wayward girls and unwed mothers in Sauk Centre, Minnesota. At the age of seventeen, Viola found herself three months pregnant, disowned by her mother and her father, and living in a home for unwed mothers in another city.

Interestingly, the church community and Viola's friends in town were told that she had suffered a nervous breakdown and was placed in the hospital in Minneapolis for her "psychotic episode". The stigma of having an unwed teenage mother in this strongly religious society demanded a cover-up, and that is exactly what her family did. Viola's reputation had already suffered, but the family needed to save face as best they could. Many people knew that she had already been sent to the Minnesota Home School for Girls prior to this round of "psychosis", so off she went again, back to familiar surroundings.

The women at the School put Viola through a barrage of psychological and mental tests. The tests revealed Viola was a very bright young woman and had many secretarial skills. They assured her that everything would work out for the best. Then they conducted the personal interview.

Viola was asked, "Who is the father of your child?"

Viola replied, "Howard Oberg."

When the interviewer asked, "Where did you meet him?"

Viola replied, "He was in the orchestra at Becker Hall. He came down from the stage and bought me a drink. We actually danced together for one song while his band played."

"What happened?" questioned the interviewer.

"He took me home after the dance," said Viola shyly.

The friendly woman asked, "Where did the intercourse take place?"

And Viola embarrassingly answered, "We stopped near Lake Salle."

"In the car?" asked the interviewer.

"Yes", answered Viola.

"Was that the only time you had relations with him?" the interviewer wondered. Viola looked embarrassed and went on to reveal she had been with Howard many other times after their meeting at Lake Sallee.

Women at the Home School believed that the young unwed mothers were often tricked into their pregnant condition by promises of marriage. Consequently, the women were very kind to Viola believing she had been tricked by this older man. They believed their

THE PATH OF DESTRUCTION

sole purpose was to form a motherly or sisterly bond with each one of the young unwed mothers, creating a warm trusting environment. The women at the Home School, encouraged Viola to get a job.

"Working as a waitress in a nearby restaurant will help you get out on your own," they told her. "Or maybe you could get a secretarial job, as your typing skills are excellent." the home school workers told her. And with her sparkly eyes and her flirtatious mannerisms, they knew she was a shoo-in for any type of work, especially since she was so bright.

One of the women told her, "Your smile and happy manner will be your ticket to help you pay your own way."

Eventually Viola did get a job and the women at the School assured her everything would work out for the best. Viola was ever so hopeful, after all she knew she and Howard were in love and would be married.

"Once Howard gets a divorce, everything will work out just fine." she thought. But sadly, Anna, Howard's present wife, wasn't about to grant him a divorce. Each time Howard and Viola met it seemed they were having more and more disagreements as to how to proceed with this stressful situation.

The Minnesota Home School for Girls in Sauk Center consisted of several cottages around a main campus. The Cottage system of Institutional Care was designed based on a theory used by the state for hospitals and mental asylums in the late 19th century. They were built in rural areas to create privacy.

CHAPTER 5

SHE'LL MAKE SOME FAMILY HAPPY

SALLY CONSTANCE CAME into this world on August 22, 1933, in Sauk Centre, Minnesota, at the Minnesota Home School for Girls. She weighed seven pounds and thirteen ounces and was named Sally for Lake Sallee, where Viola had gotten pregnant. "She's a pretty average baby," thought Viola. But as she nursed her newborn, Viola noticed that Sally's eyes were as dark and as captivating as her father's. Suddenly, the love Viola felt for Howard crept into her heart, and she felt that special love for Sally.

She was bonding with this beautiful little girl whose eyes seemed much too big for her little face. She realized she wanted to keep this baby with all her heart, but the women at the Home School were encouraging her to give the baby up for adoption. "She'll make some family very happy," they told her. But Viola wasn't budging. She wanted to keep her baby, the baby that had Howard's eyes.

The women at the Home School continued to play on Viola's emotions, "How are you going to support your baby? You don't make enough money on your own to pay for her food, let alone pay for a place to live," they told her.

Each time, Viola would say, "I can do it! I'm not alone. Howard is going to marry me!" She refused to sign any paperwork that would allow Sally to be put up for adoption. Sally was her baby, and she was going to do everything possible to keep her baby! Attentively nursing Sally for two months, Viola was able to remain at the Home School with her for that time. She even had Sally baptized in the Lutheran church in October of 1933.

In those days, unwed mothers could spend several months in the Home School, and each of the girls were expected to help perform daily tasks in the home. Along with cooking, cleaning, and laundry, the girls also worked in the garden. But the most important part of life at the Home School was being surrounded with other girls who were learning how to take care of their own babies. Infant hygiene was paramount, along with domestic chores. Having other girls in the home also offered the girls camaraderie, and the women working at the Home, hoped that the girls would learn new morals, making better choices for their babies.

The women at the Home School, fueled by pressure from the state, eventually insisted Viola go back to work. It wasn't easy to continue nursing a baby while maintaining work hours, so both Viola and Sally were placed in a state-run foster home together. Viola had just turned eighteen. "This is perfect," she thought, "I can have someone watch Sally during the day while I work, and then I can take care of her at night." And she diligently worked and paid for Sally's care for six more months. But the struggle of raising a baby alone at the age of eighteen, proved to be too much for Viola. She was exhausted all the time. She was always working or taking care of Sally, and she didn't like following the foster home rules. She wanted to be on her own, and she longed to have a life with Howard, but even that was proving to be difficult. She and Howard had more and more disagreements. Finally, Viola realized Howard was not going to get a divorce, and she called it off with him.

Regretfully, when Sally was eight months old, Viola knew she couldn't support her on her own without getting a better paying job. After all, she had watched her own mother get a better job, so now, she thought, "I'm going to have to find a better job for myself." Even though Howard was financially contributing to Sally's care, she knew she wasn't going to be able to count on Howard's money to help her. She knew Howard wasn't getting a divorce, and she knew she would have to go it alone. She had to go out and earn more money for Sally.

"Once I get a better job, I'll be able to come back and get you," she whispered to Sally one morning as she kissed her beautiful baby goodbye. Heading down the sidewalk to work, in March of 1934, she turned and whispered, "I'll be back." But Viola never returned. Although Viola consistently made payments for Sally's care until Sally turned two years old, Viola never returned. Poor Sally was left to become a foster child on her own before she turned a year old! She was just learning to crawl, facing her first separation and never fully understanding why her own mother deserted her. For many years, Sally would wonder, "Why did my mother leave me? and Where did she go?"

The Minnesota Plan of 1917 was a national triumph for the Progressive child welfare movement in the United States. It had been well established by the time Sally was in the system in 1934. Initiated for the benefit of children who were beginning life with a handicap such as illegitimacy, the plan contained regulations to strengthen and establish guidelines for abandonment, guardianship and mother's pensions. It even went so far as to establish a licensing system for child placing agencies, child caring institutions and maternity hospitals. With the Minnesota Plan in place, the state wanted to step in and ensure little Sally was not only clothed and fed, but well cared for by a good family. Their main goal with many of these illegitimate babies was to get them into a good home in hopes of breaking the cycle of illegitimacy.

The adoption process was deemed by the state in the best interest of the child, but Viola refused to sign papers allowing Sally to be adopted. In fact, Viola literally disappeared. Phillip had disowned Viola and refused to raise her "bastard child". Philip's brothers and sisters were not even approached to provide care for Sally as it was deemed none of them wanted to defy Phillip. Clara had eight living brothers and sisters. One of them from Shokapee stepped forward to adopt little Sally, but sadly, Sally's aunt was not considered wealthy enough to be financially capable of caring for her. In those days, the state looked at your bank account and your earning potential. Sally's aunt was not wealthy by any means and the state declared that she could not adopt Sally. Both families were deemed too poor to adopt, and Clara, Viola's mother, was already raising a toddler of her own with Joe Henry.

The state was looking at every option available for Sally's placement. They looked at Howard's family. Of his two sisters, one was nineteen years of age and in college to become a music teacher, and the other sister, Blanche, was twenty-six years of age and working full time as a stenographer. She oversaw teaching thirty-five other young women how to be stenographers. There was no way she could take on a toddler, nor was she wealthy enough or financially stable enough to adopt a toddler. It appeared there were no family members capable of adopting Sally, if, and when Viola signed the adoption papers. Viola had disappeared to avoid signing papers allowing Sally to be adopted.

And then there was Howard, the baby's actual father. Sadly, the state didn't believe Howard could raise a young baby either, considering his rocky marriage and impending divorce. According to their records, by February of 1933, when Viola was just six months pregnant, Howard had declared that he was the true father of her baby and he began sending child support payments to the state. He assumed this would put him in good standing with the state and Viola. But according to the state, those payments were not made in a consistent, timely fashion and Howard was deemed unacceptable to adopt his own daughter!

In those days, fathers had little options for claiming custody of their own children, especially when they were not in a situation deemed suitable by the state. Finding little recourse, Howard eventually was able to divorce his first wife and tried to pursue a relationship with Viola. He searched for her, but she had made it quite clear she wanted nothing more to do with him. He had hurt her, and she was not going back for more. Forlorn, Howard went on with his life, eventually becoming a Policeman with the Thief River Falls Police department and later marrying again.

CHAPTER 6

HOW MANY FOSTER HOMES CAN ONE GIRL HAVE?

LIFE WENT ON for Sally. At nine months of age, in May of 1934, she was placed into a new foster home without Viola. By this age, Sally was starting to talk, saying, "Dada " and "Momma", but Sally's real mother and father were not around to hear her say their names. Her new foster mother described her as a very cute baby who was exceptionally bright. "When she arrived at our home, she was very pale and scrawny", her foster mother had said. "Her big brown eyes seem much too large for her sad little face, and she looked very undernourished." Fortunately, over the next few months, Sally gained weight and her cheeks turned pink and her health improved tremendously as she gained weight. This second foster family adored Sally and enjoyed caring for the lively little girl. Their older daughter especially loved playing with this new foster baby! She loved helping her try to stand next to the sofa as the little baby tried to pull herself up. Sally was making great strides when this family got word that they would have to move out of the area due to the father's job transfer. Sadly, Sally would have to be placed in another foster home, her third home before she had even turned a year old.

HOW MANY FOSTER HOMES CAN ONE GIRL HAVE?

Sally had dealt with several separations. First, she had been separated from her biological mother and the first foster mother who had cared for her during the day while her mother, Viola, worked. Now the second foster mother and her family had to move away due to work, and Sally faced a third set of caregivers. With the third foster family, Sally settled in nicely. She had known nothing different than changing caregivers and this family did their best to make her happy. They had three older boys who adored their bright-eyed little foster sister. Interestingly enough, the boys didn't like the name Sally, so they started calling her "Connie", a nickname using her middle name, Constance. Everyone adored her and the new orphan became known as Connie.

By this time, Connie was a year old and her birth mother, Viola, had contacted the social worker for pictures of Sally. "I miss my little girl so much!" she said. "I'd love to have a picture of her!" Oh, how Viola longed to see how Sally was growing! She truly missed her precious little girl. She had taken care of Sally, nursing her for two months at the Home School for Girls and caring for her for six more months in the foster home. She had been tremendously attached to her little girl, and she wanted to see what she looked like.

The third foster mother told the social worker, "We'll try to get some photos of her during our next holiday!" but no one knows if those photos were ever sent to Viola. That momentous occasion when Sally took her first step was documented in the social worker's report. The social worker told Viola, "Sally is crawling and pulling herself up onto the furniture. She's almost walking on her own." And then the following week more documentation stated, "Sally took her first steps as we enticed her back and forth across the room, calling her by her new nickname, Connie!"

This third foster family received Connie very unexpectedly when she was only a year old. They weren't prepared to have such a young child. They had no crib, so Connie ended up sleeping in the mother's bed with her. But when Connie wet the bed that night, the foster mother realized Connie was far too young to be potty trained and needed her own bed. She immediately created a place for Connie to sleep by fastening four chairs together with several layers of blankets. This makeshift bed would serve as her crib until the family could obtain one, borrowed from friends!

This foster family consisted of a mother and father and three older boys who were very excited to have a little sister! They would each play with her and read her stories. One day the social worker visited while the mother was at a church meeting. The youngest brother, who was thirteen at the time, was babysitting Connie. She was asleep in her newly acquired crib. The son called the mother home immediately, and she sheepishly explained to the social worker, "We don't usually make it a habit of allowing our boys to babysit, but it was Connie's nap time, and she is such a wonderful baby. She never cries and she loves playing with the boys when she wakes up. She's always in a happy mood!"

It was exciting for the boys to have a little sister! They loved taking Connie to church, and their church friends eagerly helped them out with diapers, blankets and hand-me-down clothes for their new little visitor. They even loaned them a highchair and loved the fact that Connie was such a quick learner. Her new foster mother excitedly purchased a few dresses for the adorable brown-eyed baby, but when winter was approaching, the foster mother had to contact the Social Worker, Ms. Annie B. Flugum. "Connie needs a winter coat and hat," she explained over the telephone. At sixteen months of age, Connie was starting to grow out of her baby clothes and Annie B. Flugum brought along the new winter coat and hat for her, as well as a Christmas present from the Children's Home Society.

Connie immediately opened her Christmas present from Ms. Annie B. Flugum. Much to Connie's delight, it was a curly haired doll. Connie loved this new baby doll and carried it everywhere. "Thank you so much for thinking of Connie," said the foster mother, cheerfully. "We just adore her, and we love seeing her happy smile. Her eyes just sparkle!"

Connie's new family had grown very attached to her, and the

father of the family was known to be Connie's personal servant. She constantly gave him orders and he would lovingly tend to her every wish. "Up Papa, up!" she would command, and the father of the family would gladly pick her up and carry her around on his shoulders.

Connie seemed to adore all the boys and was thriving with her new foster family. In fact, the foster mother had even remarked, "We are so attached to this adorable little girl that it will be very difficult to give her up when the time comes."

Sadly, after Connie had been with this foster family for one year, the state intervened. Right before Connie's second birthday, the state deemed it necessary for Connie to be placed in an orphanage and placed for adoption. It was quite common during the depression years for many children to be given away due to financial distress, and so it was in Connie's situation. The state finally pressured her mother, Viola, to sign the paperwork releasing Connie for adoption. Luckily, Connie was not placed on one of the many orphan trains which traveled across the Midwest during the 1930's, but in July of 1935, the state decided it could no longer continue paying foster care money for Connie's welfare when she would make some family very happy.

Both Viola and Howard had paid monthly child support payments to the state to continue Connie's foster care, but those payments were sporadic and inconsistent. The state expressed its desire that it was in Connie's best interest to place her with a good family. They also stated, "Two years is long enough for Viola to prove she can support her own child." Unfortunately, Viola had not come back to prove she was a fit mother, nor did she have enough money in her bank account to prove she could financially support her daughter. On August 13, 1935, Connie was placed into the Little Red Stocking Children's Home Society Orphanage in St. Paul, MN, and became a ward of the state to be immediately placed for adoption.

When Howard was contacted to sign paperwork relinquishing his parental rights, he went to visit Connie at the orphanage. His immediate reaction was, "She looks just like her mother!" Howard was very forthright with information. He stated he had obtained a divorce from Anna and was now married to a wonderful new woman. His new wife stated to authorities, "We would love to adopt Sally and have this adorable little girl come live with us!" Unfortunately, Howard was not allowed to adopt his own daughter! Some say it was because he hadn't made consistent child support payments to the state, often making payments late or not at all. Other's guess he wasn't making enough money and couldn't afford to support Connie. While still others believe Viola may have refused to allow Howard to adopt Connie. Whatever the reason, Howard was not allowed to take his own daughter home.

Connie was just two years old when she was removed from an yet another adoring foster family. This time she was placed into the orphanage, basically, her fourth home environment where she would grow fond of caregivers. "She'll make some family very happy," said many of the workers who met the bright-eyed little girl. She was immediately placed on the adoption list, which essentially meant nothing to Connie, except she was no longer with her doting family. Little Connie, as she was now called, had so many people in her life, but no one had remained constant. Her doting foster care parents weren't there, her real mommy wasn't there and now she was with so many other boys and girls. No one seemed to talk about her real mommy or any of the other people that had been in her life. Connie knew nothing different than being shuffled from one home to the next. She had no idea this was not a normal childhood. "Where is my foster daddy" she probably thought. "I miss how he gave me horsey back rides. Where are the big brothers who played with me and read me stories? Where's my crib and my foster momma?" Connie had no idea how her life was anything but normal.

The orphanage was certainly different. She sat in the green highchair with her big brown eyes looking around the dark gloomy room. She saw the big brown steps set off against the back wall. She would later learn the steps were called the risers, upon which she would learn to walk up and down as if she were in a fashion show. The dark walls made the children who surrounded her seem bleak and gloomy.

HOW MANY FOSTER HOMES CAN ONE GIRL HAVE?

It was nothing like the bright cheery home she had come from.

One of the people who tried to cheer Connie up was the cook at the orphanage. She loved to see Connie smile. She would feed Connie oatmeal every morning and chat with her about her day. Her foster mother had said, "Connie is such a good eater. She tries everything we give her." But sadly, the cook had discovered Connie wasn't eating her peas, and she seemed to make it her own personal vendetta to get Connie to eat them! Oh, how Connie hated those green peas! The cook had even tried to trick her by serving her a mouthful of mashed potatoes and then a spoonful of green peas, thinking Connie wouldn't notice. But the taste and texture of those mushy green peas from the can made Connie gag every time.

Oh, how she missed her foster momma! Her foster momma knew she didn't like green peas and she didn't force them upon her. Connie was beginning to realize that people were coming and going in her life, and she began to remember the good people and the bad people.

Ms. Annie B. Flugum was one of the good people in Connie's life. She was a large woman who entered the room with a flourish in her flowy black dress and shiny black shoes. Along with her black dresses and shiny black shoes, she wore an enormous floppy black hat. From a two-year old's perspective, Annie B. Flugum was enormous as she floated into the room, her black skirt billowing around her. She brought with her a ray of sunshine as she whirled into Connie's life. Connie knew there was fun to be had when Annie B. Flugum came to visit. She remembered her visiting her foster home, and now she looked forward to those special days when Miss Flugum would visit her at the orphanage. Connie didn't understand why she was able to have Annie B. Flugum all to herself, but she loved it. Annie B. Flugum would take her to the playroom and there she would ask Connie questions over a wonderful tea party. Watching Miss Flugum squat down on the tiny chairs as she shared tea with Connie, gave everyone a good chuckle, but Connie loved the fun and the attention. She missed her foster brothers and how they would play with her, but Annie B. Flugum would always make it a party when she arrived.

TOGETHER ALWAYS

She'd place the tiny little saucers on the table and serve pretend tea from the miniature porcelain teapot. She'd tell Connie, "Be careful now, the tea is very hot!" as she showed the little girl how to blow on her imaginary tea to cool it down. She'd drink her imaginary tea ever so politely, showing Connie how to stick out her pinky, "Just like the queen," she'd say.

Annie B. Flugum would visit and life was always fun! Whether it was a party, or a gift bestowed for unknown reasons, she'd create a stimulating time for this two-year old's growing vocabulary. "What's a queen?" Connie would ask, and Annie B. Flugum would tell her it was a very important woman who had a crown on her head. And then there was another question, "What's a crown?" At two years old, Connie's inquisitive nature was already showing. She wanted to learn about everything around her.

Later Connie learned that Ms. Annie B. Flugum was her very own social worker and she would check on Connie quite regularly. She also learned that Annie B. Flugum had been the one to give her the baby doll for Christmas; the doll that had hair, but no clothes. Connie remembers carrying her naked doll around and saying, "Put clothes on her! Put clothes on baby!" in her most demanding voice, but during the days of the great depression, clothes for dolls were not a priority, especially in an orphanage in the 1930's! But eventually things would change for Connie!

REACH OUT AND TOUCH
Written by Sally C. Wordelman in 1968

Legal documents declare an essential fact.
A date, names, a place of birth and of first being "Smacked".
Only a necessary paper designating parent's names and ages...
Yet I remain anonymous, as I struggle thru the stages.

Growing up left me frustrated.
Who am I? Where do I come from?
Not knowing the facts, left me devastated.
A devoted adopted Father gave me more than any child could expect.

His love, guidance, and understanding taught me a deep sense of respect.
I desperately tried to forget about "before" or "What if?" and "Why?"
Yet, always having a quizzical wonderment, "Who am I?"

Was my mother a woman I could truly hold dear?
Someone to share "girl secrets" hug and hold - and wipe a tear?
Was there a Father, whose name on a paper that did exist?
Or was he someone that my Mother couldn't resist?

Who, what were they? - Would they too wonder what became of me?
As each went their separate ways, oh, who can they be?
Hesitating for so long, wanting to know my parental background...
Oh, God! Please help me seek the answers,
                    as I daily pray that they may be found.

CHAPTER 7

NOT YOUR TYPICAL TEENAGER

VIOLA'S HEART WAS broken when she had to sign the papers giving Sally up for adoption. She knew it truly would be the best thing she could do for her daughter. So, under duress, Viola signed the papers making Connie the responsibility of Hennepin County in the state of Minnesota, allowing her to be placed into the Little Red Stocking Children's Orphanage. Connie was young enough to be placed into the nursery section, being just shy of her second birthday!

But just where had Viola gone? Philip Lundberg, her father, was a railroad man and early in his career he had lived and worked in Chicago. He had many friends who still lived there. In fact, when Viola was younger, Philip had taken her and Ella to visit those friends in Chicago and had even lived there several months. He had shown them Chicago, and Viola had enjoyed her time in the big city. So, when Viola wanted to escape, she ran to Chicago. Now running away again, she and a friend headed to Chicago.

Once in Chicago, Viola, and her friend, Mary, both nineteen years old, shared a room with one of Philip's friends, eventually obtaining their own room in a nearby boarding house. Eventually both girls applied for jobs and started working. Mary took a job as a waitress in a nearby restaurant close to the railroad station, and Viola was able to obtain a position as a secretary. They lived together in Chicago for at least eighteen months, earning money, but barely making ends meet. Life was still difficult for Viola.

During 1934 and 1935, Chicago was not your typical city, the World's Fair had come to town, making the city the biggest and most exciting place in America. As the nation's transportation hub, Chicago also was known as the Midwest's primary place for small-town job seekers. It was growing by leaps and bounds, and anyone who was anyone wanted to be a part of the hustle and bustle of Chicago. It was an exciting place to be, but many were struggling financially, and Viola was no different.

Eventually, Viola and her friend Mary were able to go out dancing on Friday nights and meet railroad men who seemed to be flowing with cash. It was still the 1930's and life was still difficult, but they soon learned that these men cashed their paychecks and stashed the money in their hotel rooms, only taking what they needed for the evening. Together, Viola and Mary devised a plan to visit the railroad worker's hotel rooms while they were out dancing, and they would steal their cash. They figured the men would never know who had done it.

With Mary as her sidekick, it didn't take Viola long to get into trouble. While the men were enjoying their well-earned Friday night beers, Viola and Mary very quietly went from room to room, searching for cash. With Viola standing watch at the door, Mary searched the room. Just as Mary found the cash, Viola said, "Someone's coming! What do we do?" Apparently, there were no wardrobes or closets to hide in, so Mary headed straight for the open second story window and said, "Follow me!"

Jumping from the 2nd floor window to the ground below, Mary tucked and rolled; stood up, dusted herself off, only to see Viola following close behind. Unfortunately, Viola was not as strong as Mary, and she didn't know how to tuck and roll. Viola landed on both feet and heard something pop. Unlike Mary, Viola could not stand up and walk away! Mary ran to get help and Viola was taken to the doctor's house on a stretcher. It turns out she had broken both ankles! Viola was told she must spend six weeks on bed rest! This certainly wasn't in her plans. Without any means of earning money, Viola now found herself in need of a place to stay. With great trepidation, she contacted her mother and pleaded with her to let her come home and live with her and Joe Henry while she recovered. Mary helped Viola ride the train back to Minnesota, and Viola then spent the next six weeks at her mother's home recuperating from her "fall".

Viola was a beautiful young girl and there she lay in bed at her mother's house with both legs propped up on pillows, unable to get around on her own. Clara again was at work all day, and three-year-old JoAnn was often taking afternoon naps. The only one around the house to care for Viola was Joe Henry. Without any hesitation, Joe Henry, Viola's new stepfather raped Viola, and told her under no circumstances was she to tell her mother. Sadly, when Viola discovered she was pregnant, Joe Henry withdrew $400 from his savings account and told Viola, "Take this and get out of town and don't ever let me see you again. Your mother will never know about this. Do you understand?"

Shaking feverishly, Viola, not knowing what to do, again headed to the Minnesota home School for girls.

"You're going to have to give the baby up for adoption," they told her as she went through the initial interview process.

"I know," cried Viola. "I just signed the papers to allow Sally to be adopted and now I have to give this baby up as well." She was sobbing uncontrollable.

"It's going to be okay," they assured her. "Just tell us who the father is, and we can have him help pay restitution."

Viola vehemently refused. "I don't know who the father is," she lied.

This was the year Viola wanted to forget. In March of 1935, her brother Lloyd, whom she dearly loved, had gone missing. A huge search was conducted and for three weeks everyone seemed to be looking for Lloyd. Unfortunately, when a neighbor found Lloyd, he was sitting against an old shed a few miles from their home with a rifle lying across his lap. The detectives ruled his death a hunting accident. The entire right side of his head had been blown away, and the three weeks of deterioration of the body was an unimaginable sight. It must have been a gruesome sight. Luckily, Viola had been away when the accident happened, but she had a gut feeling it really wasn't an accident. She felt Lloyd had committed suicide, but she wasn't completely sure why.

Lloyd was such a kind soul, a true confidante for Viola. But what had been troubling him? Lloyd knew about Viola's troubles. He knew she desperately wanted to keep her little girl, Sally. But unfortunately, their strict father wasn't permitting Viola to marry Howard. Was Lloyd feeling helpless where Viola was concerned? Or did he have his own problems? No one will ever know.

Viola struggled with her brother's death. She had returned to Minnesota in March for his funeral, then immediately disappeared back to Chicago. However, her return to Minnesota did not go unnoticed by the state and they coerced her to sign paperwork allowing Sally to be adopted. She missed Lloyd. She missed Sally. She missed Chicago and now she would have to give up this baby. She started sobbing, and it felt like she couldn't stop. To say she was depressed was a huge understatement. Here she was pregnant with her second baby out of wedlock, having just signed away parental rights to her firstborn baby, Sally, and now she would have to give up another baby.

Not knowing what to do, or where to turn, Viola headed to the Minnesota Home School for Girls, in Sauk Centre, Minnesota, to have her second baby out of wedlock. She knew the state was not about to let her keep this second child in the foster care program, and she was forced to eventually place her son, Anthony Peter, up for adoption. He was born on Sept. 3, 1936. Viola patiently nursed Anthony for two months while she again lived at the Minnesota Home School for Girls. On November 14, 1936, Anthony was placed in the Little Red Children's Orphanage, the same orphanage Connie had been placed in. They had missed being together in the orphanage as brother and sister by only five months!

FEELINGS

Mother's dreams, at times, become quite real.
Sometimes children are unable to cope or to feel.

So, with tenderness and a bit of despair,
I try harder to be honest, be more than fair.

The challenge of feeling their position in each conquest,
An acquisition!

Keeps my head in a tizzy, I fret, for I too, should never forget.
I once was a teenager, a young adult, who had to learn by living and default.

Remember what Dad always had to say, "Treat all as a newborn exciting day!"
"Use fairness, honesty and trust - listen and smile, as your buns you bust!"

I've earnestly tried listening with my heart.
New acceptances of morals give me a start.

I, too, can listen, bend an ear,
But deep inside is sorrow, and I shed a tear.

Life is a chessboard, each day a new dawn.
Will I face the next move with a Knight or a Pawn?

I live for their happiness, for that is life.
But better yet, I must try harder to be a good wife!

CHAPTER 8

A LITTLE SISTER

ONE PERSON VISITED the orphanage at that time, but Connie had no idea he was there or who he was. Howard Oberg and his new wife had visited Connie when she had been placed in the Little Red Stocking Orphanage in St. Paul, MN. She was just two years old, and he took one look at her and remarked, "She looks just like her mother!"

"Connie is what we are calling her now," said one of the women at the orphanage. "One of her foster families didn't like the name Sally, so they gave her the nickname, 'Connie' and it stuck! She's such a happy little child, and we all adore her." Connie had no idea she had just seen her birth father.

Howard gave the little bright-eyed girl a huge smile, and again commented, "I just can't get over how much she looks like Viola. "She looks just like her mother with the dark hair and beautiful smile and those eyes that follow you everywhere!" And then he was gone.

Playing with the other children at the orphanage helped Connie get over missing the "big boys" at her last foster home. She had always been in a social setting where she would have to share toys with other children. But then one day, May 9, 1936, to be exact, a new family arrived at the orphanage. It was just three months before her 3rd birthday, and this family wanted to take Connie to their house. They wanted a little sister for their eight-year-old daughter. She had been at the Orphanage for almost nine months, and she was sad to be leaving the cook and the nursery caregivers who had always been so kind to her. But she wasn't sad to leave those green peas behind! Little did anyone realize this was Connie's fifth placement into a new environment and her fifth separation from caregivers she'd grown attached to. Everyone involved thought this would be Connie's forever home, as the family was eager to proceed with the adoption process.

This new mommy and daddy were very loving, but their eight-year-old daughter wasn't as compassionate! She had spent eight years being the center of her parent's attention. She demanded attention and her parents thought if they got her a sibling, it would help her be more socialized. By then, Connie, at nearly three years old, was also a strong-willed child having to stand up for herself at the orphanage for the past eight months. When these two strong willed children met, it provided the new mother with a whole new perspective on sibling rivalry.

The big sister had obviously been told she was getting a new baby sister. When the nearly three-year-old Connie appeared at the front door, the big sister was taken aback. "Where's the baby?" she'd asked.

"This is your new little sister," her parents had informed her. Unfortunately, being a bright child, Connie was very well spoken for her age and could easily express her desires. When the older sister wanted Connie to pretend playing a baby, so the older sister could carry her around, Connie would say, "I am not a baby! I'm a big girl!" But the big sister had other ideas. To her, Connie was the baby and should be the baby when they played. She'd try to carry Connie around, as if she were a baby. Since Connie was small for her age, everyone thought she was younger than she was, but she was not about to be carried around as if she were a baby. Her next recourse would be to scream, and she literally screamed as loud as she could when words didn't work!

Of course, when Connie didn't cooperate, the big sister would become outraged and throw huge tantrums, screaming as well. "Connie won't play with me the right!" she'd yell to her mother. "I

A LITTLE SISTER

want Connie to be the baby!" Pretty soon both girls were screaming.

The big sister became very possessive and would snatch toys out of Connie's hands yelling, "Those are my toys! You can't have them!"

The poor mother would try to console Connie as she sobbed, "She grabbed the toy right out of my hands."

The poor mother would have to assuage her eight-year-old daughter as the big sister yelled, "She can't have those toys, their mine!" Sharing had not been in this older daughter's vocabulary. The constant screaming, crying and fighting was more than the mother could handle. There were even days when the big sister would scream, "I hate you! I hate you! I hate you!" And of course, the shrieking of, "Take her back, I don't want her here!" brought tears to the poor mother's eyes. She was beside herself! She'd never encountered sibling rivalry quite like this! She had thought they had prepared their older daughter for the arrival of a little sister, but obviously the big sister wanted no part of sharing her things or sharing her parents for that matter.

Finally, the poor foster mother was so distraught trying to please both girls and maintain peace in her home, she said to her husband, "I can't do this anymore! We need to take Connie back!"

Within only ten days, on May 20, 1936, the mother contacted Annie B. Flugum, and explained that their older daughter was having difficulty adapting to having a new sister. Adopting Connie was just not going to work out. Connie didn't want to be carried around as a baby and their own daughter did not want to share her toys. The documents said, "The foster family's older daughter is too affectionate, and Connie doesn't like the affection." But Connie remembers it entirely differently. She didn't want to be babied and the older daughter was the first and only person to ever treat her poorly as a foster child! No one had ever been so vicious to her before!

Driving in the car, Connie remembers going back to the orphanage. She had been sitting on the foster father's lap, as he drove. She remembers him crying, "I'm so sorry, Connie. I'm so sorry! This is not your fault. You're such a wonderful little girl. I'm so sorry!" When they arrived at the orphanage, the foster father explained to the caregivers,

TOGETHER ALWAYS

"Connie is such a wonderful, happy little girl! It's not her fault at all. Our own daughter has been an only child for way too long, and she doesn't like sharing her toys with Connie. Every time she tried to pick up Connie and carry her around like a baby, Connie would scream, 'I'm not a baby!', and then our daughter would scream because she didn't think Connie was playing the way she wanted her to. It was a constant battle all day long and my wife is exhausted trying to keep peace between these two girls!" He apologized profusely and said they just weren't going to be able to keep Connie. After only ten days, Connie was again back at the orphanage and facing the effects of another separation!

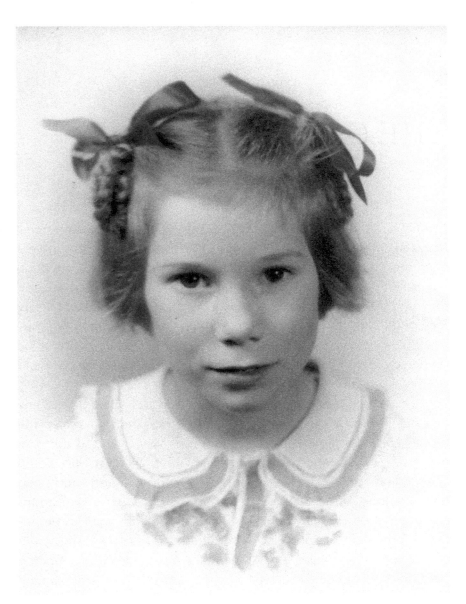

Connie - age 3 years, 1 month

CHAPTER 9

THE CHOSEN ONE

MINNESOTA REQUIREMENTS FOR adoption state that families must have the child in their care as a foster child for six months to one year from the time of placement until they can proceed with adoption papers. This family had been watching Connie at the orphanage and they had been hoping she would work out with their family. Luckily for Connie, this family didn't work out. She was relieved to be away from that nasty big sister, and happy to be back with her friends at the orphanage. She even liked her bed there, and thankfully the cook had stopped trying to feed her green peas!

Also visiting the orphanage were Mary Lee and Alfred Bates. They had put in their request for adoption in 1935 and had visited the orphanage many times. In fact, Alfred and Mary Lee had taken in two boys as foster children in hopes of finding children who would want to learn how to be farmers and grow up to be hired hands, one day inheriting Alfred's farm. The two young boys, who were brothers, worked on the farm, but it seemed they didn't want to be adopted. They didn't want to stay with Alfred and Mary Lee. They were constantly running away, and Alfred Bates spent many a time finding the boys and bringing them back to the farm. It was so frustrating for Alfred. He desperately wanted to be a father and offer these two young boys a part of his wealth. Finally, Alfred let them run away for the last time, and he and Mary Lee decided it was time to adopt a little girl. Both Mary Lee and Alfred were in their 40's and had not been able to have children of their own, so they decided adoption was their last option. They were hoping to find a child who matched their requirements.

During this time frame, many social workers were able to work to make adoption more acceptable by matching up adoptive parents and adoptees according to physical, ethnic, racial, religious and intellectual characteristics, creating adoptive families that resemble biological ones. Annie B. Flugum knew Connie's biological parents, two very musical families, one a dance band leader and the other, creative writers. She also knew Alfred and Lucille Bates, a dance band leader and a high school music teacher. Annie B. Flugum was instrumental in suggesting to Alfred and Mary Lee that she knew just the right child for them to adopt.

Each visit to the orphanage had left Alfred and Mary Lee with a feeling of emptiness. Alfred knew exactly who he wanted, and he was a patient man. He wanted a smart, well behaved child. When Ms. Flugum, the social worker at the Orphanage called telling them she thought she had found the perfect little girl for them, Mary Lee and Alfred could hardly wait to meet her. Would this be the smart well-behaved little girl he and Mary Lee had been hoping for? Was this the little girl the one they had prayed for?

Meanwhile, at the orphanage, Connie had learned about the risers which were propped against the back wall. She had been taught to walk up the three steps, turn around in a circle at the top, and walk back down the three steps on the other side. It was brought out when visitors would come to see the orphans. The orphans were instructed on how to present themselves. Even two-year-old Connie was taught to walk up the riser, turn and walk down. Then the orphans were told to walk over to the visitors who were prospective parents and wait for them to speak. After all, it was the era of "Children should be seen and not heard!" Ms. Flugum had contacted Alfred and Mary Lee Bates because she knew the Bates family well, and she thought Connie would be the perfect fit. Alfred had a good job as an Agricultural agent for eight counties and he owned three farms. He was indeed a wealthy man and could certainly afford to take on another mouth to feed. Afterall, he had just taken in two boys earlier in the year. His wife, Mary Lee, was a music teacher at Wells High School, and not only did she have a steady income, but she was a lovely woman. She knew Connie's biological father was very musical, playing in his own dance band near Minneapolis, and she knew Alfred and Mary Lee were both very musical. Alfred played the violin in a dance band in the area, and with Mary Lee's musical talents, Annie B. Flugum hoped this union would enhance Connie's chances of developing her own musical talents, if she had inherited any at all!

This June 14th visit was sure to be different for Alfred and Mary Lee! It was 1936 and almost three-year-old Sally Constance came through the door and walked across the stage. The instant he saw her, Alfred knew. He truly knew this would be "his little girl". Connie quietly walked up the three steps of the riser. She turned completely around exactly as she had been taught, and then she proceeded down the steps on the other side of the risers and walked over to the tall elegant couple. The feeling was overwhelming as a tear slowly slipped down Alfred's broad face. How little and pathetic she had looked, little spindly legs and a dress much too large for her tiny frame. She certainly fit the image of an orphan! Sally Constance displayed a delicate head of cropped auburn hair and a wide smile almost too big for her small thin face. He thought to himself, "She's the one!" and their eyes met. Oh, those dark brown eyes that looked at him with such a forlorn, child-like innocence.

Alfred shook his head to clear his mind and tried to listen to what the social worker was saying, "Connie's mother has tried to keep her, but the state has had to intervene. They feel this child must be placed for adoption. Her mother now realizes she cannot financially support the child and has signed the papers to release her for adoption. Connie has lived in several foster homes and was recently returned by another family. It seems Connie was overly affectionate, and their older daughter was becoming very jealous of the attention Connie

THE CHOSEN ONE

was getting. The mother felt that there would be problems later." Alfred had a hard time concentrating. He was watching Connie!

As Connie walked toward Alfred, he instantly knew there would be no more searching. This little brown-eyed girl had made the choice for him. Tugging on the tall man's coat, Connie timidly asked, "Are you my new daddy?", knowing full well she shouldn't speak! Alfred scooped her into his bear-like arms, and she giggled as he tickled her ribs. "Why yes, little Connie," he told her. "I'll be your daddy and we'll be together, always!"

"Always! Always! Always!" thought Connie. This was a new word for her almost three-year-old vocabulary! "What did it mean?" wondered Connie. She had no concept of the phrase, "Together, always," but the big man had said it so kindly and the words sounded so comforting. Connie later learned that the word "always" meant forever. She thought about forever. "Always together meant that she didn't have to go to a new home! She'd be with Alfred and Mary Lee forever! Together, always!" she said in her head. She loved the sound of those two words. And she would be reminded of them constantly throughout her life, "Together, Always, and "Always Together," it was a pact between her and Alfred Bates, her new daddy!

The usual papers were signed and Little Connie, as she was often called, walked with them to the car. Oh, how she loved hearing her new mommy and daddy use her name. And oh, how she loved watching these two new people in her life: her new mommy and daddy! They seemed so sweet and soft spoken, and they had chosen her! She was chosen out of all the other children at the orphanage! She was hand-picked! They had wanted her! And they told her this often. Her new mommy and daddy had sweet smiles.

The small group, Alfred, Mary Lee and little Connie said their goodbyes to Anne B. Flugum, and Annie B. bent down to reassure Connie she would see her again soon. As they drove away from the orphanage, Connie was so excited! Alfred and Mary Lee had said they were taking her to her new home. "A home!" It seemed to be another new word for her new vocabulary. Even at this age she loved words. Over three hours of driving from St. Paul to Wells, Minnesota, provided Alfred and Mary Lee plenty of time to spend with their new little girl. They told her about the farm and the animals she was going to meet, and as they drove through the warm summer afternoon, Mary Lee and Alfred talked to her so sweetly. Connie knew this was going to be a wonderful adventure!

"Home" turned out to be a farm, complete with cows and chickens and even a pony for Connie to ride, as well as a new Collie puppy who bestowed her with lots of sloppy kisses. But when the car stopped, and everyone got out, a strange man rushed up to greet them, anxious to meet the new family member. Connie, being a bit scared, reached for her new daddy. Was this man going to take her away from her new mommy and daddy? "It's okay, little one," daddy was saying, "This is my best hired hand! He's our friend." Connie soon realized that this stranger would become one of her friends, too, as daddy proudly introduced her to his best hired hand. "This is Connie, our little girl!" Connie liked the sound of that!

The first night was so frightening for this frail little child. There were crisp white sheets on the bed. And what a big bed it was, not like the cot she had slept in at the orphanage. The room was painted a light pink color and beautiful floral curtains adorned with lace decorated the edges of the windows. Never had Connie seen such opulence. Everything was so beautiful! The smells were different, too. Unfamiliar aromas from the farm filled her nostrils. She was scared that first night, and Connie clung to her new daddy, afraid to have him leave the room. He gently assured her, "The door will stay open, and I'll be right outside the door." But little Connie cried, with a simple plea, "Daddy!"

"Hush little one." Alfred had said as he gently stroked her back and began to softly sing to her. "Amazing Grace, how sweet the sound, that saved a wretch like me..." Never had anyone sung to her and rubbed her back. And if they had, no one had ever sung to her with such affection. His deep bass voice softly sung this magical song. His love poured into her, and the warmth of his gentle hand on her back felt so good. It had been so long since Connie had felt the warmth of someone close. Slowly she relaxed and drifted to sleep with a childlike peace, and Alfred tenderly pulled the covers around her small little frame. Again, he felt the welling of tears in his throat. "My little girl!" he thought, "Oh, how I need this little girl in my life!" But could Alfred possibly give her what she needed? Wiping the tears from his cheeks, he quietly tiptoed out of the room, leaving the door wide open, never realizing the challenges that lay before him!

Alfred Emery Bates and Mary Lee Yaeger with Connie, 1936

CHAPTER **10**

LIFE ON THE FARM

CONNIE'S DAYS WERE so full of growing and learning. There were so many things to see and do on the farm. There were cows to milk early in the morning. And there were chickens to feed, and eggs to collect from those chickens. And there were pigs. Oh, how they stunk. Daddy and all the adults on the farm told her never to go near the pigs, as they were "the meanest animals in the county!" There was a pony to ride and a dog to play with, and she spent all her daylight hours grasping all that she could see on the farm. Everything was so new. Everything was interesting, and everything was a learning experience for Connie. Alfred couldn't believe the eagerness she showed in her busy little body, discovering all the farm had to offer, and how quickly she learned.

"Why do the chickens lay their eggs in there?" "Where do the cows sleep?" "Can the puppy come into the house?" "Why daddy? Why?" She was filled with so many questions!

"My God!" Alfred thought, "will I ever be able to keep up with all the energy of this curious little child?" She was a bright little girl and so eager to learn, and he knew he had his work cut out for him raising this little one!

Alfred always took time to explain the answers to her questions with his deep melodic voice. Firmly, he took Connie's hand as they moved together to explore her new world. First, he showed her the puppy. Lady was her name and she was a beautiful Collie. Connie and Lady soon became friends as Lady quickly licked her cheek.

Next Alfred took her to see the cows, the most important part of his farm. He showed Connie the Holsteins and the Guernsey's and how they each had their own stalls. He showed her how the cows needed to be milked every morning. He even had her sit on the tiny stool as he showed her how to get fresh cow's milk! He showed her how the cows needed to be fed each day. And then he showed her the bull. Connie stared up at the huge creature, and Alfred warned her to stay far away from the bull. "Bulls can be very dangerous," daddy said, you mustn't go near him without a grown up."

"What's dangerous?" asked Connie.

"Bulls are very mean and can hurt you. You must stay away from this bull! Do you understand?" Alfred replied very sternly, and Connie got the message from the tone of his voice!

Off they traipsed across the yard with Connie wearing her new overalls and boots. Hand in hand Alfred took her from building to building. "Let's go see the chickens in the chicken coop," he said, as they came up to the next building.

"What's a coop?" asked Connie.

"A coop is what we call the chicken's house," explained Alfred, "it's a place for the chickens to sleep and lay their eggs. He answered all her questions, explaining Connie's job would be to look for eggs every morning. Then he showed her how to look for the eggs. "You just lift the chickens like so," Alfred stated and showed her where to find the eggs. Then he showed her how to feed the chickens. Connie was learning that each building on the farm housed a different kind of animal, and each animal's building had its own smell. And each animal had to be tended to with loving care, even the pigs!

The pigs seemed to be the smelliest creatures she had ever met! She was so amazed when she watched her father pick up a little pig with one hand and hold it tightly. Oh, did it ever squeal, and the sound was loud. Alfred warned her in his sternest voice, "Now you must make sure you stay away from the pigs. They can eat you!

They are just as dangerous as the old bull!" Connie got the message loud and clear and nodded that she had understood. "Stay away from the stinky pigs," she thought, "that won't be too hard!" After each building had been explained, they went back to the house where she could take off her overalls and play with Lady.

One day, no one could find Connie. Everyone, including the hired hand had stopped what they were doing and began to look for Connie. "Connie?" they called, "Where are you, Connie?" Suddenly, someone saw her little red hat trampled in the pig sty, and everyone feared the worst as they came running, still calling, "Connie! Where are you, Connie?" Knowing full well she wasn't supposed to even be near the pig sty, she didn't want to answer. She knew she would be in trouble. She had only climbed up on the fence to look at the pigs when her foot had slipped, and she had fallen in! Afraid to call for help, Connie lay very quietly in the mud scared to death! Much to everyone's relief, Alfred reached her in the nick of time and saved her from the fate that could await any small child falling into the mud of the pig sty with vicious pigs! Connie never went near the pigs again!

Another animal Connie wasn't fond of was the pony. Everyone was excited for this three-year-old to have her first pony ride, but Connie was very apprehensive. From her viewpoint, the pony looked like a huge horse. Daddy swung her high in the air and plunked her up on top of the pony. The pony's legs started to prance back and forth in place, scaring Connie. "Don't let him go anywhere!" she said with a petrified look on her face! As the pony continued to dance, Connie cried, "I can get down now!" wanting nothing more to do with the pony. Her legs had been splayed wide open across the pony's back and she had nothing to hold onto. Fear gripped her as she clung to her daddy when he lifted her down, and from that point on, Connie hated the pony and never wanted to ride him again!

Learning new words, she could barely pronounce, or even understand, the now three-year-old learned one emotion in Alfred and Mary Lee's home, and that emotion was love. She felt that love as she looked up into her father's warm hazel eyes. He was such a big strong man. His height was overpowering, standing over six feet tall to her tiny little frame. But with her small hand in his firm grip, she felt safe with this gentle giant, and together they walked to see the new calf in the pasture. There, in the pasture with the mamma cow nearby, Connie saw a small brown and white calf wobbling on her four unsteady legs as she began to stand. Connie watched in amazement as the baby cow wobbled over to the mamma cow to nurse. "This baby cow is called a calf," said Alfred, and Connie repeated the new word, "Calf." She was thoroughly absorbed in the small wonders of the farm and loved learning about everything the farm had to offer.

"And what's a baby pig?" asked Connie.

"A baby pig is called a piglet" explained Alfred.

"And the baby chickens are called chicks!" said Connie proudly. She was certainly learning everything she could about the animals on the farm.

But there was more to life on the farm than just the animals. Fishing was Alfred's favorite hobby, and he couldn't wait to share his love of the water with little Connie. There she was standing next to her daddy, just having turned three years old, proudly displaying a big smile as she displayed her new fishing coveralls with the zippered front. Alfred stood next to her, proudly displaying his fishing pole in one hand and a bucket for the fish in the other. Friends from Blue Earth had come along to capture Connie's first fishing trip on their camera.

Gentle giant that he was, Alfred always liked to stand up in the boat to cast his line, not realizing how he usually rocked the boat. This day was no different. As Alfred stood up to cast his line, the boat began to rock back and forth. Back and forth it went, and back and forth Connie went. She tried to hang on for all she was worth, but she had been caught unaware. It was no use, as Connie grasped for the edge of the boat, it rocked just enough, and she went head over heels into the lake.

Connie certainly hadn't learned how to swim, and under she went, gasping and sputtering. Luckily, one of the friends from Blue

LIFE ON THE FARM

Earth reached into the water to retrieve the terrified little girl, but she was thrashing so much they couldn't get a hold of her. As he grabbed for her again, Connie felt herself going underwater, sinking once, and then twice! She was gasping for air and choking. There wasn't even time to cry. And then, just as she was sinking further towards the bottom of the lake, she felt the powerful grip of Alfred's hand as it seemed to grab her from the depths of despair. "Air", she thought, but then suddenly the zipper on her overall went down and her body lurched forward again, and down into the water she went. This time she found herself sinking and struggling to get out of the water. She didn't know she was drowning!

Finally, Alfred was able to grab her scrawny little body and lift her back into the boat. As he hugged her tightly, he said, "I think we're done fishing for today!" He felt terrible that she had to experience fishing under these pretenses. The look on the terrified girl as he took her home told him that fishing was probably not something she cared to do again. Even though Alfred held her tightly on the way back to shore, the fear of the water never truly left her!

The days passed with Connie enjoying everything the farm had to offer. One day their dog, Lady, a beautiful brown and white fluffy Collie had puppies. Connie had been called to watch the birth. What a miraculous event for this now almost four-year-old to see. Seven puppies had come out of the mommy's tummy. She had counted each puppy with her mommy as they entered the world. Connie loved to watch the puppies snuggle up to their mommy to nurse.

One day when Annie B. Flugum came to visit, Connie was eager to show her the new puppies. "I named them all!" said Connie as she grabbed Miss Flugum's hand to take her outside to show her all the puppies.

"Well, I just bet you did," said Annie B. Flugum as she willingly went along with the vivacious four-year-old.

Connie and Annie B. Flugum sat down to play with the puppies and Lady, the ever-protective mother, jumped up and bit Connie on the face, cutting her lip. She learned a valuable lesson that day, and the next time Annie B. came to visit, Connie said, "We can't touch them right now! If you touch them while Lady is nursing, she'll bite you!"

"Oh, I see!" said Ms. Flugum as Connie chattered on, "I'm glad you remember when she bit your face. It looks like it is healing nicely."

"Yes, Daddy said mommy dogs don't like anyone touching their puppies, especially while they are nursing!" replied Connie.

"My goodness! That was certainly a learning experience!" said Ms. Flugum. She was a regular visitor to the farm, just as she had been at the orphanage. She was Connie's social worker from the Minnesota Foster Care system and she regularly checked on Connie's progress. She was impressed with how well Connie was fitting into life on the farm, but more importantly, she was impressed with how well Connie was thriving, living with Mary Lee and Alfred. She had made several visits to the farm over the past year and was always impressed with how Connie had grown and developed. She was no longer the scrawny little waif she remembered seeing at the orphanage.

As the grownups met in the living room, they all chuckled as they secretly listened to Connie chattering away in the next room. She spoke using her first name, and it seemed to preface everything she talked about. "This is Connie's home!" she would exclaim. "This is Connie's doll!" and "This is Connie's chair." Everything was Connie's. One day a visitor came to the farm, and Mary Lee overheard Connie talking to herself. "Miss Walker coming to get Connie. No! No! No! This is Connie's home! Connie's staying here!" She had most undoubtedly found her place on the farm with Mary Lee and Alfred, and they were tremendously enamored with Connie as well.

By the time she had been with them for six months, they were so impressed with this little imp who had entered their lives, Alfred and Mary Lee decided they wanted to start adoption proceedings. They spoke with Annie B. Flugum, the Social worker from the Children's Home Society of Minnesota, saying they were ready to adopt Connie. She was now just three months past her 4th birthday. "She's such a talkative little girl," said Mary Lee.

"Maybe that's an understatement!" Alfred jokingly commented, "She sure does ask a lot of questions!"

"At first, when meeting visitors, Connie is very shy, but once she gets acquainted, she becomes quite animated." said Mary Lee. "She loves reciting Bible verses, singing songs and conversing with friends." Both Alfred and Mary Lee spoke with pride about her participation in weekly Sunday School classes and how she is very fond of Bill, a neighbor boy who lives on the next farm over from theirs. Alfred and Mary Lee also were amazed by her imagination, "She loves having tea parties with her dolls." said Mary Lee.

"She has such a sunny disposition," commented Alfred, "And we're very eager to make her a part of our family." So, during the fall of 1937, Connie was officially adopted by Alfred and Mary Lee Bates, and she continued to learn more and more about life on the farm.

That summer Alfred and Mary Lee traveled to Decatur, Iowa, to introduce their new little girl to the Bates family. They were so proud to announce Connie's adoption was final. Several relatives were there, but Connie remembers Grandma Polly Twitchell Bates and Grandpa Will Bates. It was a huge gathering and Connie was amazed by all the grownups who came to meet her. How they all were related was something she would have to process!

"Isn't she adorable!" one lady remarked.

"You're going to have to fatten her up, Alfred!" said another.

"My goodness! Just look at those scrawny little legs! You'll definitely need to feed her!" joked another friend.

Later that summer, they went to visit Mary Lee's parents in Riceville, Iowa, where Grandma Margaret Yager and Grandpa Oliver Yager lived. "This is your Grandma and Grandpa," said Mary Lee.

"Grandma and Grandpa", repeated Connie. More new words to add to her brain! She had never known a grandma or grandpa in her life before and this summer she had met two grandmas and two grandpas! They had to explain that a grandma was mommy's mother or daddy's mother and a grandpa was mommy's father or daddy's father. These people were just as sweet as her mother and father, and it was easy to warm up to their kind souls. Grandma and Grandpa Yager doted on Connie and her eagerness for life. They laughed at her constant chattering and incessant questions. They loved seeing Alfred and Mary Lee so happy! Everyone adored Connie's animated gestures and sweet demeanor, and she loved being the center of attention! Even though Grandma Yager was ill during the time of their visit, she hated to see them go home. She had grown very fond of Connie in just one short week's visit. It was with great sadness the little family said their goodbyes. Later that winter, when Grandpa Yager became ill and passed away. Connie was happy to have Grandma Maggie come to their house for an extended visit!

Mary Lee, Connie and Alfred

GOD's HAND

Morning dew drops glisten atop blades of grass,
Creating a prism radiating a spectral mass.
Gentle rays of dawn capture God's loving caress.
Wonder of wonders I marvel at His tenderness!

Grandma and Grandpa Twitchell

CHAPTER 11

MATCHING RED DRESSES

MARY LEE HAD been a music teacher at Wells High school when she married Alfred Bates in 1928. She was a phenomenal vocalist and had studied at the Minneapolis School of Music, after spending a year studying music in Chicago before obtaining her degree in Music Education at the University of Minnesota. She married Alfred Bates in 1928 and gave up her career as a public-school teacher to give private piano and voice lessons in her home. She showed Connie the names of the keys on the piano and taught her how to play simple songs. Connie loved sitting on the piano bench next to Mary Lee. The closeness they shared felt so good. Eventually Mary Lee and Connie could play little songs together and sing together. Mary Lee was impressed that Connie accurately sang on pitch at the age of three! In fact, she even though Connie might have perfect pitch!

Mary Lee's voice students came to the house every week for lessons and Connie knew during those times she had to be very quiet and not disturb Mary Lee. Each night Connie was allowed time to practice the names of the notes with her mother and she diligently struggled to play just the right keys. When she made a mistake, it didn't sound right to her ears, and Mary Lee would patiently show her the correct fingering.

Connie loved Sundays when mommy and daddy would take her to church. They would often sing duets together, standing behind what was called, the communion rail. The railing had a beautiful red velvety curtain which ran the entire length of the rail at the front of the church. It was just Connie's height. The first time Connie attended church with them, they took her with them up to the front of the church, behind the communion rail. They took their places and instructed Connie to sit right smack dab between them on the floor while they sang their song.

Oh, they had amazing voices! In fact, some would say Mary Lee had the voice of an angel and Alfred's bass was as smooth as buttery chocolate. Connie loved listening to them sing! As they each took their place, they had intended for their well-behaved little girl to sit quietly right between them and listen to them sing, as they had practiced. However, out of sight, out of mind, or so Mary Lee and Alfred thought! As they began their duet, the congregation began to snicker. This was an unusual response to their solemn Sunday duet! No one had chuckled or laughed at them during church before, at least not while they were singing such a serious song! Trying to figure out what the congregation was snickering at, Alfred glanced down to see Connie lifting the curtain and peeking out at the congregation. Her curiosity had gotten the best of her and she had wanted to see who was watching. Although the congregation was amused, Alfred was not. Everyone in the church adored this little girl who had come to live with Alfred and Mary Lee, but Alfred believed that children had to learn respect and Connie very quickly learned she was no longer allowed to lift the curtain and look out at the congregation! In fact, she was banished from sitting behind the curtain, and was sentenced to sit in the front pew and act like a lady while her parents sang their duet! There, they could keep their eyes on her! They expected and demanded obedience!

One day there was a huge party at the church. It was Connie's adoption party and included friends and family from near and far. Everyone gathered around for a lovely picnic, even Grandma and Grandpa Yager had come to the picnic! It seemed like a birthday party to everyone else, but Connie had never had a birthday party before.

"Why is everyone here, and why am I getting presents?" Connie asked her mother.

"They're celebrating your adoption, Connie!" said Alfred. "You are now officially our little girl, and your name is now Sally Constance Bates, but we'll still call you Connie." Connie was amazed at this outward pouring of love. The church friends bestowed Connie with a little wooden rocking chair just her size, while others gave her new clothes. Life for this little girl, who had been hand-picked by Alfred and Mary Lee Bates was certainly changing. Connie loved them and they loved Connie. Final adoption papers were signed in 1937 when Connie was four years old.

Life went on quite evenly over the next year. Connie had learned to feed the chickens and gather the eggs. She had learned to milk the cows and steer clear of the pigs. She had learned Bible verses at Sunday School and learned to play the piano, albeit the playing of a five-year-old, but still her musical talents were starting to shine.

And then events started happening in the house which Connie couldn't understand. What was going on? So many people were coming and going to the house, and it wasn't the piano students and voice students. The piano students and voice students had stopped coming! Why were so many other people visiting their house? Connie knew her mother had gotten sick. It was very strange not to hear Mary Lee sing around the house.

And then momma went away. "Where is Momma going?" asked Connie.

"She's going to the hospital." said her friend, Dr. Barr.

"But when will she be back," Connie cried.

"She'll just be gone for a little while," said Dr. Barr. "Your Momma will be back soon." But a little while seemed like an eternity to Connie. When Mary Lee finally returned to the house, she couldn't talk. Connie had learned that Mary Lee's voice box had gotten sick and they had to take it out. She had laryngeal cancer, or cancer of her voice box. Mary Lee could no longer talk, let alone sing! How devastated she must have been as a performer and voice teacher!

MATCHING RED DRESSES

They gave Momma a little silver bell. The shiny little bell sat on the dark wooden nightstand on top of a beautiful doily Momma had crocheted herself. It was right next to her bed. Eventually, when momma felt better, she would ring the little bell. Momma would give that little bell a jingle whenever she needed something, whether it was a drink of water, a book to read or her crochet needles. Someone would always run to Mommy's room to see what she wanted. Momma would write down what she wanted on a piece of paper and the helpers would run off to get what Momma wanted. Connie wanted to help Momma, too, but poor Connie couldn't read or write yet. She had just started school and was only in first grade. But then Connie had an idea. She was good at drawing pictures and Momma loved seeing Connie's pictures, so off she went to draw Momma pictures. Mary Lee would smile sweetly at Connie, but she could never say anything. Momma's throat cancer had completely taken away any way of her talking to Connie. Connie watched as mommy and daddy wrote notes to each other. Every day they would tell each other how much they loved each other. Every day they would share what had happened and Connie would watch the love that her mother and father shared. They had a truly special relationship.

Dr. Barr came to the house many times over the next few months to check on Momma. Mary Lee seemed to be spending all her time sleeping in the bedroom. "Shhh!" Doctor Barr would say to Connie, "Your momma needs to rest." The hours turned into days and Connie was taught to be very quiet in the house. "Mamma needs to sleep," daddy would say. Some days Connie had gone home with Doctor Barr after he was finished with his house call checking on Momma. He was a strange gruff man, but he always spoke ever so tenderly to Connie. And then when her momma had gone into the hospital again, she had spent many days with his family. She hated to admit it, but she really did enjoy being with the Barr family, playing in their basement with all their toys.

One day Connie asked, "What is a hospital?"

Daddy explained, "A hospital is a place where they make people well." So, Connie anxiously awaited the time when momma would come home, after the hospital made her well. How strange it felt to have her mother in the hospital. She was used to going to church on Sundays and snuggling between her momma and her daddy. They had all been in church together every Sunday for the past few years. She had listened to her momma sing. Momma had the voice of an angel, and Connie missed hearing that beautiful voice next to her on the piano bench after dinner.

They had gone shopping together, buying red velvet dresses that matched. And they had just worn their matching red velvet dresses to church. It was only a few weeks ago. Was it only Thanksgiving?

Music was such a special part of their home and without her mother there, the piano lessons had stopped, and the voice students no longer visited. Connie didn't even feel like playing the piano herself without Momma. "Why has everyone stopped coming to lessons?" Connie asked. "Where is Momma?"

Daddy kept telling her "Momma is in the hospital. She will be home soon." Daddy had told her they would always be together. "Together always, and always together," daddy had said, but momma had never come back.

When Mary Lee had been brought into the house for the viewing, men had come into Momma and Daddy's bedroom and taken down the big bed. Daddy explained to Connie that the men were from the funeral home. After they had taken down the bed, they had set up a strange metal stand. Then they removed the window. It seemed like a very strange thing to do in the middle of winter in Minnesota. There had been a gaping hole in the bedroom. And then they brought in a large wooden box, right through the window. Daddy called it a coffin. He said that Momma's body was inside the coffin! When they opened it up, Mary Lee's body lay motionless inside the coffin. Daddy had tried to explain the complexities of death and funerals to Connie.

That afternoon, many people were at the house. Connie had been dressed in her red velvet dress and it wasn't even a Sunday. As she wandered through the crowd of people looking for her daddy, she wondered, "Where is he? Why hadn't he told me what was going on, and why were there so many people in their house?" Finally, she found daddy in the darkened living room. She wondered why the room was so dark. Then she saw that Daddy was crying. Sobs were racking his entire body. He was sitting there, sobbing with his head between his hands. This wasn't her daddy. Connie felt so lost. In her little voice she asked, "Daddy, why are you crying?"

"Oh, little one," he sobbed, as he opened his big arms so wide, enabling Connie to run into them. He clung to her and Connie felt his internal strength. His tears were so wet as she crawled into that familiar lap, completely enveloped by this gentle giant. She always felt so warm and safe with him. His love poured into her. Daddy had always made her hurts go away. Hadn't he just told her the other day when she skinned her knee, "Big girls don't cry."? Yet here he was, her daddy, crying real tears. She didn't know how to stop this hurt.

"Where does it hurt, daddy?" Connie asked.

"Oh baby! We've lost her. Your Momma won't be here anymore. The hospital couldn't make her well." Tenderly, he held her as he spoke to her, pouring out his own deep sorrow. Several times Alfred had to stop. The words were there, but the tears seemed to come too fast, and he couldn't speak. Through his sobs he told Connie how much he had loved Momma. "She's not coming home to us ever again," he said as tears streamed down his cheeks, "But we'll still love her. She was a wonderful mother to you, little one!"

"But where is she, daddy?" Connie asked.

"With God," he answered. "She'll always be with God. But I have you, and no one will ever take you away from me. No one! You're mine, Connie, and mine you'll always be. We're a team, Connie, and we'll be together always. Always together!" Then Alfred said, "We need to go say our goodbyes to your momma."

Daddy had taken her hand as the two of them later walked into the bedroom that memorable day to say goodbye to her Mother. Her Momma was so beautiful! The funeral director had dressed Mary Lee in a beautiful red velvet dress; the same dress that she and Connie had picked out together when they last went shopping together, a matching red velvet dress that Connie now wore. No words were spoken as daddy tightly held her hand, almost too tightly it seemed. Connie stood motionless as her father leaned over and kissed Mary Lee. Connie didn't want to say goodbye. This was not how her story was supposed to end. She truly loved Mary Lee and wanted to be with her always.

"Why is she in that box?" asked Connie.

"She's sleeping," daddy said, trying to assuage her fears.

"Can't she sleep in her own bed?" Connie had asked. "Why is she like that?" Connie kept asking questions. So many questions were running through her head. "What's a funeral? Will she stay there forever?"

Soon everyone left their house, even the funeral men had come and taken Momma's coffin back out through the window and then carefully replaced the window. Daddy explained to Connie that he had to leave for a couple of days. "Leave!" She had just seen her Momma leave and now daddy was leaving, too! "No, daddy! No! Don't leave me!" she cried.

Alfred spoke softly, "Connie, I have to be gone for a few days, but I promise I will come back to you." Hadn't they just taken her Momma away and now her daddy was leaving her, too?

Connie couldn't understand. She felt cold and shivered as she asked daddy, "Why? Why? Why?" But daddy said he had to go, and he would be back.

"You have to trust me, little one," he said. "I promise you I will come back, and we'll be together, always. You'll just have to stay with the Barr's one more time." When he was gone, there wasn't anyone to give her the answers she so desperately needed to hear. She watched from the safety of their warm house as the hired hand hitched a pair of horses up to pull the funeral coach down the driveway out to the main road. She watched as daddy followed in his truck close behind. The cold Minnesota winter had left mounding snow drifts across the driveway. Later, Connie would follow her parents through the snow as she was taken over to stay with Dr. Barr and his family, but she had never felt so alone in all her life!

Mary Lee was buried December 1940, in Riceville, Iowa, when Connie was just seven years old. Alfred had accompanied Mary Lee's body to her final resting place, buried next to her father. He realized that someday, Connie would have to be told the entire story. He'd tell her about his love for Mary Lee and their oneness together. He'd tell her how much they truly wanted Connie together. He was slowly feeling the impact of the loss, but he still had Connie. He'd made a promise to Mary Lee and himself, and to Connie, "No one will ever take her away from me." he had said. Alfred stood tall and looked straight ahead as they lowered Mary Lee's body into her grave. He knew what lay ahead for him and he knew what he would have to do.

CHAPTER **12**

A ONE ROOM COUNTRY SCHOOL

FEROCIOUS MINNESOTA WINTERS were unbearable! The wind would howl across the plains, the snow would swirl, and the temperatures would dip, sometimes well below freezing. Without any domestic help with Connie's care, Alfred would often take her along with him on his trips to the farms as an agricultural agent. One such trip to a client's farm took place during one of these cold winter days. The snow had already piled itself halfway up the telephone poles, but Alfred knew this farmer needed help. As the snow kept falling, the wind started blowing, and severe blizzard conditions soon made the roads impassable. When Alfred discovered he and Connie were stuck, he got out and started shoveling. He always kept a shovel in the back of the truck. "You stay inside," he told her. "I don't want you to get too cold." As he shoveled, he started sweating. And the more he sweat, the hotter he gets. The hotter he gets, he starts taking off his clothes, article by article, until he's shoveling snow in his underwear! Connie sat inside the truck trying to read, but she was giggling so hard she could barely follow the words as her book bounced up and down on her belly. When Alfred finally gave up, he opened the door of the truck to start putting his clothes back on. Once he was all dressed, he walked around to the passenger side of the truck, picked Connie up and carried her to a nearby farmhouse where they were invited to spend the night.

Heading to bed that night, Connie had to sleep in her clothes, and she could barely stand the stench of urine from the smelly bed she had to share with the farmer's daughter. In the morning, the farmer's wife cooked them eggs and sausage for breakfast, and then the farmer helped daddy pull the car out of the snowbank with his tractor. Connie was never so happy to be heading home, back to her clean house and delicious food. Luckily, daddy was a good cook!

At six years old, Connie was going into first grade, and she had to walk to school. But before she could even start walking down the country roads to the school, she had to walk the three-quarters of a mile lane that led to the main road. Just getting to school was exhausting.

Every morning the teacher would be ringing the school bell as the students arrived at the old white building. And every morning, the teacher greeted the students as they entered the building through the huge schoolhouse door, greeting each of them by name. "Good morning, Connie," she'd say. Connie like that. Once inside, the students would hang their coats on the metal hooks in the cloak room and place their tin metal lunch boxes on the floor under their coats. During the winter months, snow boots would be lined along the walls under the windows and mittens would decorate the floor around the old potbellied stove which stood in the middle of the room. One of the big boys, who sat in the back of the room, would have to keep the stove stoked with wood throughout the day.

At the front of the room was an old dusty black chalkboard. The teacher's desk also sat at the front of the room with a long bench next to it. There, the teacher could meet with small groups of students while others sat at their own desks and worked independently. This one room schoolhouse contained desks of every size facing the teacher's desk, and since Connie was the smallest student in the school at the time, she sat in the smallest desk at the front of the room. As winter approached, she was thankful her desk was near the stove as she didn't mind getting too hot from the stove, because she had gotten so cold and wet on her way to school!

Getting to school and back was the most difficult task of the day during her first year of school. First, she had to walk down the lane and turn onto the main road. There, she would meet other students who were on their way to the old one room schoolhouse. One neighbor boy, Ralph Piper, had a pony, and he would ride his pony to school, but Ralph was a bully and he would allow the pony to bite Connie whenever it got near her. You do remember, Connie wasn't fond of ponies! Ralph thought it was great fun to use the pony to tease her all the way to school. "Ha ha, Connie, the pony's going to get you!" he would taunt, and poor Connie would escape being bitten by the pony by running into the ditch filled with snow! When she thought she had run far enough ahead, she would come up out of the ditch, but along came Ralph and his pony, and down into the ditch Connie would run again. It seemed like an endless game of cat and mouse all the way to school; walk the road, down into the ditch, up onto the road and back down into the ditch, again and again. By the time Connie arrived at school, she was usually soaking wet and shivering with cold, not to mention, exhausted. Ralph seemed to take pleasure in tormenting her, and told her, "Don't you dare tell anyone, Connie! If you tell", he said, "I'll let the pony eat your hat and mittens!" Poor Connie. She believed Ralph, so she never told anyone until one day when daddy was waiting for her to get home from school. He noticed how wet she was and how she shivered with cold.

"What in the dickens are you doing on your way home from school to get so wet?" daddy asked her, and he demanded an explanation.

Connie finally had to tell her daddy what had been happening. "Ralph Piper is letting his pony bite me. I run down into the ditch to get away from him, and then he speeds up when I come back out of the ditch and I have to run back down into the ditch again to get away," she breathlessly explained. She told daddy everything! "He does it in the morning on the way to school and he does it every afternoon on the way home from school," she cried. "Every day I get soaked! He told me if I told anyone he would let the pony eat my hat and mittens!"

Alfred was aghast! He stood up and said, "Well, we'll just have to see about that!" He put on his jacket and hat and headed out the door. He went straight over to Ralph's house, just down the road and returned shortly. Connie never knew what was said, but the next day, the "pony teasing" ceased, and Connie no longer had to deal with getting soaked going to and from school.

Attending school in a one room schoolhouse meant that there were students of every age in the school, from first grade all the way through eighth grade. Connie just happened to be the smallest student in the whole school. That same year, two sixth grade boys and three eighth grade boys kept teasing Connie about being a slow eater. "Connie's a slowpoke," they would taunt. "Why are you always the last one done?" they chided. Every day they would bully her about how slow she ate her lunch. Unfortunately for Connie, the teacher was always inside the school and never heard the boys taunting her. It seemed that Connie never finished eating her lunch by the time the bell rang for everyone to go back to class. One day, the boys physically picked up the scrawny little first grader and carried her behind the outhouse. There, someone had pounded a huge nail, and one of the boys lifted her up and hung her up on the big nail by her blue denim overalls. There she hung, screaming and hollering, but everyone was inside the school and there was no one to hear her screams.

It wasn't until the teacher finally discovered Connie wasn't in her desk when she asked. "Where's Connie?" No one seemed to know. Finally, the teacher went outside, only to hear Connie yelling for help. Her tiny little voice screaming for all she was worth. Connie was mortified. She had had to go to the bathroom so badly that she had soiled her pants, and she was so embarrassed. The teacher caringly lifted her down and took her inside and helped her change her clothes. Connie never knew if those big boys got into trouble for their antics or not, but she sure hoped they did!

Mary Lee had passed away on December 6th and the first Christmas without her was just around the corner. Connie was looking forward to what Christmas would bring. Daddy had cut down a tree from the grove and brought it up to the house. Together they made popcorn and cranberry strings to decorate the tree, after Alfred had shown her how to use a large needle to thread each piece of popcorn and each cranberry onto the long string. He also helped Connie hang her stocking on the doorknob to her bedroom. After decorating their tree and hanging Connie's stocking, Alfred and Connie headed off to the little schoolhouse for the annual Christmas program. It was to be Connie's first solo, singing "Jolly old St. Nicholas". She loved the part that said, "Suzie wants a dolly," because she truly wanted her very own dolly. She knew she wouldn't forget the words, for she had practiced them diligently, over and over.

Just as she finished singing her solo, everyone heard a loud, "Ho! Ho! Ho!" from the front door. The entire schoolhouse full of students and parents turned to look. Santa had arrived at the tiny one room schoolhouse. He seemed like a huge man, dressed in a red suit and hat and he had a white beard. A large gunny sack was slung over his should, loaded with candy and nuts. Santa scooped Connie into his big arms and said, "Have you been a good little girl?"

"Yes! Yes! Yes!" Connie squealed, recognizing her very own daddy's voice!

"Shhh!" whispered Alfred, "Don't say anything about who I am, and we'll have a very special present of our own at home!" As he set her down, Connie beamed with pride. Oh, how she loved learning Santa at the schoolhouse was very own daddy!

First grade was finally over; ditches, ponies, potbellied stoves and hooks on the outhouse were all in the past, and Connie was ready for life to move on though she missed Mary Lee ferociously!

CHRISTMAS IS - - -

Lots to eat! Friends to meet!
Bells that ring while carols we sing.

A tree to trim with lights,
A cozy fire for chilly nights.

Presents to wrap and mail.
It's late, better shag my tail!

Christmas is love and caring,
With so many, it's great to be sharing.

The candles are lit, the tree's aglow,
Santa's arrival makes a hit! (He really exists, you know!)

I shed a few tears for loved Ones I miss,
But fond memories, for all the years

Bring a smile and good cheer.
I love every minute and look forward to another loving year!

Connie in first grade with Alfred and Lady.

CHAPTER **13**

LIFE GOES ON

THE FIRST SUMMER, after Connie's mother, Mary Lee, had passed away, was so different for Connie. It was hot and humid in Riceville, Iowa, where daddy had taken her to stay with her Grandma Maggie. She was Mary Lee's mother, and she would take care of Connie while her daddy worked, crisscrossing eight different counties in Minnesota for his agricultural seed business. It was the kind of summer where your clothes stuck to your skin, and all you wanted to do was sit.

Grandma Maggie adored Connie, and the feeling was mutual. Her house was filled with the aroma of lavender, and it seemed wherever Grandma Maggie went, she left a wafting scent of lavender behind her. Sometimes, Connie would just follow her around the house, sniffing her, hoping Grandma Maggie wouldn't turn around and see her sniffing! She loved the lavender scent wafting from Grandma Maggie's dresses, and Connie imagined that every pocket and dresser drawer was filled with satchels of lavender. Connie loved the smell of lavender from that time on!

At night, Grandma Maggie's old house creaked and groaned, and Connie was scared. She felt so alone. Daddy wasn't there to tell Connie everything would be all right. Daddy wasn't there to tell her not to be scared. And most of all, daddy wasn't there to sing her to sleep. She knew daddy expected her to be a big girl, but sometimes she would cry herself to sleep in her pillow, no one hearing her muffled sobs! She desperately missed her momma and now, her daddy had left her, too.

Sadly, Grandma Maggie had no idea Alfred would sing Connie to sleep when she was scared. Actually, Grandma Maggie had forgotten what little girls needed. It had been a long time since her own daughter, Mary Lee had been small. Losing Mary Lee just six months earlier left Connie missing her mother, and Grandma Maggie still trying to cope with the loss of her only daughter. She didn't have any other grandchildren, and subsequently had no dolls, or toys for little girls to play with. She didn't think of having a tea party with Connie, and she didn't even have books for Connie to read. So that summer, the two of them sat beside each other by the hour, with a mantra of "Knit one, pearl two," as Grandma Maggie patiently showed Connie how to maneuver the long knitting needles between her fingers. The feel of the soft yarn gliding along the inside of her hand reminded Connie of petting the sheep on the farm, and the gentle clicking of the needles was soothing to her soul. Grandma Maggie patiently encouraged Connie as she taught her to knit a blanket for her doll. Connie was so excited when daddy arrived at the end of the week, she couldn't wait to show him the blanket she had made!

"Daddy look what I did!" she squealed as soon as her daddy walked in the door.

"Wow! You two have certainly been busy," daddy exclaimed, as he examined the little yellow blanket Connie had knit all by herself.

"Grandma Maggie helped me," Connie said, "And she showed me how to make these cute little dolls, too. Let me go get them," she yelled, as she excitedly ran to the porch to retrieve the hollyhock dolls, she and Grandma Maggie had made. Returning with several flowers, Connie breathlessly explained, "Grandma took one flower like this, and she turned it upside down, and then she took another flower and attached it like this. All of a sudden, we had a little doll!

Aren't they cute, daddy?" She was so excited to show her daddy what she had made.

"I see," said daddy as he gave his little girl a big hug. "Grandma Maggie is a good teacher!" he said.

"What's in the bag?" asked Connie eagerly.

"Root beer floats," said daddy.

"I love root beer floats!" Connie exclaimed, as she intently watched Alfred pull the ice cream container and root beer bottles out of the brown paper bag. Grandma Maggie got the scoop for the ice cream and three tall glasses with three spoons. Then, the three of them sat down to enjoy root beer floats together. The cool ice cream felt refreshing as it slid down their throats, followed by the fizzy bubbles of the root beer as it tickled their noses. She was glad one of the hired hands had shown her father how to make root beer floats. Every weekend that summer, when her daddy came to visit her at Grandma Maggie's house, he would bring root beer floats for a treat. They tasted so good on those hot, humid summer days in Riceville, and they were exactly what Connie needed to let her know her father had been thinking of her.

Daddy also loved to buy oranges, and he even smelled like oranges! He would often buy a bag of oranges when he stopped for soda pop, and as he drove along the country roads, he'd peel the oranges and pop individual slices into his mouth. The next morning, sure enough, Alfred produced a bag of oranges for breakfast, and the aroma made her want to hug him. She loved the smell of oranges, but more importantly, she loved her daddy!

The weekend Alfred arrived to help Connie celebrate her 7th birthday, he announced that the two of them were going home, back to the farm. "Oh boy!" said Connie enthusiastically, "We're going home, and I can sleep in my own room!" She was ecstatic, but then Alfred dashed her excitement.

"We're just going for a visit to check on how things are going," he said. "We won't be staying there long. We're going to get your things, and you will be living with the Grangers during the school year," said daddy matter of fact. Alfred had arranged for Connie to spend her second year of school with the Grangers, a family who lived in town. Daddy further explained, "Arthur Granger is the Superintendent of Schools and Bernice Granger is a wonderful lady. They have a daughter named Polly, who is just two years older than you are. She'll be like a big sister. You'll love it there, and I'll be able to visit often."

CHAPTER **14**

LIFE AT THE GRANGERS

CONNIE WAS LEERY of this new situation, apprehension filling her with a new kind of fear. When she arrived at the Grangers, she was re-introduced to Polly and her parents, Arthur and Bernice Granger. She had known them as acquaintances from church, and they seemed nice enough. She and daddy would each have their own rooms while they lived at the Grangers. She met their housekeeper, Deena, who cooked new and wonderful different kinds of foods, and she and Connie became the best of friends.

Before Daddy, he assured her that he was not leaving forever. "This is just temporary while I work during the school year. In the summer we'll go back to the farm." he explained. Then he further added, "I'm a traveling salesman, and I have to travel for my job, but I'll visit you often." He tried to impress upon her that he was not abandoning her and if she needed him, she could always reach him on the telephone. "Remember, together always!" he had said and waved his hat goodbye.

Connie had taken her favorite belongings to the Grangers house. She took her doll, her cherished rocking chair, and a tea set for tea parties with Polly. She also took along her very own pewter dish, and her own spoon. Just like her daddy, Connie had a pewter dish and spoon tucked into the glove compartment. Alfred would often stop for ice cream when they were out driving on the weekends, so Alfred made sure Connie had her own spoon and dish, also. She also loved to use them for tapioca pudding, cereal or applesauce. Her favorite possessions were the piano books Mary Lee had given her.

Polly Granger was nine years old and going into the fourth grade when Connie came to live at the Granger's home for the start of her second-grade school year. Polly played the violin, and Connie loved to watch her. Since Connie had learned some piano from Mary Lee, she quickly showed Polly the piano keys and how to play songs on the piano. Together they sang songs and enjoyed playing their instruments for each other. Connie loved having a new sister to play with!

When Daddy came home and heard the two of them playing together, he said, "I think it's time for Connie to learn how to play the violin, too!" Daddy and his brother and sister played the violin when they were little, and Daddy knew just what to do. He gave Connie his old violin; the one he used when he played for street dances in Iowa. Then he made arrangements for Polly to take Connie along to her violin lessons. Connie would start violin lessons from the same teacher Polly was using. Little did Connie know this violin would change her life forever!

Living with the Grangers opened a new world for Connie. The Granger family lived in a duplex connected to the Christianson family. They had several children and that meant built in playmates for Connie. Walking to school was nothing new for Connie, but now she no longer had to deal with Ralph and his pony or the one-room schoolhouse bullies. She loved her new lunch box and proudly set off for second grade, content to know she had a family to live with, friends to play with and a daddy who loved her very much.

Connie and Polly had become like sisters, sometimes fighting and sometimes getting along like best friends! Connie enjoyed the beautiful hand-me-down dresses Polly had to offer, but she secretly longed for brand new pretty dresses of her own. Polly's stature was much larger than Connie's small, thin petite frame, so Connie would often have to wait for Polly's dresses to be altered.

After school, Connie and Polly would practice piano and violin before playing outside. There were so many kids in town to play with and every girl had so many dolls. It made Connie's head spin. The Schultz's down the street had nine children, and everyday there were tea parties, games and friends to play with. It was an interestingly new time in Connie's life. Luckily her daddy visited often.

For her eighth birthday, Daddy gave Connie a brand new two-wheeled bicycle! "Thank you, daddy, thank you!" she cried! Oh, my was she eager to learn how to ride her new blue bike. Her birthday was at the end of August, and by mid-September, the training wheels had been taken off, and Connie discovered a whole new world. She loved riding around the little community of Wells, Minnesota. She would ride to Wells Park and back every day, and she would ride by the church, the high school and all around the neighborhood. She had never felt such freedom!

Connie's 2nd grade picture.

Polly Granger and Connie Bates

CHAPTER **15**

THE BULL AND THE BARN

AS AN AGRICULTURAL agent for eight counties around the Wells, Minnesota, area, Alfred felt bad about leaving Connie. After having her stay with Grandma Maggie, the first summer after Mary Lee passed away was very difficult for both father and daughter. He missed Connie terribly. But then leaving her with the Grangers during her second school year was even more difficult. He couldn't bear the thought of leaving Connie again, so he decided to have her spend the summer with him, riding along as he made his County Agricultural visits. During the day they would travel from county to county as needed, and at night they would go back home to the farm and Connie would sleep in her own bed.

Connie loved these summer trips around Minnesota. They'd have mashed potatoes and gravy every night if they wanted, and after their evening meal they both loved having ice cream while they listened to their favorite programs on the Old Philco radio! "Only the shadow knows…," Connie would whisper in her scariest voice.

Daddy had his favorite ice cream spoon tucked away in his glove compartment so if he wanted a treat during the day, he could stop and each get ice cream anytime, anywhere! Daddy loved ice cream! He had even gotten Connie her own spoon to join him in devouring his delectable treats as they spent their summer days on the road.

As Connie grew older, she learned her multiplication tables during their summer road trips, with daddy patiently listening to her recite all her times tables. She loved being with daddy, just the two of them sharing their days together on the open road, talking and singing. One of her favorite songs was learned with daddy while they were traveling. He taught her one of his favorite songs. They sang "His Eye is On the Sparrow and I know He watches me," together. It was their favorite song to sing together because Daddy taught her how to harmonize while they went down the Minnesota highways and byways. With her perfect pitch, she quickly caught on to harmonizing and soon they were singing many other songs he and Mary Lee had sung together. She loved hearing his deep bass voice singing the melody while she learned to sing the alto or tenor parts.

Sitting in the truck while Alfred went into the agricultural offices gave her plenty of time to read, and fortunately she loved reading. In fact, reading was an adventure in and of itself for Connie! She loved learning new words and visiting new places through books! And when Daddy got back into the truck, she loved telling him about the places her books had taken her. The Nancy Drew series was one of her favorite series to read. Like Connie, Nancy Drew had also lost her mother, and like Nancy Drew, Connie was a confident and independent young girl! She was destined to be a superwoman, at least her father encouraged her, telling her she could accomplish whatever she set her mind to! So, Connie's summers were filled with ice cream, mashed potatoes, Nancy Drew mysteries, multiplication tables, songs and adventures around the eight different counties of Minnesota. Traveling with her father provided her with a multitude of favorite times and fond memories and three months of sleeping in her own bed!

During the summer, she and daddy would head to the farm in the evenings. Alfred had other side jobs to tend to on the farm. He did most of the artificial insemination for the county as he had the bull for the cows, and the "hawg" for the sows as he used to say. The old hand-cranked telephone on the wall would constantly ring with people requesting the services of these two "gentleman donors".

TOGETHER ALWAYS

Connie would don her overalls and rubber boots, and she would ride along with daddy on his "insemination trips", learning another aspect of life on the farm.

The County Inseminator position job became quite a large job, so Alfred hired a German immigrant to help retrieve the semen from both the males. This man's name was Yogi Pusch. Connie would always giggle when she heard Yogi's name. To her, it sounded funny! But something else fascinated Connie about Yogi. He refused to take a bath! He told Alfred, "Pigs wash in a tub, and I'm not a pig! I need a proper shower!" This caused quite a dilemma for Alfred.

"How in the world is he going to get clean?" Connie asked her father when she found out that Yogi wouldn't use a bathtub. She had grown up taking a bath several times a week, so Connie was quite worried Yogi would start smelling like the pigs he worked with! Soon she watched with devoted admiration as her daddy built a shower in the barn. Never having seen a shower before, Connie was totally intrigued with this new bathroom facility. "How does it work, daddy," she asked.

Daddy explained that Yogi would stand under the shower head and running water would pour out over his body. Then Yogi would use soap and running water to wash his body. Connie was amazed. Luckily, Yogi loved his new shower. He hated smelling like the pigs and once the shower was installed, he never entered the house smelling like the cows or pigs like some of the other farmers in the area. Connie was glad Yogi insisted on always being clean, and she was very impressed with the new shower, although she was never brave enough to try it herself!

Connie always went along when daddy and Yogi would head out for an insemination job. She loved nestling between these two large men as they rode along in the truck to their next job. Once, when daddy went into a local farmer's house for a cup of coffee after the insemination, Connie followed right behind him. As she entered the kitchen behind her father, she saw a huge pig hanging from a hook. Right there in the kitchen was a huge pig, hanging upside down with

THE BULL AND THE BARN

one hoof wrapped in rope, suspended from a hook in the kitchen ceiling! A huge washtub sat below the pig, and the blood was dripping right into the washtub. The room was filled with a yellow cloud, and it smelled like fat frying in the pan. The farmer's wife was rendering the lard to be used for cooking as they butchered the pig. The farmer, seeing Connie's eyes wide as saucers, explained, "The blood dripping into the tub is going to be used for sausages, and then the sausages will be packed into the pig's intestines." Connie gulped as the farmer went on, "The fat from the pig is boiling on the stove to make lard. I bet you've used lard to cook at your house, haven't you?" he asked rather matter of fact.

Connie nodded her head as she secretly thought, "Oh my God! They are going to eat this stuff!"

As Connie made her daily trips to the barn to milk the cows, she noticed an odd-looking item hanging on the wall of the barn. Sitting on the little stool, gave her plenty of time to peruse the landscape inside the barn. This bag had weird looking pipes coming off from it. "What's that?" Connie asked her father when he came in to see how she was doing.

"That's a set of bagpipes," replied Alfred, knowing full well there would be a barrage of questions! "They belong to your grandpa William Bates. This used to be his barn."

"What are they for?" asked Connie.

"They make music. They're from Scotland." replied Alfred quite matter of fact, hoping to stave off any more questions.

"Can I make music with them?" asked Connie.

"No," said Alfred. "They're not for little girls."

Connie knew not to push her daddy any further, but every time she went out to the barn to milk the cows, she would longingly look at those bagpipes and wonder how they sounded. Sadly, Grandpa Will passed away before she ever got to hear him play those bagpipes.

The insemination phone calls were constant, and Connie loved going along. Each farm trip provided new experiences at every turn and she learned so many new things, but sadly, every time they had to go on an insemination trip, they had to get the bull into the truck. It seemed they were always trying to get the bull up the chute, down the chute or out of his stall or into his stall. The bull was a very stubborn animal with huge horns, and he was most definitely a challenge to maneuver around, so taking him to another farm was always a challenge.

One day the bull decided he wasn't going to stay in the barn anymore. He bolted, taking the barn with him! Away he ran, making his escape, his large horns catching the sides of the fragile old barn, taking it right along with him! It was the funniest picture anyone on the farm had ever seen. There was Dad and the hired hand chasing the bull all over the farm, through the garden, down the lane, to the gravel road, up through the grove, and back into the pasture!

"Leave him there!" puffed Alfred as he came back from his adventure. "I'm too tired to force him back up to the barn. He'll come when he's hungry." And sure enough, daddy was right. When the bull got hungry, he made his way back to what was left of the barn. Everyone slept well that night; Dad and Yogi were exhausted from chasing the bull all over the farm and Connie was exhausted from laughing!

The very next day Alfred ordered lumber to build a new barn! As soon as the lumber arrived, Daddy and Yogi proceeded to build a new barn! They poured concrete footings and then they made the concrete floor which included manure runs. The new manure runs were the same width as a shovel which made it so much easier to clean them. They put stanchions in so that each animal had their very own stall. Every single stanchion locked at the very same time, by flicking one switch! Connie was thrilled to see how easy it would be to lock the cows into their own stalls, all at the same time. She no longer had to go along and lock each cow into its individual space. What a delight to just pull one lever and see all the stanchions close at the same time!

The concrete block walls were next and stood eight feet high followed by the wood above, forming the final walls with the hay loft above. "I love it daddy!" Connie cried, looking around at all the truly

THE BULL AND THE BARN

modern state of the art equipment her father had put into the new barn. It was incredible for a barn of the 1930's. Alfred had built the best. Secretly, Connie wondered where the bagpipes had gone. She never asked about them and no one mentioned them again. But the best thing about the new barn was that the bull never had to leave the barn again! All the semen extractions were done in the barn. Alfred had built the bull his very own area surrounded by three brick walls. Artificial insemination had made its way to the Bates farm.

It was a chilly fall morning, just after the barn was complete, when Daddy announced that Uncle Arthur, his brother, was coming to visit. Uncle Arthur owned one of the farms, but daddy and a hired hand were the caretakers. Uncle Arthur was arriving by train, traveling all the way from Pasadena, California, to Mankato, Minnesota! Daddy took Connie with him to pick up Uncle Arthur at the train station. When Arthur stepped off the train, he looked like a big teddy bear, dressed in an enormous black fur coat and a fur cap which had flaps over his ears. His black-rimmed glasses framed his face, and his voice sounded identical to daddy's voice. Uncle Arthur had the same soft deep bass voice, and when he smiled, his whole face crinkled up! Connie loved his laugh. It was so infectious everyone would start to laugh with him. Affectionately, he'd pick Connie up and carry her around on his shoulders, occasionally throwing her up into the air. Then he'd give her tummy a tickle, and the two of them would end up having a raucous laugh together. Oh, how they had laughed together! Uncle Arthur would laugh, and Connie would giggle, and then everyone around them would join in until the room was filled with laughter. Uncle Arthur was probably her most favorite adult in the whole wide world.

Uncle Arthur said, "Connie, I heard that you play the violin like your daddy. How about if you play a song or two for us?" Connie quickly went to get her violin to play a song. Daddy and Uncle Arthur were so proud of Connie when she was able to step forward and play her violin for them, taking the perfect stance and holding the bow properly, she impressed her new audience. "You're very good!"

Uncle Arthur said, and Connie beamed from ear to ear. She wasn't afraid to play in front of others. In fact, she loved it!

"Thank you." she said, accepting the compliment graciously.

"You did a wonderful job," said daddy, "but now it's time to say good night." Connie was exhausted and told Uncle Arthur and daddy good night. Sadly, that was the last time Connie ever saw her Uncle Arthur.

Alfred and Arthur had a huge argument that night and never spoke to each other again. The brand-new barn had been a huge bone of contention between the two brothers. Their parents had given their three farms to their three children. Alfred and Mary Lee had lived on the farm they had inherited from his parents, along with Connie. Arthur, his brother, and Helen, their sister, owned the other two farms. Hired hands lived on Arthur and Helen's farms because they both lived in California. Alfred, who lived in Minnesota, managed all three farms with the help of three hired hands who lived on the other two farms. The three Bates children shared the income and expenses from the three farms. When the bull destroyed the barn, it was Alfred who made the call to upgrade the barn. Arthur had disagreed with Alfred's state of the art upgrades to his new barn and felt Alfred was spending too much of their money on his own barn. Arthur had refused to pay his share of the cost for the new barn, thus creating the huge argument between the two. Sadly, the two men never spoke again!

Connie begged her daddy to patch up the hard feelings with Uncle Arthur. "Please daddy!" she begged. "Please tell Uncle Arthur you're sorry. I want him to come back!" She loved Uncle Arthur, and desperately wanted to have this fun man in her life. But daddy was a proud, stubborn man, set in his ways, and he refused to concede to Uncle Arthur's demands. She continued to plead with her father over the years to put his animosity aside, but her father refused. It made Connie so sad. She never saw her Uncle Arthur again. But one day, right before her high school graduation, Connie received a letter and a package. Uncle Arthur had sent Connie a gift with a very long letter enclosed, encouraging her to continue to use her wonderful talents and always keep her beautiful smile and infectious laugh! She still adored Uncle Arthur.

THE BULL AND THE BARN

When Connie was nine, some neighbor kids were visiting the farm. They all went out to look at the new barn. Everyone decided to swing from the hayloft rope, jumping down into the cattle yard below. Connie was little for her age and she was apprehensive as she watched the others swinging and jumping, but when someone double dared her to jump, she decided to give it a try. She grabbed the rope, swung out over the cattle yard and dropped. As she landed with a thump, she thought. "Oh, oh! Something is very wrong!" She hobbled around for two days, limping here and there when finally, daddy took her to the doctor's office to see what was wrong.

"She has broken both arches," said the doctor. "She will have to wear these special orthopedic arch supports in her shoes. And I hate to tell you, the only shoes to support these orthopedic arches are these orthopedic shoes."

"Ugly, grandma-looking shoes!" Connie moaned. "I don't want to wear those ugly shoes!" Oh, how she hated the dark brown oxfords the doctor suggested her father buy for her. She prayed and prayed for her feet to heal quickly and grow so she could wear different shoes, but at nine years old, her feet didn't grow much more! Alas, she was stuck with those ugly grandma looking oxfords throughout her entire school days. Every time she went to the shoe store, she would longingly look at all the cute new styles. She saw all the different colored shoes and adorable boots, but sadly she was stuck with her "gramma" shoes until high school graduation. Right before high school graduation her father took her to the shoe store. How excited she was when he told her she could buy any pair of shoes she wanted! Connie picked out a pair of white high heels! What glee she felt when she walked down the aisle to "Pomp and Circumstance" for graduation wearing those white high heeled shoes!

Alfred loved spending time in his new barn, and one day Connie encountered Daddy pacing back and forth, up and down the alleyway of the new barn holding a book. He seemed to be talking to someone, but there wasn't anyone around. She wondered. What on earth is he doing, and politely she asked, "Daddy, who are you talking to?"

Alfred chuckled. He explained to her, "I'm practicing. I have to recite the Masonic rites at a graveside service for a friend who is a Mason."

"What's a Mason, daddy?" asked Connie, very perplexed. She'd never heard that word before.

Alfred replied, "Well now, that's a serious question. Let me see..."and he paused to think a minute. "I'd say a Mason is a person who believes in God and wants to be a good man who helps others. The man who died was a Mason and I'm going to recite this speech at his graveside service after his funeral." He had worked at memorizing the entire service and Connie was so impressed with her father as he paced back and forth in the barn, reciting the Masonic rites. She was also impressed with her dad's love for God and his dedication to help others. Over the fifty years he was a Mason, he received many honors and awards, rarely missing a meeting! Connie adored his spirit towards this society and how he shared his knowledge with others. In her mind, he was the wisest man in the world!

One constant in the Bates home was the blare of the Philco radio. The announcer would report the prices for pork, beef and corn! Some days dad would say, "It's time to load up the calves and take them to the slaughterhouse, Connie." Other days corn prices would be high, and Daddy would say, "Connie, get your coat! We need to load up the truck with corn and go to the elevator." High prices on corn meant loading up the truck and she was amazed at how the corn came pouring out of the chute. She loved to ride along to the local elevator just as much as she loved riding with her father on insemination trips. It was fascinating for her to watch as they weighed the large truck with a load of corn and then weighed the empty truck after the corn was offloaded. It was Connie's job to calculate how many bushels of corn were sold. Simple math came easy to her and she offered to do calculations for the other farmers who were waiting in line. Dad thought this was a very meaningful task for her and he would proudly tell everyone around the elevator to have Connie do their calculations!

Connie after having her appendix out at 15.

CHAPTER **16**

STORIES WITH DAD

ALFRED GREW MUCH of their own food, whether it was in the garden or from the trees and bushes he had around the farm, but with all this food came harvesting, pickling or canning for use during the winter. As each crop was harvested, Dad and Connie would get to work canning or pickling. There were cucumbers, which were then pickled. Connie was responsible to put the pickles in the big clay crocks and store them in the basement for winter. She had fun burying the potatoes and carrots in the cellar to keep them fresh throughout the winter.

Getting the apples down from the tree was always a challenge, but the pies they made were worth the effort. The smell of fresh baked pies was amazing, and so was the aroma that wafted through the house when it was time to make strawberry and raspberry jams! Although it wasn't easy, Connie knew eating the jam was worth the effort!

Some afternoons she would trot through the ditches looking for asparagus and cut the stalks and bring them home to be canned. She learned how to can peaches, pears and chokecherries for pies, but along with the wonderful aromas came the job of washing the fruit jars and their lids. Everything was then put into the pressure cooker. The sugar beets were plentiful and brought them lots of sugar during the harvest. Corn and peas were never ending and what they didn't need, they sold to a canning factory on the edge of town. The worst part of canning was making sauerkraut and pickled pig's feet. Those pungent aromas were not as pleasant as those from baking pies, and Connie hated looking at those jars of pickled pig's feet stored on the shelves of the cellar.

There was always one time of year when Connie was ecstatic, and it wasn't her birthday! When the circus came to town with its big tent and carnival stalls Connie was the happiest. The most exciting part was the fact that the harvesting and canning had to be halted for the day! The entire day's work stopped! Off she and daddy would go to visit the big top. She loved hearing the calliope playing its music, as if it were calling her right down to the big top, itself. There were all kinds of animals to see with the ringmaster calling out the acts. The cotton candy was scrumptious, and she loved the hustle and bustle of the people smiling and enjoying the summer, but the best thing about the circus coming to town was the fact that canning and pickling ceased, even for just a day! No pickling, no washing and no dealing with the hot steam from the pressure cooker! The best part of summer was when daddy would take her to the circus!

In between haying and thrashing, Dad would fill the sprayer and head out to the corn fields to spray the mustard weeds. Connie would tag along, learning another aspect of farm life. Together they would eat their lunch sitting alongside the road, spending hours chatting with each other throughout the summer. Alfred would tell Connie about his childhood, growing up in Decatur, Iowa. He talked about his family and about the long trip his family made when they moved from Iowa up to Minnesota. They had loaded all their belongings into a covered wagon and made the arduous trip together. Now just a three-and-a-half-hour drive for the 243 miles between Decatur, Iowa, and Wells, Minnesota, but back in the early 1900's, in their covered wagon, it had taken his family seven days! They carried their own food and water, with his mother cooking on a camp stove every night. He told Connie about the bed that he slept in. It had been taken apart and then loaded onto the covered wagon and brought to Minnesota. All of them had slept on the mattress laid out in the covered wagon. He also told her about the dresser with the marble inset. It was their original kitchen cutting board and storage center.

TOGETHER ALWAYS

Connie treasured these stories, because she knew the actual furniture daddy was telling her about. It was now in the farmhouse she lived in. His trip reminded her of the stories she had read in a book called, "Little House on the Prairie." She loved reading about Laura Ingalls and her family and her very own daddy had lived it.

Alfred shared with her the fact that his family had a dairy farm at the edge of town, and every Sunday, he and his brother Arthur, would get up early to make homemade ice cream. Then, the two of them would deliver all the orders for ice cream early Sunday morning. "We had to get up awfully early to make that ice cream, deliver it to our customers and still be back in time to go to church!"

"I'll bet that's why you like ice cream so much!" said Connie, enthralled with his story.

"That's for sure!" he said. "Most people had an ice box by then, and the ice blocks were delivered on Saturday afternoons. That meant when we delivered ice cream on Sunday mornings, their ice box would be cold and waiting for our ice cream delivery!"

One day Alfred told her about the street dances, and how he used to play his violin with his brother and sister. "Oh! We had so much fun playing together!" he chuckled. The stories her father told her were tremendously intriguing now that she had learned to play the violin. She could only imagine that she and Polly could have so much fun! Connie's imagination soared. Oh, how she had wished she could have heard his family sing and play!

Her dad's stories of WWI were fascinating, and Connie always had questions, wanting to know more and more explicit details about his times growing up, and his time serving in the war. One night, after finishing catechism class at the church, Dad and Connie came home and turned on the radio to hear President Roosevelt announce, "We are at war!" It was December 8, 1941. Connie was just 8 years old and she watched as her Daddy sat right down on the couch and cried. This was only the second time Connie had seen him cry, the other time was when he told her that Mary Lee had died. She knew her daddy must be very, very sad. He explained, "America will never be the same, baby! I wish I wasn't so old; I would re-enlist and go fight this war!" He was such a proud veteran! Every Veteran's Day and Memorial Day, daddy would march in the local parades, and Connie would stand along the road as proud as could be to see this great man's pride in his country. He'd always marched in the front row of every parade with the other WWI Veterans. He instilled a deep sense of patriotism in Connie, which would run as deep in her as her love for him. Together they loved their country.

Even though Daddy loved America, he had learned to speak both high and low German, so Connie learned a few words of each language. Yogi, the hired hand, was married to a lovely German lady and she taught Connie to sing "Silent Night" in German. "Stille Nacht, Heil'ge Nacht" she would sing. "Alles schlaft; einsam wacht." The words of this sweet song were used for many Christmas Eve church services to come. And every Christmas, this song, along with the red poinsettias and the beautiful candles made Connie think about her Christmas with Mary Lee when they were supposed to wear their matching red dresses. And then her mind would wander to her biological mother, the mother that gave her away. What was she doing now? Did she have other children? And then the ever-present question would surface, "Do I look like her?"

Daddy's deep bass voice would bring her back to reality. "Manners, manners, manners!" Daddy would say, always demanding she act like a lady. "Sit up straight!" he would say. "Don't talk with your hands. Keep your elbows off the table." Connie would get so exasperated. He was always fussing at her about how she presented herself. "Sit still," he'd chide. "Listen quietly." he'd whisper. He never ceased to amaze her in his attempt to turn her into a lady. "Remember who you are!" he'd say, constantly fussing over how she behaved.

"But why?" thought Connie, "I'm not a lady yet! I'm only eleven years old!" Connie knew she had to keep her thoughts to herself. She knew she could never tell her father her innermost thoughts. She knew his answer would be, "Remember who you are and who you represent! You are a very special child and you have been handpicked!"

Connie age 16.

CHAPTER **17**

THE WICKED WITCH OF THE WEST

THE SUMMER CONNIE turned twelve had many new experiences which proved difficult for her. Having been around the cattle and horses all her life, Alfred now felt she was ready to help on the hay wagon. The wagon itself was a twelve-foot-long flatbed trailer. It had a wooden lattice and a wooden ladder at the front of the flatbed which enabled the driver to climb high above the horses and look out in front of the horses. This is where the driver would hold the reins. With the hired hand as her guide, Connie had watched as he easily controlled the horses. They had stopped to load bales; Connie was watching as the bales were hurled up onto the flatbed of the wagon. Suddenly, the hired hand yelled, "Connie, it's your turn! Take 'em up to the corner and stop!" As she climbed up onto the ladder and grabbed the reins, the sleeping horses became startled and took off at full speed. Without her even making a sound, the team of horses bolted, going through the fence, into the ditch, over the road and into another ditch. Connie screamed as the team broke loose from the wagon, and the hired hand yelled, "Let 'em go, Connie! Let 'em go!" The wagon immediately came to a full stop with Connie hanging on for dear life. The team of horses kept right on going down the road!

In horror, Connie watched as the horses galloped away at

breakneck speed. Luckily, she wasn't thrown off the wagon or too badly hurt. However, the bruises she received on her arms from hanging onto the reins were rather tender. They seemed to be a "dead giveaway" that something wrong had happened, but she never discussed the truth about the wagon and the horses with her dad! It seemed to be her secret with Yogi, unless the he had secretly told her father. Her Dad just thought Connie was limping because she was exhausted from heaving those heavy bales. Truth be told, her limping and the bruises were from hanging onto the reins for dear life. Thank goodness the hired hand had told her to let go when he did, or she would have been in much worse shape!

That summer Dad also announced, "It's time for you to start cooking for the harvest team! Twelve extra hands will be eating dinner with us today," he said. "Here's the chickens!" He plopped six chickens on the counter and headed out the door.

The big meal of the day was at noon when the extra hands required their nourishment to continue working for the rest of the day. All the people who came to help with the harvest would expect to be fed at noon. Dad had wrung the necks of six chickens and plopped them on the counter. Connie looked at them and thought, "I can do this, I've watched Mrs. Parriott do this before!" So, she put the chickens into the pot of water and waited until she could pluck them. She started peeling potatoes and snapping beans, feeling rather proud of herself! When the chickens were thoroughly boiled, Connie took them out of the boiling water and plucked them all by herself. Feeling even more confident in her cooking expertise, she took out two large roasters and started the stove. She plopped three chickens in each roaster and put them in the oven. As she continued to peel potatoes, Mrs. Parriott stopped by to check on Connie to see how she was doing with her first meal alone.

Opening the oven, Mrs. Parriott gasped, "Oh my goodness sake! You haven't taken the innards out of the chickens!" Closing the oven door, Mrs. Parriott quickly grabbed some potholders and took the roasters out of the oven. Then she proceeded to take the chickens out of the roasters with her bare hands and set them on the counter! She made quick work of cutting the innards out of the chickens, plopped them back into the roasters, and silently slid them back into the hot oven! "There!" she said as she dusted her hands together. Then she took Connie, and the chicken innards outside, and together they buried the chicken innards in the grove behind the house!

"Oh my," said Connie, "you've certainly saved the day! Do we have to tell daddy?"

"Absolutely not!" laughed Mrs. Parriott! "Your father will never know!" Thank goodness Mrs. Parriott had arrived when she did. Connie's learning experience would never be forgotten! Many years later she told her father how Mrs. Parriott had saved her during her first cooking experience for the hired hands, and she and her dad had a good chuckle, but at the time Connie and Mrs. Parriott had their own little secret!

Mrs. Parriott was a wonderful resource throughout Connie's growing years. She lived on the next farm around the corner and was delighted to have a "daughter" to nurture. It seems she was always there when Connie needed help. She taught Connie how to cook and bake while Mrs. Purdy taught her how to sew. Between Mrs. Parriott, Mrs. Purdy and Mrs. Granger, Connie had a wonderful group of role models to guide her throughout her life. Even though she never grew up with a mother of her very own, Connie had many special women in her life who taught her many wonderful skills.

Mrs. Parriott was also Connie's Sunday School teacher. Connie and Billy Parriott were very good friends, often holding hands under the table during Sunday School. But sadly, Mrs. Parriott remarked one day, "Don't you think you can marry my son. We can't have him marrying a bastard child!" Connie had not known what Mrs. Parriott was talking about. She'd heard the word growing up, but here was Mrs. Parriott using that word. Not realizing what it insinuated, Connie went home to ask her father what a bastard was.

"Oh, my goodness!" Alfred was taken aback. One of the people he had so completely trusted with Connie's care, had called her a horrible name. He explained to Connie, "A bastard child is an illegitimate child. That means your birth mother and father weren't married when you were born." Alfred had always told Connie how special she was and that she had been his chosen child. He explained, "There are people who don't understand that we wanted you and you are very special. I'll have to speak to Mrs. Parriott."

Of course, the incident with Mrs. Parriott only brought Connie's questions to mind, but they were questions she could never ask anyone. "Who do I look like? Where is my real mother? Why did she give me up?" Alfred had always told her she was adopted and how special she was, but that didn't stop Connie's mind from wondering, "Who do I look like?" All her friends looked like their mothers. Connie kept wondering what her mother looked like. If she met someone on the street, she'd wonder, could that lady with auburn hair be my mother. Now she had to contend with the fact that she was a "bastard child" and may never know who her mother was!

Just after her twelfth birthday, Daddy surprised Connie and said, "I'm getting married, and we'll be moving back to the farm! You won't have to stay with the Grangers anymore!" Connie was excited to move back into her own room for the school year, and she was excited to ride the school bus. She was happy to be able to go into town to go to school. She'd been spending school years with the Grangers, and she loved them. For five years Connie had spent the school years living at the Granger's house. She had spent the summers and weekends traveling with her father and helping him on the farm. Although the Grangers were very good to her, she was truly excited to be on the farm full time again. But Connie was also excited about a new woman coming into her father's life. Alfred had been dating Cora, a local beautician. Connie also knew Cora's sister, Minnie, who was Dr. Barr's nurse. Dr. Barr had taken care of Connie's mother five years earlier when she had gotten esophageal cancer. Minnie was always so sweet to Connie, so she figured Cora would be just as sweet!

Unfortunately, Cora, the new woman in Alfred's life, wasn't at all like Minnie, and she certainly wasn't sweet like Minnie! In fact,

THE WICKED WITCH OF THE WEST

Cora wasn't at all what Connie had hoped for, or expected. Connie had grown to love Minnie, with her sweet voice, and Mrs. Parriott with her kind patient ways, showing her how to cook and bake, and she loved the soft-spoken Mrs. Granger and her lovely tea parties. But Cora! Well, Cora fit the epitome of the wicked stepmother, immediately demanding Connie call her "Mother". Cora very easily could have played Joan Crawford in the movie "Mommy Dearest", a woman who was tremendously callous and abusive to her adoptive daughter. Connie knew Cora wasn't her mother. Mary Lee had adopted her, and Connie had called her mother. She wasn't about to call Cora, "Mother". In fact, Cora's demeanor made Connie wonder even more who her mother was and what she looked like. In fact, Cora taught Connie one of the most important lessons of her life; she learned what she never wanted to be when she became a mother!

Cora was very jealous of the relationship between Connie and Alfred. Over the nine years Connie and Alfred spent together, they had become quite the duo. To say they had a close relationship was an understatement, and Cora did not want to share her new husband with this twelve-year-old child. Sadly, what Cora didn't realize was the bond between father and daughter was far greater than she would ever understand. They had been best friends, supporting each other through life's major calamities, growing and learning about life together. Cora would nag at Connie about every little thing, and then one day Cora told Alfred that Connie had lied. Alfred, being the very wise man, he was, listened to the events unfold. Listening to Cora, he said, "I need to talk to Connie about this!" After listening to Connie's story, Alfred went back to Cora and said, "I believe Connie is telling the truth and you are lying to me!"

Cora became unhinged and angrily exploded, screaming, "You believe her, over me?"

And so, it went, every time Cora would tell Alfred Connie had done something, he would listen to both their stories, and invariably, he would believe Connie, trusting she would never lie to him. He knew she would always tell him the truth when she was confronted, and eventually he figured out that Cora would lie to try and get Connie into trouble and out of her life! She was mad because Connie refused to call her, "Mother."

One day Cora confronted Alfred and demanded the adoption papers be amended to have her listed as "Connie's owner!" Alfred explained to Cora, "Slavery has been abolished in the United States for years, and you are not going to be Connie's owner! There are no owners in this household!" He further explained that he was Connie's "father", and the original adoption papers would stand as written. Mary Lee was the adoptive mother and that would not change. This made Cora livid! She wanted legal rights to be able to control Connie. She had no love for Connie, and Alfred began to understand that fact. He also began to realize what a controlling, conniving woman she really was. This argument over ownership was truly the beginning of the end of Cora's relationship with Alfred.

Being able to live at the farm during the school year presented its own set of obstacles. Every morning at 4:30AM, Connie would get up out of bed and start her day. Oh, how she hated the smell of the barn in the wee hours of the morning! First there was the manure and then the acrid smell of DDT, a pesticide that was used to keep the bugs off from the cows. It was sprayed all over the cows and it smelled like gasoline. The smell of the barn in the morning certainly held its own aroma, and it was putrid! After milking the cows, it was Connie's job to bring the milk to the house for pasteurizing. While the milk "cooked" in the pasteurizer, Connie would get ready for school and then she would practice her violin. When the milk was done cooking, she would make her daddy a huge breakfast! Daddy had made their own lard and butter and Connie loved the smell of the lard as it heated in the pan. "There's nothing like the smell of bacon as it sizzles in the pan," she thought, getting a dozen eggs ready to be scrambled in the large cast iron skillet. She was amazed at just how much her father could eat every morning. While she scrambled the eggs, she sliced bread from the loaf she had baked the day before. It smelled so delicious all by itself, but the best part of breakfast was fresh strawberry jam she had learned to preserve. She set the jam on the table for her father. They loved sharing breakfast together. After eating breakfast with her father and washing the dishes, Connie would head to the bus stop. She was always the first one to get on the bus in the morning and the last one to get off at the end of the day.

After school she would do her homework before going out to help get the cows back into the barn for milking! After milking, she would start the evening routine of practicing her piano and violin lessons while the milk "cooked" in the pasteurizer. After supper and the dishes were done, if time permitted, she would join daddy to listen to the radio. They often listened to mysteries or comedies if they weren't listening to the news. It was a grueling routine which happened, rain or shine, sleet or snow, but Connie didn't know any differently. Her days were always busy! She only saw Cora in the evenings while they listened to the stories on the radio.

Somehow the Bates family still managed to attend several church meetings in between their jam-packed days. They were always at both Sunday morning and Wednesday evening services, and even some events in between. Somehow, she managed to finish her chores, do all her musical obligations and be at church on time! Connie loved being busy and she loved the routine. In fact, she thrived on the routine of the farm and being with Alfred!

But Cora wasn't thriving on the farm! She grew tired of her daily drive into town on the gravel roads to her beauty shop in downtown Wells, Minnesota. Eventually she insisted they all move into town. She owned an apartment above the Red Owl Grocery store. Her beauty shop was down one landing from the apartment, over the store. People would go through the door on Main Street and climb a flight of stairs leading up to the beauty shop. From there, Connie and her father would have to turn and go up another flight of stairs to their apartment. It had two bedrooms, one for Alfred and Cora and one for Connie. This would become their home for several years while Alfred was married to Cora. And there, Connie no longer had to be the one up at the crack of dawn to milk the cows, but she did have to get up at the crack of dawn to practice her violin.

Wanting a well-rounded woman, Alfred took Connie on a canoe trip from Grand Portage, Minnesota to Kakabeka Falls, in Ontario, Canada. She learned how to launch a canoe, paddle a canoe, pick up the canoe and carry it over her head. It was a wonderful experience spending time with her father and his friends. The days were busy and sometimes wet, while evenings were spent drying off by the campfire. Meals cooked in that old iron skillet were extra special. The homemade lard turned the freshly caught trout into a gourmet feast! The tall pine trees provided a beautiful canopy over the open fire, sometimes swaying in the breeze. Alfred, or one of the tour guides, would tell scary ghost stories as they all huddled together around the campfire. Connie would shrink down farther into her jacket and snuggle closer to her father as the stories got more and more scary. And then they would sing campfire songs. She loved to listen to her father's voice as it gently soothed her to sleep. She truly treasured this special time spent with her dad in the woods.

When they returned from their camping trip, Yogi, the hired hand, decided Connie was now old enough to start herding the cows. After all, she was thirteen heading onto fourteen years old. Surely, she would know what to do. She had been helping him get the cows home every night. Herding cows back to the pasture seemed to be the next step in learning about farm life. Not knowing exactly what this job entailed, Connie figured it couldn't be too difficult since she had watched Yogi do it many, many times. Off she went, bravely herding the cows down the road. Regrettably, Yogi had neglected to show Connie how to turn the cows around the corner. The Bates farm was located on a corner, and when the cows smelled the fresh new corn in the neighbor's field at the end of the road, they headed straight across the road and into the cornfield and started chowing down on the neighbor's corn! There was no fence to stop them, so Connie ran to get her dad and Yogi. "Dad! Dad!" she cried, "The cows have gone into the cornfield across the road!" Daddy, Connie and Yogi jumped into the truck, and the three of them drove the old truck right down into the cornfield, going through the corn in order to turn those cows around. It was quite a fiasco with much arm waving and yelling involved!

Oh my! Those cows were so sick from gorging on so much corn! They were physically bloated, and each cow had to be treated individually. It took Daddy and the Yogi a long time to get all the cows treated and back to feeling normal. Yogi never let Connie forget about herding cows! He'd teasingly say, "Hey, Connie, it's your turn to herd the cows!" and then everyone would have a good laugh. Connie also had a good laugh, but she also learned how to turn those cows at the corner and they never let them get into the neighbor's cornfield again!

During her teenage years on the farm, Connie continued violin, voice and piano lessons. Her first concerts were performing as the entertainment for the Masonic Lodge. She felt so privileged to be able to perform in such a prestigious location. One time when she was nervous about performing, her father told her, "Just imagine the audience is naked!" Connie giggled. Daddy always had a good sense of humor.

Sometimes daddy would drive her to Albert Lea, Minnesota, for private voice lessons, while he went to a Masonic Lodge meeting. When she was a junior and senior in high school, she would ride the train the 31 miles from Wells to Mankato, and back again, all by herself to have private violin lessons. When she was asked to play with the symphony at Gustavus Adolphus College in St. Peter, she was ecstatic! Having won her regional high school music contests, she was sent to Minneapolis to try out for the All State Orchestra and there she became the first chair violinist and concert mistress! Her dad was so proud of her, and Connie was so excited. She was to stay in Minneapolis for the rehearsal day and the evening concert, which meant she would get out of her chores on the farm for at least a day! Performing in Minneapolis with the orchestra, Connie was truly in her element and loved every minute of it! Alfred hoped that she would someday pursue a music career because she was indeed talented.

Piano lessons, however, were a different story. Piano lessons took place at the convent in town with the Catholic nuns administering the weekly lessons. Many people have described lessons with the nuns.

"Nuns are tough," they would say. "Nuns are mean!" others would report, but those people didn't know Cora. Cora, Connie's stepmother, was far nastier and malicious than any of the nuns! She was a strict taskmaster, who demanded perfection.

On one occasion, one of the nuns asked Connie, "Why do your knuckles look all red and sore? What on earth have you been doing?"

Connie shyly explained, "When I'm practicing, my stepmother stands over me and watches. When I make a mistake, she cracks my knuckles with a ruler and makes me start the song over. I try to play the song perfectly, but when I don't, she is always there to crack my knuckles! This week's lesson was tremendously difficult, so my knuckles were cracked more than usual!"

Another time, the nun asked Connie, "What's wrong with your hands, dear? Why are they all red and blistered?" The nun was very concerned and thought maybe Connie needed to see a doctor. Luckily, Alfred was the one who picked Connie up from her piano lesson at the convent that day. When Alfred arrived, the nun approached him, "I think you'll need to take Connie to the doctor. Her hands have been badly blistered." Alfred looked at Connie and demanded to know how she had gotten her hands blistered.

Sheepishly, Connie showed her dad her blistered hands and explained, "Cora didn't want me to use her dish towels on the black cast iron skillet, but I forgot. As soon as I had started to use one of her dish towels on the skillet, I realized what I had done, and stopped using that dish towel right away, but Cora saw what I had done. She started yelling at me. I told her I had forgotten, and that I was sorry, but she didn't believe me. She said I had ruined her dish towel on purpose and that I would have to clean that towel all by myself. She made me use straight liquid bleach and scrub the towel on the old washboard until it came clean." By now Connie was in tears and Alfred was appalled! When they got home, he immediately confronted Cora.

"Why do you think Connie's hands are all red?" he asked Cora.

Cora replied, "Well, you know those nuns, Connie has been whipped for lying before. This time she obviously put her hands behind her back, and they got blistered along with her rear end! You know Connie always lies!" Knowing the truth about the dish towel and liquid bleach, Alfred confronted Cora with her lie.

"You're the liar here," said Alfred! "You know she burned her hands in the bleach cleaning your precious dish towel."

"How dare you believe her over me!" Cora screamed! It was as if WWI had started all over again with the yelling and screaming that ensued! Cora left that night, storming out of the house screaming, "You seem to love her more than me!"

The next day Cora got her revenge. As the campfire counselor for Connie's troop, she drove to each home of the campfire girls in her troop and told each girl and their mothers that Connie was a liar. She said Connie wasn't allowed to be in her campfire troop anymore. Cora single handedly alienated all of Connie's friends and their mothers! Then, she proceeded to come back to the house and get Connie's Campfire bolero. Next, she began to destroy all of Connie's achievement badges. Connie had sewn each badge onto her campfire bolero by herself and was very proud of her accomplishments, but Cora plucked each one of the badges off and began cutting them up. Connie was devastated and ran out of the room! "How could anyone be so cruel?" she thought to herself. She never participated in campfire girls again, and Cora resigned as a counselor that fall.

Cora's marriage to Alfred lasted five long years, from the time Connie was twelve, until she was seventeen. Five long years of dinners where Cora would say, "Connie, tell your father to pass the mashed potatoes."

Five long years of her father saying, "Connie, tell Cora to pass the gravy." Five long years of daily arguments! Five long years of constant hassles! And five long years living with a wicked stepmother! Connie wanted nothing more than to escape this woman's cruelty. Finally divorce papers were drawn up and Cora was on her way, but she wasn't entirely out of the picture.

Connie started working for the Vernig brothers; Dr. Mark Vernig and Dr. Dick Vernig. They had their private practice in Wells,

Minnesota. Connie started by babysitting for their children. Once they got to know how responsible and intelligent Connie was, they started having her work in their office as well. When Alfred started divorce proceedings with Cora, Connie was going into her senior year of high school. Due to Alfred's job as a traveling agricultural agent, Connie no longer wanted to live with Cora in her apartment over the Red Owl Store, and she couldn't stay at the farm without any transportation. She no longer wanted to live with the Grangers as she felt too mature for that! She needed a place to stay in town so she could attend high school and work for the Vernig brothers. Dr. Vernig had helped Connie get a job as a nurse's aide at the hospital, working evenings, but she still needed a place to stay.

Luckily, the Purdy's had a room above their photo studio on Main Street and offered Connie an opportunity to rent the apartment during her senior year of high school. This presented itself as the perfect place for Connie to live, being able to walk to the high school and to the hospital. The Purdy's were a wonderful family and were very understanding of Connie's situation. They knew Connie's situation with Cora.

Courageously, Connie worked several nights a week from 11PM-7AM and then attended high school during the day! Both doctors were instrumental in helping Connie earn her way. They knew her dream was to become a nurse, and they knew she had been accepted into the Nursing school in Albert Lee, MN. They knew all the arrangements were made for Connie to live in the dorm in the fall when she went to nursing school there.

Everyone who had known Connie while she was growing up in Wells, went out of their way to help her. Everyone except Cora. Cora knew about Connie's intentions of attending nursing school in Albert Lee, so she rented an apartment there. Then she contacted the nursing school behind Connie's back and cancelled Connie's reservations for the dorm. Next, she called Connie and insisted Connie come and live with her in her apartment in Albert Lee while she attended nursing school. Connie firmly stood her ground and refused to stay with Cora, but she quickly found out the damage had already been done. Her reservation for a place to stay in the dorm had been cancelled. Sadly, she decided she didn't want to live in the same town with Cora and continued to live in the Purdy's apartment throughout that summer after she graduated. Unfortunately, her dream of attending nursing school was thwarted by Cora and her finagling ways.

CHAPTER 18

A TORNADO VISITS WELLS

ON AUGUST 17, 1946, Connie had just received her new piano, which was supposed to be her thirteenth birthday present. This would enable her to practice her violin in the morning and her piano in the afternoon while they lived in Cora's apartment. Unfortunately, the weather had a different birthday present in store for the town of Wells, Minnesota. It was early Saturday evening, and many of the farmers had come to town to do their usual Saturday evening socializing, going from car to car visiting with each other, and chatting about their week and how things were going. Many others were in the theater across the street from the Red Owl store. Still others were in Cora's beauty shop getting the final touches for their Saturday evening festivities. A few clients were still in the beauty salon, some had curlers in their hair, while others were just getting a fresh comb out before going out to a Saturday evening on the town. Everything seemed quiet. In fact, it was too quiet.

The rain was not unusual for that time of year, but the hailstorm that came up changed the weather pattern. When the hot humid air in Minnesota meets with the cold air coming down from Canada, it destroys nature's equilibrium and causes a tornado. Luckily, the rain and subsequent hailstorm forced many of the Saturday evening visitors to seek shelter in nearby basements. Deena, the cook who Connie had grown up with at the Granger's, was now cooking for

Cora and Alfred. She had just finished the evening meal and was doing the dishes. As she looked out the window over the sink, she noticed the sky turn an awful chartreuse green. Then she saw the black storm clouds heading their way. But it wasn't just any storm clouds she saw. She came running out of the kitchen yelling, "There's a tornado coming this way! We've got to get to the basement!"

Connie and Alfred quickly followed her as she scrambled down the topflight of stairs. As they reached the landing where Connie's bike had been parked, Connie watched in horror as the wind whisked her brand-new bike straight up into the air and out of sight. Seeing Connie frozen, staring wide-eyed at her disappearing bicycle, Alfred grabbed her arm, and the two of them hustled into the beauty shop. There, Deena had already announced the approaching tornado, and Alfred and Connie helped to scoot ladies out from under dryers, or out of chairs, and maneuvered them towards the basement. They could already hear the screaming of the people from the street below.

Before they rushed out of the beauty salon, Connie had a bird's eye view of the green skies and approaching black funnel cloud. It was heading straight towards the theater across the street. Alfred called for Connie to get away from the window and they hurriedly raced down the final flight of stairs, Alfred making sure everyone was ahead of him as they scurried to get to the basement of the Red Owl store. Hurrying as quickly as they could, they found themselves trapped in the stairwell as the sound of a locomotive train passed over their heads. They all hunkered down together. The tornado was on top of them and was ripping a destructive path through the little town. The screaming from the people below rang in Connie's ears as the tornado's locomotive roar passed over them. They felt the entire building shudder as they huddled together in the stairwell. Silently they each wondered, "What's happened? Would the building collapse on top of them? Would they survive?" And just as quickly as the locomotive sound swept over them, it was gone. But the screaming from the people in the street continued to ring in Connie's ears.

Everything had an eerie feeling as they ventured outside to look around at the destruction. They saw the roof of the movie theater collapsed on top of the movie screen, and the front brick wall had been destroyed. Later Connie read that Bill Heath, the theater manager and Gordon Danks, a police officer, had been standing in the doorway of the theater when they saw the storm approaching. According to the Wells Mirror, the local newspaper, some 300-400 people had been inside the theater watching "Night Train to Memphis", unaware of what was going on outside. When Bill and Gordon realized what was happening, they raced inside the theater, yelling for everyone to take cover under their seats. By the time they reached the rear of the theater, the lights had gone out and they were all in total darkness. Luckily, Bill and Gordon were able to keep people from running towards the lobby where a wall of bricks was being thrown about by the high winds. Once the sound of the locomotive had passed, they used their flashlights to look around, and discovered amazingly, no one in the theater was killed, though several were injured.

As Connie and her dad looked around, they saw cars stacked on top of other cars, and a wooden two by four board had been stuck directly into a tree trunk. Bricks and glass covered the cars as well as the street. The little town of Wells looked as if it had been bombed. The entire Main Street was cluttered with pieces of buildings on top of cars with bricks and broken glass strewn everywhere. There wasn't a business in town that hadn't been destroyed. And if those businesses didn't lose merchandise during the tornado, they lost most everything that night from the subsequent rain that followed, due to all the roofs having been ripped off during the tornado.

Alfred took Connie upstairs to look at their apartment where they discovered a portion of the cornerstone from K.C. Hall had been carried the length of two entire city blocks and dumped onto Connie's bed. The shudder they had felt while huddling in the stairwell had been the cornerstone landing on top of their building, caving in the roof. If the tornado had occurred two hours later, Connie would have been killed while sleeping in her bed! Her brand-new piano had been placed up against an inside wall and only received nicks and scratches, but with the subsequent rain that followed the tornado, her brand-new piano was destroyed.

Without a roof on their apartment, Alfred knew they had to find shelter somewhere else, so the little family headed over to the Granger home. As they were walking, the power went out and the night became completely black. Connie had never seen the little town so dark. Alfred carefully led the way through the dark rainy night, precariously skirting their way around fallen trees and electric wires knocked down by the tornado. By the time they arrived at the Granger home, the Bates crew was soaked to the bone, and shivering from the shock of their ordeal. The Grangers were prepared to welcome their good friends. They had already retrieved lanterns stored in the basement for just such occasions and had hot chocolate heating on the stove. Since the Bates family had been frequent guests in their home, Alfred knew they had room for them to snuggle in for the night.

As the family headed to their own beds, Connie shakily asked, "Will we have any more tornadoes tonight, daddy?"

Realizing his young daughter was terribly frightened about another tornado on its way, Alfred assured her, "Since it has started to rain, there will be no more tornadoes tonight! Get some sleep and we'll see what we find in the morning." Connie, however, wasn't convinced and remained leery, struggling to get to sleep that night, with the screams of the Wells citizens still ringing in her ears.

The next morning the National Guard was called in to guard the town. The cleanup was completed quite quickly as the entire town seemed to pitch in and cut away trees and move debris to the side of the roads. No outsiders could venture down Main Street, but as business owners, Cora and Alfred were able to go inspect their apartment and the beauty salon. On their way back to the apartment, they found Connie's bicycle nestled under a car about two blocks from Main Street. It was still rideable, and Connie was elated! Everywhere they turned, trees were uprooted, and cars were overturned. "How in the world did we get to the Granger's house last night?" Connie wondered.

TOGETHER ALWAYS

As they reached Main Street in the daylight, it was even worse than the evening shadows had made it seem the night before. Going back to the beauty shop, they found their canary, amazingly still in its cage, although it had been blown from the front window to the back porch. Upstairs in their apartment they discovered Connie's little dog, Chita, who had been placed securely in the bathroom of the upstairs apartment, was gone and the bathroom window was open. During the storm, Chita had been sucked out of the bathroom window and carried several blocks across town. She was found cowering in the corner of Mrs. Beckman's porch. Fortunately, Mrs. Beckman knew Chita belonged to Connie and they were reunited Sunday afternoon.

At the age of thirteen, Connie was fascinated with the power and destruction a tornado could cause. She had never seen anything like it in her life, nor did she ever want to experience one again! She saved every single newspaper article she could find and collected many pictures from the Wells tornado of 1946, making quite the journal of her experiences. The fear of the green skies, the quiet stillness of the trees, and the sound of an approaching locomotive still draw her back to the memories of that tornado. Remembering that fateful day in Wells, Minnesota, just before her thirteenth birthday created quite a memory.

Cars were parked on top of each other.

CHAPTER **19**

AN UNEXPECTED BIRTHDAY PRESENT

DURING HER TEEN years, Connie was sent to Campfire Girls Camp at Camp Tanadoona in Chanhassen, Minnesota on Lake Minnwashta. Alfred hoped she would learn to swim, especially after the memory of her falling out of the fishing boat and nearly drowning! She did finally learn to swim her last summer there. In fact, she learned how to swim, dive and even retrieve a cup from under the water, but somehow the fear of drowning never left her, and she always remained apprehensive around water.

Right before Connie's fifteenth birthday, Connie had a horrible stomachache. Finally, fearing the worst, Alfred took her into Dr. Barr only to discover that Connie needed her appendix out. After the surgery she experienced a side effect from the anesthesia; her hair around her hairline started to fall out. Unfortunately, for Connie, she ended up having a second dose of anesthesia when she broke open the scar while running hurdles in high school track and field meet. She was very dismayed with her ninth-grade picture which showed her hair falling out!

On Connie's fifteenth birthday, Alfred decided she was now mature enough to learn more about her biological parents. "I have an envelope for you," said Alfred. "I think you are old enough and mature

AN UNEXPECTED BIRTHDAY PRESENT

enough to learn about your birth parents." Connie slowly opened the manilla envelope and took out the papers. Her daddy had always told her she was adopted. "Handpicked," he had said. He had always told her she was special. She had always known she had another mother and father, after all, this was the reason Mrs. Parriott had called her a bastard child. But now, right here in front of her, were the papers that would tell her who her birth parents were. She looked at it apprehensively. Questions about these people flooded her mind and now, here in this envelope were the answers to her questions. The envelope said, Minnesota Children's Home Society, St. Paul, Minnesota. It was addressed to Alfred E. Bates. As she opened it, she read, "File #7671". There it was in black and white, information about her birth mother and her birth father and all their relatives. All her relatives!

"Sally's mother was seventeen years of age when Sally was born. She was of Swedish and Norwegian descent and Protestant faith. She went through eleventh grade in school. A mental test given to her rated her as being "bright". Her parents separated when she was a young child, and she has been shifted around from one place to another. As a result of this she became rather unmanageable. Persons who have known her, speak highly of her ability. One person described her as being a very good worker, faithful, dependable, willing, clean, pleasant, honest and truthful. At one time she was given a test which was supposed to show clerical ability. She rated as having superior ability, and as having a high degree of speed and accuracy. She has dark brown hair, blue-gray eyes, is five feet, five inches tall and weighs 140 pounds.

Sally's mother had a brother who completed high school and then did odd jobs. He died accidentally at the age of twenty-two. A sister is twelve years of age and a half-sister is two years old. These people have always been in good health.

Sally's father was twenty-eight years of age when Sally was born. He is of Scotch-Swedish-English descent and was a protestant by birth, though he has just recently become Catholic. He was raised on a farm. He finished high school. He took a pre-medical course for a few years and later took up nursing in a private school. He has worked as a nurse in doctor's offices. He plays the violin in a dance orchestra. He has always been in good health. He is of medium height, slight build, has dark hair, dark eyes and seems to be an intelligent person.

Sally's father has two sisters. The elder, twenty-six years of age, attended college for two year and is now in charge of thirty-five stenographers at a large bank. The younger sister, who is nineteen years of age, is in her sophomore year at a state university studying to be a public-school music teacher."

On and on Connie read about her maternal grandmother and her family, and then her paternal grandmother and her family. She finally had physical descriptions and nationalities. The papers even told her what many of them were doing for a living, but she was still haunted by the one question she couldn't shake; "Who do I look like?"

"Thank you, daddy!" she whispered, but she knew he would never know the deep yearning in her heart to know who her mother was and what she looked like. She could never tell him how much she longed to know more. There were no pictures, only descriptions. She desperately wanted to see a picture of her mother. All her friends seemed to "look like" someone in their family and no one had ever said, "You look just like your mother!"to Connie. She still had the nagging question gripping her mind.

Alfred leaned over and said, "I want you to know, you are my daughter and you are loved more than you will ever know. No one will ever replace you, but I know someday you will want this information. It isn't much, but hopefully, it will answer some of your questions." He gave Connie a huge hug and she tearfully put the papers in a safe place. She and her dad truly shared a special bond, and he was giving her as much information as he had available to him. This was truly an unexpected birthday present.

Connie at 17 – Graduation picture

CHAPTER **20**

SHATTERED DREAMS

DURING CONNIE'S SOPHOMORE year, she started dating Jimmy Wordelman, but he was very shy and introverted, and not at all Connie's type, so they broke up. Then in her junior year, Jimmy's older brother, Rex Mitchell Wordelman came home from college, and he started pursuing Connie. Rex was a college sophomore who was studying Medical Science at the University of Minnesota. He was more serious in his relationship with Connie than she was. He had been called home from college by his father. It seems his father, who was a funeral director, needed a certificated mortician to keep his funeral business up and running, so he asked his son, Rex, to change his major from Medical Science to Mortuary Science. All Rex needed to do at that point was complete a course in Mortuary Science and pass the test for certification, which he promptly did. Rex had been engaged to a girl named Janet for two years and it seems he was jilted by her about the same time as he was called home to Wells. He came back to his hometown, where he became a substitute bus driver for his father, as well as the mortician for the Wordelman Funeral home. He was just 19 years old and Connie was just 16. His dream of becoming a doctor had been shattered by his father's request to return home, so he decided to make the best of it.

As the substitute bus driver for his father's bus route, Rex would kindly greet Connie every morning, "Good morning, Connie! How was your evening?" he'd say. And every afternoon as she got off the bus, Rex would say, "Have a nice evening." Enjoying the attention from an older boy, Connie thought she knew Rex well. After all, she had dated his younger brother, Jimmy, who was one year older than her in school, and she had gotten to know Mary Kay and Garry, his younger sister and brother, as well. Jimmy had been very quiet and tremendously shy, but Rex was just the opposite. He was outgoing, friendly and chivalrous, making sure she was well looked after. She was the first one to board the bus in the morning and the last one to get off in the evening, so she watched him as he politely greeted and said goodbye to all the other students.

One Sunday, he drove a school bus for the church youth group who were going to the roller-skating rink. That evening while at the roller-skating rink, Rex insisted Connie skate with him the entire evening. She knew it was because she was an excellent skater, even able to go backwards when others she was with were not as skilled. They looked like quite a cute couple as they rhythmically skated together during the couple's skate. Eventually he asked her to go out on a real date. He seemed fun to be around, always willing to impress her. He was always clean and didn't smell like some of the other country boys who lived on farms. He was also a skilled swimmer and a football player when he was in high school, and she knew he was a good student because he had been attending classes at the University of Minnesota to become a doctor! He'd also scored the highest on his test for Mortuary certification. But what Connie didn't realize was that sadly, his dream to become a doctor had been shattered when his father called him home to become a mortician for the family funeral home. Instead of becoming a doctor, Rex had completed the Mortician's certification his father had wanted and was never able to finish medical school as he had hoped.

It was 1950, the Korean War was raging. Rex didn't want to go to war like many of his friends were doing. He had joined the ROTC at college in Mankato and was afraid he would have to go fight in Korea, too. Unbeknownst to Connie, Al Wordelman, Rex's father, suggested he marry Connie and get her pregnant as quickly as possible. "That way," he explained, "you can get a deferment and you won't have to go to Korea." Rex had threatened to move to Canada to avoid the war, which would have put his father and the funeral home in a bind, so his father's plan was set in motion.

Rex immediately requested Connie's hand in marriage after she graduated from high school. "Can't we please get married?" he begged. "Can't we?" He continuously begged Connie to get married. Over and over he would ask her. Sadly, for Connie it seemed like the perfect solution. Her father, due to some unrealistic course of action on Cora's part during the divorce, forced her father to not be in Minnesota during the week. He could only visit Connie on Sundays. For Connie it meant she could get away from Cora's demanding and menacing eye. After all, if she were married to Rex, Cora couldn't stand in her way, and Connie wouldn't have to pay for her apartment, plus she could continue working at the hospital. Although Connie had no idea about Rex's motivation to rush the situation, her depression over living arrangements, nursing school, and Rex's constant coercion to marry him, made an early marriage seem like the perfect solution! For Rex, the fact that he might be able to avoid going to war seemed like the easy way out.

Connie had wanted to become a nurse, giving up a very magnificent music scholarship in the hopes of pursuing a nursing degree. After all, she was an outstanding violinist for her age, and a scholarship to Gustavus Adolphus was waiting for her. In fact, the biggest argument she ever had with her father occurred over that music scholarship! It broke her father's heart to know she wasn't going to pursue a music degree! Oh, how he wanted her to use that music scholarship and follow in the footsteps of Mary Lee. He knew she was an excellent violinist and pianist and she would make a wonderful music teacher just like Mary Lee. But with nowhere to go after graduation, and Cora upsetting the dorm arrangements at the nursing school, Connie decided to escape by marrying Rex.

After his divorce from Cora, Alfred had gotten a job in Ames,

Iowa. Due to the Minnesota divorce laws at the time, Alfred refused to sell the three farms and liquidate his assets in order to keep Cora from taking everything. Cora was livid, thus trying to get Connie to live with her. With the divorce finalized, Alfred was not allowed to be within the state borders of Minnesota, except on Sundays for visitation with Connie. So, one Sunday, Connie explained to her father that Rex had been begging, "Dad, Rex keeps begging me to get married. He keeps saying, 'Can't we please get married?'. He's constantly begging me, and I've finally agreed! The wedding is planned for Sunday, August 26, so you can be there and give me away!" Connie would turn eighteen on August 22! She had three months to plan the wedding!

All their friends stepped up to help make the wedding plans. Money was exchanged and plans started rolling. Connie's friend, Joannie, helped Connie find a wedding dress in Albert Lee. It was a beautiful tea-length lime green dress with a delicate tulle overlay. Joanie purchased a bridesmaid's dress in a rosy pink color and Connie made her own lacey hat with a small veil to cover her face as she walked down the aisle. L.D. Parriott, Jr. was Rex's best man. Polly Granger, who was like a sister to Connie, played the violin before the service, during the service and after the service while Beverly Lovelace played the organ. Connie walked down the aisle of the Evangelical United Methodist Church in Wells, MN, to beautiful organ music, and all the ladies from the church, who'd known Connie her entire life, planned a reception for the young couple. Connie wore her first pair of white high heeled shoes that were purchased for her high school graduation, which had only taken place just three months prior to her wedding!

It all happened so fast, it felt like a big blur to Connie. There she was on August 26, 1951, standing at the back of the church with her father, ready for him to walk her down the aisle. Her mind was spinning. What would it be like to have her mother here? Would her mother let her go through with this whirlwind marriage? With uneasiness creeping in, she told her father, "I can't do this, dad. I don't want to marry him! I don't think I truly love him, and everything is moving way too fast. My gut is telling me to run!"

"Everyone gets cold feet!" dad had explained, and he chided her into going through with the wedding. "Everyone's here," he said, "and it's all set up." Proudly, he escorted her down the aisle while Polly played, "I LOVE YOU TRULY" on her violin.

On their wedding night, the two newlyweds had gone to a beautiful restaurant. Connie had ordered her dinner and before all the food was gone, Connie told Rex that she was too full to finish her meal. "It's so delicious, but it's just way too much food for me to finish!"

"You'll sit here until you've eaten the entire thing," Rex commanded, saying "In my family we don't waste food." This was certainly different from the way her father had treated her! This certainly wasn't the kind-hearted dates she remembered having with Rex. This man had turned into a tyrant overnight. Stuffing herself to the point that she felt she was going to burst, she then headed to the hotel room where she had to submit to his demands for sex, even though she was already physically miserable and exhausted. Their honeymoon was a disaster with Rex constantly controlling her every move. Right then and there, Connie knew she had made a mistake, but hoped that she could change him.

Their first home was on the old Wordelman farm. They lived in a brand-new trailer, which was about 12 feet long! Small and compact, the little trailer was stuffed with wedding presents and all their belongings. Connie worked nights at the hospital, while Rex drove a school bus and took care of the farm, performing mortician duties at his father's funeral home whenever needed.

During those first couple of months of marriage, Connie realized that Rex had a terrible temper. Not only did he cuss and swear when things didn't go right, he took his violent temper out on her. She'd grown up with so much love and praise from her father, that being subjected to this verbal and physical abuse left her with a feeling of betrayal. No one would listen to her accusations, except her father-in-law, Alvin Wordelman. Connie went to Alvin whenever Rex was out of control. Alvin would attempt to calm Rex down because he truly needed Rex to stay in Wells. He needed a licensed mortician and funeral director for his funeral home to stay operational. Rex would apologize to Connie and say he would never act this way again, but of course, life only changed for a few days, and then Rex would be back to his old ways. He continued to verbally and physically abuse Connie! Shattered dreams were crumbling around all those involved in this relationship. Rex had wanted to become a doctor, not a mortician. She had wanted to be a nurse, not abused. "Was living a life someone else had planned, causing all of his anger?" Connie wondered.

Rex continued his National Guard commitments and then promptly set course to get Connie pregnant. He never became a doctor, and Connie never became a nurse. Their hopes and dreams were shattered, but they trudged on as any young married couple would do in the early 50's, trying to hold onto their dreams!

During this time in her life, Connie continued to play her violin, which proved to be her saving grace from all the turmoil she faced. Her dear friend, Arthur Granger, was being honored upon his retirement as the Superintendent of Wells Unified School District. "This is Your Life" had become a popular radio show and new television show during that time, and the school district thought it would be clever to do a fun show for Mr. Granger, saying "This is Your Life, Arthur Granger!" Connie was invited back to Wells to perform with her violin. Never afraid to perform in front of a crowd, she stepped onto the stage wearing her lime green, tea length wedding dress and white heels, and played one of Arthur's favorite songs called "Fiddlin the Fiddle". Then confidently walking over to Arthur and Bernice with other dignitaries seated on the stage, she spoke to Arthur about the wonderful times she remembered living at his house throughout her elementary years. After speaking to Arthur, she stepped back to her spot on the stage and again played her violin without anyone accompanying her. The "Orange Blossom Special" was quite the hit as she gallantly played the entire piece by memory. Yes, music was the ticket to get her through the hard times.

Connie played and spoke for Arthur Granger's retirement program, "This is Your Life, Arthur Granger," 1952.

CHAPTER **20**

ONE – A MOTHER WITHOUT A MOTHER

THOSE FIRST YEARS of their marriage were tremendously difficult for Connie. She was not used to being criticized and constantly put down. No matter what she did, Rex was quick to condemn her, cursing and swearing at her for what seemed like no reason at all. She felt constant tension in this new marriage. Her life with her father had been filled with praises and accolades. He had always given her positive feedback and would tell others about her talents, abilities and choices. She had learned to walk tall and proud with her father's constant love and praise, but suddenly Connie felt the tension in this new relationship with Rex. She was afraid to make a move for fear she would be sworn at with vehement phrases or worse yet, hit! During those early years, friends from high school would stop by to see how she was doing, noting the change in her behavior, but eventually those friends all went off to college and Connie was left alone with Rex, escaping when she could to work at the hospital.

Living behind closed doors was extremely painful for Connie, who loved the social activities she had grown up with. She loved all her music activities and church activities. Rex had seemed to change overnight from the fun-loving man she had dated. He was now very critical of her. She didn't seem to do anything right. He found any

ONE – A MOTHER WITHOUT A MOTHER

little thing she did as a way to verbally attack her. In fact, she often thought of the day she stood at the back of the chapel and told her father, "I don't think I should marry this man. Dad, something doesn't feel right." She wished with all of her might her father hadn't encouraged her to go through with this marriage. She was truly being beaten down, mentally, emotionally and physically.

As anticipated by Rex and his father, Connie became pregnant very quickly! Connie, not knowing a pregnancy was in the plan to help Rex avoid military service overseas, was beside herself. How could she tell Rex they would have another mouth to feed? She avoided telling him until her third month. She had expected him to explode.

But one day before she could confront Rex, his father asked, "Is Connie pregnant, yet?" Connie's head quickly snapped around as she looked at Rex.

Rex replied to his father under his breath, "Shut up!"

Alvin asked again, "Is Connie pregnant, yet?"

Again, Rex replied, "Shut up!" to which Connie looked at Rex. And then it dawned on her. In her mind she was listing all his friends who were serving in Korea.

"Did you got me pregnant so you wouldn't have to go to Korea?" she asked. She knew she had no recourse, but at least he wouldn't explode at her for being pregnant, if that was his goal! Connie was devastated. She should have realized at that moment in time that Rex truly didn't love her. He had used her! Oh, he was enamored with her, but he truly didn't love her. Now here she was, eighteen years old with a new baby on the way and an abusive husband. She finally realized he had married her and purposely gotten her pregnant so he would not have to go to war in Korea!

The doctors at the hospital were so excited about Connie's news. They encouraged her to work right up until she delivered her baby. The day she felt those first pangs of imminent childbirth, Rex was out combining peas to be sold to the Green Giant factory in LeSuer, MN. Connie diligently fixed lunch for the twelve morning workers, and then prepared a huge chicken dinner for the evening meal, as she knew the men would work right on through until sunset and then be hungry. Potatoes were peeled and ready to be boiled, the chicken was in the oven, rolls had been baked and vegetables were waiting to be served. She knew she would need someone to help finish up the evening meal, so she quickly called her dad and asked him to go get Connie's mother-in-law, Alice, who lived in town. Dad brought Alice out to the farm to finish the dinner Connie had started. Alice and Dad would then stay at the farm and serve all the afternoon and evening workers, while Connie drove herself to the hospital.

Stopping out at the pea stack on her way to the hospital, Connie jumped out of the car to run and tell Rex she was in labor. "You go ahead," he yelled. "I've got to finish up with the harvest. I'll be there later." He never offered to take her to the hospital or comfort her. He was more interested in getting his crop of peas harvested. Feeling more contractions, Connie jumped back into the old 1948 Cadillac and sped down the gravel roads to get to the hospital in town. She felt like she was driving 90 miles an hour as rocks and gravel flew past her!

Dr. Vernig, who knew her well, told her she was better off working on the floor, helping to keep her mind off from the labor pains. So, Connie began working on the maternity floor where the doctors and nurses could keep an eye on her, periodically checking to see how the labor was progressing. Finally, they insisted she lay down in the delivery room, and at 7:00PM, with both doctors in attendance, Connie gave birth to eight-pound, nine-ounce Caryn Lynn. Rex arrived two hours later still in his "pea-pickin'" clothes and smelling to high heaven. He hadn't even taken time to clean up before coming to the hospital. "But knowing Rex," Connie thought, "he would never think to clean up on his own!" Connie often had to coerce him into the bathtub, at least once a week to get him cleaned up. He was quite the opposite of her dad in more respects than one!

The next day, Rex never showed up and Connie drove herself and the new baby back to the farm after spending the night alone in

ONE – A MOTHER WITHOUT A MOTHER

the hospital. By this time, they had moved from the little trailer into the old farmhouse, having gotten everything situated in November. Caryn Lynn was born on June 30th, 1952. Sadly, no one was there to greet Connie and the new baby, and she promptly sat down and wept buckets of tears. "What had she gotten herself into?" she wondered. And then those thoughts crept into her head. "What would my mother do? Do other young mothers return home to an empty house? What does she look like? Where is she now? Does she ever think of me, like I think of her?" Connie's brain was going a mile a minute and she made herself even more distraught. Unbeknownst to Connie, she was overwhelmed with postpartum blues from the lack of love and support from Rex, which she so desperately craved and needed.

Still working nights, along with nursing a new baby, Connie was the epitome of the tired new mother! But she knew for Caryn's sake, she had to carry on. Luckily, the doctors allowed Connie to bring Caryn to work with her. They knew the hospital was the best place for the two of them to be. Not only was Connie safe there, but she learned so much working with the nurses. Both doctors taught her delivery room procedures and a wealth of information on how to care for a newborn baby. They taught her how to measure the new babies from head to toe and measure the circumference around their heads. They showed her how to add eye drops, bath the newborns, as well as feed and burp them. She even learned how to use the incubator on premature babies or put those babies with jaundice under bilirubin lamps. What great experiences she was acquiring as a new mother who had never had a mother of her own.

Although she was a pretty baby, Caryn was covered with a cradle cap and eczema. The doctors made many visits to help Connie take care of this skin affliction. Eventually they were able to have Connie take Caryn to Mayo clinic to have allergy tests. As it turned out, Caryn was allergic to all 120 items she was tested for. Watching the doctors place forty needles across her daughter's back three different times, brought tears to Connie's eyes each time, but she kept thinking it was in Caryn's best interest. The doctors told her that Caryn was highly allergic to dust and grass and they suggested Connie take extra time to wet dust her house often. Diligently, Connie dusted the entire farmhouse every morning with a wet washcloth, making sure the dust was not going to cause any eczema outbreaks for Caryn. Being a fastidious woman, this announcement only enhanced Connie's need to be in a clean and tidy environment.

While nursing her own baby, Connie again wondered about her own birth mother. "How in the world could my mother have given me away?" she pondered looking down at Caryn. "How do you give away your own flesh and blood?" She loved nursing, and she loved being a mother. She loved singing to her little one and watching Caryn make faces and start to coo. It certainly brought up those old feelings of wondering what her own mother was like. "Just who was my mother? What did she look like? Did she nurse me like I'm nursing Caryn?" Connie wondered. Although she never mentioned these haunting questions to anyone else, Connie held them deep in her heart.

As she settled into motherhood, Connie wanted to make her home a special place for her new baby and so it was only natural that she wanted to get some things that were rightfully hers. It was about this time Connie decided she wanted to get Mary Lee's German Haviland china for the farmhouse. When Mary Lee and Alfred had gotten married, Mary Lee's parents, Grandma and Grandpa Yager, had special china shipped over to the United States from Germany as a wedding present. Connie was supposed to inherit the china when Mary Lee passed away, but since Mary Lee passed away when Connie was so young, the china was kept in storage until Connie was old enough to inherit it. Unfortunately, Cora had gone to Uncle Arthur and Aunt Mildred in California and told them she wanted to send the china to them for safe keeping. As it turned out, she had absconded with the china, and refused to give it back. In fact, Alfred had to take Cora to court to get the China back, and when it arrived from California in the two big china barrels, most of it was broken, including all the glass stemware. Connie also had to fight to get her piano back. Her father

ONE – A MOTHER WITHOUT A MOTHER

had given her the piano for her 13th birthday, but Cora had kept it at her house. Grandpa Yager had also been a gemologist and had made wedding rings for dad and Mary Lee. Sadly, Cora didn't want to give those back either. Cora wanted to keep anything she could to keep Connie coming back to visit her. Luckily, through the courts, the judge decided that Connie should have the china, the piano and the rings. Connie was able to get the broken china and piano, but not the rings. Nothing ever was easy where Cora was involved.

The doctors assured Connie she wouldn't get pregnant while nursing, so Connie and Rex didn't use any kind of birth control during Caryn's first year of being nursed. Sadly, Connie learned this adage was just an old wife's tale! "Oh my God!" she thought, "I'm pregnant again!" Breastfeeding a new baby while being pregnant took a toll on her tired body, and she truly had to eat for two! She packed away tons of food, gaining nearly 50 pounds on her small 5'2" frame. Only one year and seven days after Caryn was born, the little family welcomed the arrival of another baby girl. Cathy Lee was born on July 7, 1953, in the Wells Hospital, and Connie was 20 years old. Weighing over eight pounds, Cathy arrived with a beautiful smile and black eyes like her big sister. Delivery was easy for Connie, thanks greatly to Dr. Vernig and his staff! And since she knew the doctors and nurses, they took good care of her in the hospital.

In those days, hospital costs were approximately $100 for the delivery room and a one day stay in the hospital, so Connie had to return home the next day, having spent less than 24-hours in the hospital's care. Paying for the doctor's visits throughout the pregnancy was expensive, and now the delivery room cost seemed like a huge added expense for the little family. Times were difficult in the money department. As a farmer, Rex didn't make much money, so he supplemented his farming income with driving a school bus and performing the embalming work at the mortuary. With two babies, Connie now had to give up her job at the hospital and become a full-time mother, so money was tight!

It was during this time that Alfred, finally free of Cora, became good friends with Lucille Foster, Bernice Granger's sister. Connie had grown to love Lucille as an aunt when she had lived with the Grangers during all her school years. And of course, Alfred had grown to love her, too! When Lucille's husband passed away very unexpectedly, she was teaching school in Loveland, Colorado. Alfred started courting Lucille, and they were married the same summer that Connie gave birth to Cathy. It was wonderful to see dad so happy again, but it meant that he would be moving to Colorado and Connie would be struggling with two babies, alone.

Caryn 2, Connie 21, and Cathy 1, in Wells, Minnesota

CHAPTER **22**

A NEW COMMUNITY

TIME MOVED ON and Connie did her best to raise her daughters under the controlling eyes of her husband. Her main goal at the ripe old age of twenty-one was to be the best mother that she could be to her two beautiful daughters. She and her dad talked every single Wednesday evening and he would bolster her up and encourage her to go on for the girl's sake. She would hug and kiss her daughters, and Rex would become angry. Hugs and kisses were sexual to him and that type of affection was not to be given to the children, but only to him! He was a very jealous man! He also insisted that she not tell the children she loved them. He didn't like her doling out any praise or kudos to her children, and yet this was what Connie had grown up with. Her father was always so positive and had lavished her with many kudos and praises. She had grown accustomed to this behavior and anything different was foreign to her. But, according to Rex, the girls were to be raised with the strict Norwegian upbringing he had experienced, with no love or affection openly demonstrated between family members. This crushed Connie's heart. She had seen mothers over her years in foster care and growing up and she tried so hard to do her best, but eventually, she could no longer stand the control and abuse from Rex.

Eventually, Alvin and Alice Wordelman purchased a furniture store in Fulda, Minnesota, and expected Rex and Connie to move

A NEW COMMUNITY

their young family with them. So, in 1955, Connie was forced to leave the support system and friends she had grown up with and move into the bottom floor of a large house on the outskirts of the little town called Fulda. During the move, the girls were left with Grandma Alice Wordelman while Alvin, Rex and Connie, along with Rex's brother Garry, did all the moving. As Connie met new friends and neighbors during the moving process, she was so excited to describe her two little girls who were staying with grandma in Wells. "They are two and three years old and they have the cutest little blonde pigtails! Their hair falls in ringlets and I can't wait for you to meet them!" Connie had excitedly explained!

Unfortunately, when Grandma Wordelman heard that Connie had accidentally broken three fingers on her right hand when they had gotten slammed in one of the car doors, she thought, "How can Connie possibly take care of these pigtails?" Grandma Alice, thinking she was doing Connie a favor, promptly cut the pigtails off from Caryn and Cathy, leaving Connie's adorable little girls looking like they had been butchered by some insane barber! Connie had been so excited to show off her adorable little girls to her new friends in Fulda only to find out they didn't have their adorable little pig tails! Oh, how devastated and angry she was when she discovered Alice had cut off those cute little pigtails! She had yelled at Alice! Never had Connie yelled at anyone, but this time she yelled. She screamed at her mother in law. All her anger came out, and then she cried. How could this be happening? It seemed no one in this family was on her side. That was when she gave her two little girls their first Toni Permanents to give their hair some curl and help the "just butchered" look of their new haircuts!

One memorable evening, the little family was working at their new furniture store when the fire siren blew. Rex, being a volunteer fireman for the small town, ran off to the fire station, leaving Connie alone with the girls at the store. Connie quickly ran outside to see if she could find out where the fire was! Gerdie, another storekeeper, was standing outside watching the fire engine roar down main street.

Connie hollered across the street to Gerdie, "Where's the fire?"

Gerdie, looking stunned, yelled back, "Why... why... why, it's at your house! The fire trucks just headed there!" Gerdie was located directly in the center of Fulda and all the fire calls went into her local shop number. She was knowledgeable about everything that went on in the little town!

"Oh, my goodness!" Connie exclaimed and then yelled at Caryn and Cathy, "Jump in the car!" Off they went to the house. Once they arrived at their house, Connie told Caryn and Cathy to go see Herman and Laura Lemmerman, the next-door neighbors, who were watching everything unfold. Connie then went running up to the house to see what was burning. They were living in a huge two-story house which had been divided into two separate two-bedroom apartments. Delores Swan and her husband lived upstairs. Doing their duty, the firemen would not let Connie get anywhere close to the house, even when she explained, "This is my house! I live here!"

"I'm sorry ma'am," said one of the firemen, "We can't let anyone in there!" The small fire had been discovered by the family who lived upstairs when smoke had begun to roll up through their heater vents. When the firemen wouldn't let Connie near the house, she joined the girls at Herman and Laura's, who gladly entertained the girls with beautiful wooden puzzles while Connie paced back and forth outside. Apparently, Cathy had put a little flannel doll blanket over a lamp in their bedroom when the family headed to the store to work for the evening. She didn't want her dolls to be afraid in the dark! It didn't take long for the small lamp to start smoldering the old baby blanket, and the flannel quickly burst into flames. The fire had attacked the bedroom wall, but the smoke quickly warned the Swan family and the fire didn't do too much damage. However, the entire house had to be opened and aired out. Luckily, it was a warm spring evening and there wasn't any major damage.

Eventually, Rex's father bought the Reusse Funeral home in Fulda, and turned it into Wordelman's Funeral Home. Rex worked at the furniture store and helped with the funeral home. He would do the embalming and sales of vaults and caskets and readying the showroom floor for those mourning clients. He was now a funeral director. Connie took care of the children and was expected to help at the furniture store when needed. She was also forced to help at the funeral home, applying makeup, curling hair and dressing the dead bodies, making them presentable for viewing! Together the family seemed to have it all together, attending church every Sunday morning with Rex volunteering to be a youth group leader and Deacon, while Connie sang in the choir and eventually became the Sunday school superintendent. However, things were not what they seemed! Connie was suffering from loneliness and a lack of love. She didn't experience any togetherness from her husband, and her opinion was never sought out. No one realized Connie was struggling with depression.

Connie and her father had always remained close, talking on the phone every Wednesday evening. Her dad, knowing their financial situation, often secretly sent Connie money on the side. She would stow it away for special needs, maybe to purchase a new toy or new fabric to sew clothes for herself or for the girls, or maybe just put an extra meal on the table. She never told Rex about the money and eventually, when Connie had enough money stowed away, she decided to escape. She knew for her own sanity, she needed a break from Rex's controlling abuse, so secretly she had a friend drive her to the bus station in Worthington, where she got on a bus to Denver. Her father had been married to Lucille for a few years and they were settled in Loveland, Colorado. They welcomed Connie with open arms, but alas, after many phone conversations, Rex drove out to get her and bring her back to Minnesota, again convincing her that he would change!

Perhaps another baby would help the marriage they thought, as Rex demanded they needed to have a boy. Not realizing at the ripe old age of twenty-four, a baby doesn't make a better marriage, but along came baby number three. The strain this baby put on the marriage and the relationship was immense, and sadly, this baby was not meant to be. Connie miscarried very early in the pregnancy. That loss brought on more depression, but Connie had no choice in the matter and found herself pregnant with baby number four. This baby, too, had a sad ending.

It was Easter Sunday when Connie's father and Lucille had come to visit from Colorado. Knowing most of the southern counties in Minnesota and wanting to do something different, Connie's father and Lucille suggested taking the family over to Laverne for a Turkey dinner at the Blue Mound restaurant famous for their Sunday turkey dinners. Alfred also wanted to secretly save pregnant Connie the work of preparing a huge Easter dinner for eight people! Afterwards, someone decided it would be fun to take the grandchildren over to the Okoboji Amusement park. There they were, Rex's mother and father, Alice and Al Wordelman, Connie's father, Alfred and his wife, Lucille, all crammed into the old four door sedan, with the two little girls sitting on their grandma's laps in the backseat with pregnant Connie in the middle!

All eight of them made the trip to Laverne for lunch and then on to Okoboji in Iowa! But the adventure grew alarming when they reached the amusement park. Caryn and Cathy, dressed in their brand-new Easter dresses sewn by Connie, with little white lace anklets and new black patent leather shoes, headed in the direction of the park! Unfortunately, safety standards were not what they are today. The little train, which ran around the circumference of the park didn't have any guard rails or fencing around it, protecting people from being on the track at the same time the train was moving. The conductor swore he blew the whistle, but no one in the little group remembers hearing a whistle of any kind. As Connie climbed out of the car, she saw her two little girls standing on the track with the train heading their way, she raced over to the railroad tracks to shove them out of the way of the miniature train barreling towards them. She pushed them so hard their shoes were still on the track as the train went by! But the cow catcher at the front of the train caught Connie, who at the time was seven months pregnant. The little train dragged her body down the tracks and when the train finally stopped, Connie couldn't walk. They rushed her over to the manager's house and called the doctor.

The doctor assessed the damage and explained that she had suffered two broken kneecaps. Both legs were put into casts for the summer and she was placed on a bed which was out on the screened in porch as it was a terribly hot day. There, she spent the night all alone. She laid back to think about her day. The men in the little group had been arguing with the park officials as to whose fault it was. The grandmas had been caring for the girls, who had retrieved their new shoes from the tracks. Everyone left Connie resting peacefully, while they all drove back to Fulda without her.

During the night, Connie started to miscarry baby number four. The pain from this miscarriage was excruciatingly more difficult than any of her other deliveries as the baby was stillborn, having been killed during the train accident. Without the help of the baby, the birth was tremendously agonizing, and she had been left alone. The next day Rex came to get her and sadly she had to tell him their beautiful little boy had died in the accident. Rex made arrangements for the baby to be buried in an unmarked grave at Okoboji, Iowa. Connie spent that summer on crutches, using knitting needles to scratch the horrible itching from the casts! There was no help for her depression as she faced the fact that they had lost their little boy. She was miserable beyond belief.

Rex demanded they continue to try to have another little boy, but intimacy was not a part of their marriage Connie looked forward to. Instead, their sexual encounters were more like consensual rapes. Being the dutiful wife, Connie acquiesced to Rex's advances to keep the peace, wondering if all marriages were like this. If she complained, she was told that divorce was out of the question, and so she obediently became a cold fish, submitting to him in silence.

Connie with Cathy, 4 and Caryn 5, in Fulda, Minnesota.

CHAPTER **23**

MORE CHILDREN

EVENTUALLY CONNIE WAS pregnant for the fifth time with another baby! This induced birth was scheduled by the doctors in Worthington, Minnesota. They didn't want to miss their vacations, so on July 14, 1959, Connie's last baby was delivered. It was an unbelievable day! Connie arrived at the hospital at 7:00AM to have labor induced. Her water was broken, and the birth was as easy as could be! Out came Lisa Annette, the most beautiful little baby girl. She was adorable! She had the softest creamy white skin, in fact it was pure white skin, along with beautiful brown eyes complimented by her dark auburn hair. Neither Caryn nor Cathy had been born with hair, let alone dark hair, so this baby was quite a surprise!

But as beautiful as this little baby was, when Rex was told he had a girl, he went berserk, and threw a huge fit, ranting throughout the hospital, blaming the doctors for not producing a boy! He had desperately wanted a boy and was furious to have another girl. He was so obnoxious and angry that the hospital had to call security and have him escorted out. He was told not to return until Connie was ready to be dismissed. He did bring Caryn and Cathy by to see their mother, but they could only stand outside her 2nd story window and wave at her! Rex was not allowed into the hospital at all. Looking down at these two adorable little girls she wondered, "Where is my mother and what would she be saying if she could see her three beautiful granddaughters?" After Rex took the girls home, Connie sadly padded off to her hospital bed feeling very alone and terribly sad.

Loving words and language, Connie loved the alliteration of Caryn, Cathy and Connie. She wanted her new baby to be called Cindy. At the time, several other babies in the Worthington hospital were named Cindy, so Rex chose the name, Lisa Annette! It was so feminine sounding and suited this beautiful baby so perfectly. But in the same breath, Rex informed Connie, "I will not be changing any diapers on another girl!" He emphatically stated, "I'm going to make this baby my boy!" Luckily, Connie had her faith to fall back on and boy did she need it as she headed home.

When Connie arrived home with Lisa, she discovered much to her disappointment that Rex had chosen this time to build a room addition to their house. His intentions were good, but it was poor timing. He had wanted to give the little family a real bathroom, complete with two sinks, a toilet and a tub. Up until this time, Connie had to bathe the girls and herself in the kitchen sink! Alas, as Connie knew, Rex did not clean up after himself, so when she walked in the door, she was greeted with saw horses, sawdust, tools and wood scattered all over the dining room. Rex had hoped to have his project completed before Connie returned home, but unfortunately, he didn't meet his deadline! The new mother, fearing for Caryn's allergies became very distraught and a battle ensued until the room addition was complete and the house was again back in order! Rex, of course, felt that Connie didn't appreciate anything he did!

Baby Lisa had two doting sisters and one doting parent. Her father wanted nothing to do with her for about two weeks, until he realized what a beautiful intelligent baby she was! Everyone wanted to play with her. And because she was so intelligent, she picked up everything very quickly. Connie had learned how to be a wonderful mother to her older two girls, and she immediately implemented those tools with Lisa. She loved reading stories to the three of them, and making the characters come to life as she changed her voice to match each character represented in the story. Naptime and bedtime were sure to find Connie reading stories, with a Donald Duck voice or a squeaky little mouse voice coming from the bedroom. The girls would plead, "Be a duck, mom! Be a duck!" And then you'd hear that infamous "quack, quack, quack" coming from the bedroom! Connie also loved to sing with her girls. Every night before story time, they would gather round the piano and Connie would sing songs with them, teaching them musical nursery rhymes and various folk songs, just as her mother and father had done with her.

By 1962, the older girls were learning to play the guitar, which Connie had taught them, and they were learning how to sew and iron. Rex, needing to show his Christian deeds outwardly, decided the family could earn extra money by being a foster family. Knowing that Connie had been in foster care herself, he felt she would be excellent at caring for other foster children! However, what he didn't comprehend was the mental toll being a foster parent takes on the caregiver, as well as the entire family. All the daily care as well as housework fell into Connie's lap. The first baby arrived. Little Lori was only two days old when she came to live in the Wordelman household, and as such, she needed constant care. The older girls were more than happy to help hold Lori and entertain her and feed her a bottle during the day, but the night-time feedings were up to Connie. Waking every few hours to give Lori her bottle was exhausting, along with keeping the house cleaned doing the laundry and fixing three meals a day. Everyone adored Lori and loved it when she began to smile and coo. But, as with many foster families, someone stepped forward to adopt Lori and at three months old she was removed from the Wordelman home and given to her adoptive parents. This crushed Connie as she had grown quite attached to this little baby in those few short months. Depression was growing at every corner, but for the sake of her girls, she knew she had to keep going.

Thinking what was needed, Rex again, requested another child be placed into the Wordelman home. Michelle was a small little baby with dark skin, soft curly brown hair and big beautiful brown eyes. Connie decided to nickname her "Shelly". She was just a few months old when she was placed into foster care. She had a very white Swedish mother with blonde hair, and a very black African American father who was stationed at the Chandler Air Base, not far from Fulda. Shelly was even more fun for the Wordelman girls than Lori because Shelly could sit up and was beginning to crawl and talk. Unfortunately, Shelley had hip dysplasia which was discovered when she started to walk. She had surgery and was placed in a cast from her hips to ankles, requiring her to be carried wherever she wanted to go. She required a tremendous amount of attention, and the girls loved to play with this gorgeous baby, including all the neighborhood girls, but not Lisa. Lisa was having trouble sharing her time with this new attention getter! "When is she going home?" Lisa would ask. "I don't want her here anymore!" she'd constantly tell Connie. It seemed that Connie was being pulled in two directions, pleasing her own daughter, and taking care of her foster daughter. Was this history repeating itself Connie wondered, thinking back to when she had a "big sister" who didn't like her when she was in foster care.

When the family took their yearly vacation to Colorado to visit Connie's dad in Loveland, it became apparent that Connie was being ostracized for having a black baby in her care. In fact, Connie was holding Shelly in the Ben Franklin Store in Loveland, and no one would wait on her. The salesclerk literally turned her back on Connie and refused to speak to her or acknowledge her presence at the cash register. "Let's go!" said Connie quietly to her girls, as they left their items lying on the counter.

It was the summer of tremendous racial unrest, and segregation seemed to be alive and well all over America. Martin Luther King, Jr. was giving his "I Have A Dream" speech and the country was full of racial tension.

"What happened mommy?" asked one of the girls.

Connie explained quietly, "Some people don't like people with dark skin."

"But we do, don't we mommy?" said one of the girls and Connie knew she was right.

"Yes! Yes, we do!" said Connie, reassuring her daughters. "In our family we look at how people act and not how they look. Everybody is the same on the inside. The outside doesn't matter if they are kind people. We look at how they act."

"That lady didn't act very nice, did she mommy?" said one of the girls.

"You're right. She didn't act very nice, but we have to just smile and move on," replied Connie, and off they went to the park.

Returning to Fulda, Connie thought, "Maybe Shelly needs to be with other black people, so she doesn't face being ostracized in this small white community. Maybe living in an all-white community isn't fair to her." She told Rex, "Maybe Shelly needs to have boys of her own race to date when she's older. Maybe she'll feel self-conscientious being the only black person in town. I think we should give her up now before it gets even more difficult to lose her later. I'm growing too attached to this adorable little girl!" So, with much sadness, Connie explained to the Social worker, Mrs. March from Slayton, Minnesota, that she could no longer be Shelly's foster parent. It was just emotionally too difficult for her having to give these children away. After Shelly was placed in a home in another town, Connie would walk around the house saying, "Shelly, where are you?" forgetting Shelly was no longer there. She missed Shelly terribly and it took Connie months to deal with the loss of this beautiful little girl, but she knew it was in Shelly's best interest, as well as her family's best interest, for her to be raised with another family.

Being a foster parent brought Connie full circle to the times when she was a foster child. Although she never knew the ladies who had taken care of her, she was thankful for the people who had stepped up in her life and helped her; ladies like Mrs. Parriott, who took her to 4-H meetings where she learned to sew; and who was her Sunday School teacher; and Mrs. Granger, who'd been invaluable to her education as a mother; and Mrs. Purdy who had given her a place to stay when she didn't want to stay with Cora. Not only had they provided religious education, they had taught her to sew and cook. Here she was making her own little girl's dresses, and even sewing them beautiful doll dresses, as well. One Easter she made matching coats to go along with the girl's dresses. They looked so adorable in their little white hats and gloves with the matching dresses and coats. All these women had stepped up to help her become the mother she was today. Even though she never knew her own mother, Connie always tried to be better than any other mother she had known, and these women were wonderful role models. But still in the back of her mind, especially now after being a foster parent, she couldn't shake the questions that constantly flooded her mind; "What does my mother look like? And where is my mother now? What would she think of my accomplishments? What would she think of me as a mother?"

Caryn, 12, Cathy, 11, Lann (Lisa) 5 in Fulda, Minnesota, 1965.

CHAPTER **24**

MRS. MINNESOTA AND BEYOND!

BECOMING A DEVOTED member of the little town of Fulda, Connie grew to know a lot of people. She was an active member of Mrs. Jaycees, as well as the Civic Chamber of Commerce. She was also very involved in the First Presbyterian Church, singing in the choir, playing the violin and organ for various church services, teaching Sunday School, and eventually accepting the job as the Sunday School Superintendent. One morning a week she would participate in the Ladies Aide circle at the church, a Bible study with other women who met every Tuesday morning. She enjoyed the camaraderie of the other young mothers in the Ruth circle. Monday nights found her in the bowling league at Lanoe's Cafe and Bowling Alley. She was a champion bowler and as a winner, she often had to buy a round of drinks for her teammates, even though she didn't really like to drink! Wednesdays she would practice with the adult choir in the evenings, and as Caryn and Cathy got older, she loved to be able to assist her friend Carol Phelps with the children's choir Wednesdays after school, priding herself in helping the church purchase and sew all of the little red bows for the children's choir robes which they proudly wore during their Sunday morning performances. Rex had been a founding member of the Maple Lawn Nursing home in Fulda, and Connie became a member of the Pink Lady Auxiliary, volunteers who worked at the Nursing home. Many days Connie would be at the furniture store, dusting and vacuuming the three floors of furniture, as well as watching the store and working with customers while Rex delivered furniture. She eventually knew all the local merchants and supported the little town as best she could. She was very social and needed those friendships.

The Fulda Water Festival was an event she supported. There was an annual parade which marched right past their house on Lafayette Avenue with the carnival setting up on Main Street. The little town became filled with people looking to participate in all the festivities during the Water Festival in July. During this time, Connie realized many other little surrounding towns had a beauty pageant for their high school girls. The town Queens then promoted the town by riding in the local parades. The pageants promoted poise, public speaking and a way to gain confidence through sharing their talents. It also offered young high school girl's money for scholarships. Eventually, Connie felt that Fulda needed a beauty pageant, so she approached the Chamber of Commerce and requested that she be able to start a beauty pageant in Fulda. The pageant itself was quite a well-attended event and the queen was then invited to ride in the local parade and attend the Water Festivities as royalty. Connie organized the pageant for several years and loved working with young high school girls who were vying for the title of Miss Fulda.

One day the local Red Owl grocery store owner, Clifford Mansmith, challenged Connie, "Look at this! I've got the paperwork for the Mrs. Minnesota pageant. How about if you try your hand at being in a pageant yourself?"

"What is a Mrs. Minnesota pageant?" Connie had asked. "Misses? Really?" she said.

"Well," said Mr. Mansmith, the grocery store owner, "It's a pageant where married women display their homemaking skills. It says here they compete in cooking, child rearing, sewing, and other talents. I really think you should enter!" he said, "Come on! I dare you!"

"As long as I don't have to trounce around in a bathing suit!" thought Connie! Cliff gave her the paperwork and she read, "Women in the Mrs. Minnesota pageant have to be extremely intelligent women, who are community volunteers."

"Okay," she said as she took the paperwork. "I'll look it over when I get home!" and promptly walked out of the Red Owl store, taking the papers with her. As she began to fill out the questionnaire, she became excited about the prospect of sharing her goals and her dreams. It had been a long time since she had competed for anything. As she completed the essay she wondered, "What am I getting myself into, and what will Rex say?" Questions came flooding into her head, and she realized she needed to take the bull by the horns and make some decisions. She had never done anything quite like this before.

Not only was she going to be judged on what she cooked, but on her shopping ability as well. She also knew she was going to be judged on how she served her meal. "Prepare an economical meal for your husband's boss," the instructions had read.

"Oh my," she thought, "I'm going to be judged on my economical shopping abilities, the cost of the entire meal, the table setting, how the meal tastes and what I wear, plus how I interact with the judges, who will be portraying my husband's boss!" Connie's head was spinning as she thought, "What can I fix? What should I wear? How can I decorate the table and what should I talk about?" She knew this competition was judged on being a housewife and a mother. She had been a housewife and mother for thirteen years and her husband never had a boss, unless you count her father-in-law! The only meals she had prepared were for hired hands on the farm and all the holiday meals with the Wordelman family. This whole idea was making her extremely nervous! "Who else would want to do such a crazy competition?" she asked herself.

"One thing at a time," she chuckled to herself, "Don't get too far ahead of yourself!" Being a very methodical person, Connie sat down and made a list of what she would need just for cooking her meal. She decided to cook her children's favorite meal, Shepherd's pie. It was a very economical meal and was well liked by her entire family. She included fresh baked rolls and their favorite strawberry Jell-O with fresh strawberries, cool whip and marshmallows. For dessert she included the family's favorite, her cherry and marshmallow layered dessert with a graham cracker crust.

"There!" she said to herself, finishing the list of all the ingredients she would need to make her meal. But then she thought, "What in the world am I going to wear? I don't have an evening gown, and what in the world do you wear for an evening serving dinner to your husband's boss?" Connie headed straight over to ask her friend, Dolores Swan. "What do I wear for this competition?" she asked her neighbor, after explaining what she was about to do!

"I've got the perfect outfit!" exclaimed Dolores. "This brown tweed suit will fit you perfectly. All you have to do is hem the skirt a little higher because you are so much shorter than I am!" Dolores also had a brown satin blouse to wear under the brown tweed suit, and Connie was set for her dinner, but she still needed an evening gown.

She headed over to her friend Ruthie's house. "Don't worry, I've got you covered! I know just the dress for you!" exclaimed Ruthie Hoffman, and she explained to Connie she would call another friend! After much alterations, Connie was blessed with a beautiful copper colored evening gown for the competition. It had come from one of Ruthie's friends who owned the implement shop out on the highway. Connie knew she could count on her Fulda friends to help her out.

Feeling confident she had thought of everything, she completed the form and returned it to Mr. Mansmith at the Red Owl store, along with the required application photo. Now, all she had to do was tell Rex she had entered the competition! She knew he would react favorably if he'd receive free publicity for the furniture store and funeral home. Rex's reaction floored her. He said, "Sure, why not!"

Now, all she had to do was pack an outfit to display her sewing abilities and be ready to display her hair styling abilities, which wasn't too difficult. After all, she had helped Cora in the beauty shop, and she had been cutting and perming her daughter's hair for years!

She had also been sewing their clothes and her own clothes for years. As she readied herself for the trip to Minneapolis, Connie felt she was providing her own daughters with a marvelous role model. Win or lose, they would see the strong, talented independent woman their mother had become. She had never had a real mother of her own and she wondered what her own mother would think of her entering a competition to display her talents as a mother. Connie was apprehensive, but confident as she and Rex headed to Minneapolis for the competition on August 12, 1965! When she met the other nine contestants, she knew she had her work cut out for her! Each one of the nine women were incredibly talented, intelligent women.

The two-day competition was filled with a luncheon, a hair styling competition and interviews throughout the day. For their cooking competition, the women were provided with a budget and a two-hour time limit to shop and prepare their meals. Connie loved shopping for food and fixing her children's favorite meal! The Shepherd's Pie was always a hit with her children, and the red Jell-O with fresh strawberries was another favorite. After all, you didn't go to anyone's house in Minnesota during the 1950's or 1960's without being offered Jell-O or a hotdish! "Shepherd's pie and Jell-O are just as much a staple in the Minnesota household as meat and potatoes," she thought! And to top it off, Connie incorporated those green peas into her shepherd's pie, and served warm dinner rolls on the side. For dessert she made her infamous creamed marshmallow layered cherry dessert with a graham cracker topping and crust. Watching her budget proved to be no challenge for Connie in the competition. She knew how to pinch pennies since she and Rex didn't make much money in the furniture store or the mortuary business, of which Rex had now become a part owner with his father.

Connie proudly wore her friend's brown two-piece tweed suit with a chocolate brown satin blouse tucked neatly into the skirt as she entered the dining area to serve her dinner. Borrowing every stitch of clothing she wore for the competition created a bit of anxiety for her. Getting new panty hose on during the muggy August weather in Minneapolis was nerve wracking, and a bit of a challenge, too. As she removed her jacket to serve her dinner, she felt like the slippery, chocolate colored satin blouse was constantly creeping out of her panty hose! She worried she would look too disheveled and appear somewhat discombobulated! But as she passed her homemade shepherd's pie and rolls, along with the Jell-O salad, she confidently carried on a conversation about her views on foster parenting, supporting her husband in his business and her endeavor to be an active member of their community. Once dinner was finished, she was ready to head on to the final portion of the competition.

For the evening gown competition, Connie had borrowed a gown from a friend who owned the John Deere implement shop in Fulda. The bodice was a shimmery copper color with an empire waistline, and the bottom of the gown was a flowy chocolate brown color, which accented her auburn brown hair. Connie simply glowed on stage. The questions involving child rearing were easy for her. As a member of 4-H in her younger years and Speech and Debate clubs in high school, she was adept at public speaking. Her many musical competitions had also instilled in her a strong sense of well-being on the stage, which enabled her to speak with knowledge and confidence about her ideals on parenting. At just thirty-two years of age, she had learned a tremendous amount of the kind of mother she did and did not want to be.

She was the only one who had gone through the foster care system and her philosophies on child rearing impressed the judges. At the end of the evening, August 12, 1965, Connie was crowned Mrs. Minnesota! She immediately called her father to thank him for giving her the confidence to stand on that stage alone. She wanted him to know his guidance and support had provided her with the confidence she needed to win this competition. "I won, dad! I won! Thank you for giving me the confidence to do it!" she said. "Thank you for encouraging me and supporting me all of these years through all of the violin lessons and solo competitions! I couldn't have done it without you!" Her dad had given her the kudos and praise she needed. Now, her dad, on the other end of the telephone in Loveland, Colorado, beamed from afar!

"Very well done!" said Alfred. "Very well, indeed!" He was so proud of the young woman she had become!

"I'm going to San Diego next week to compete in the Mrs. America pageant, dad!" She had excitedly said.

"You'll be wonderful!" he assured her. Her first phone call had been to thank the man who had raised her and made her who she is today. "Just remember who you are and who you represent!" he chuckled, and Connie smiled to herself.

"Same ole dad!" she thought! "I love you!" she said out loud. "I'll let you know how I do next week in San Diego!"

The little town of Fulda, Minnesota, along with her hometown of Wells, Minnesota, were bursting at the seams with pride. Each business in the little town of Fulda painted words of encouragement on their store windows. Rich Gilbertson from the Skelly Gas station even painted his building saying, "Fulda, Home of Mrs. Minnesota, Mrs. Rex Wordelman". The Probst Jewelry store painted their window to read, "Congratulations, Connie! Mrs. Minnesota, Our Mom of the Year!" while Les Speckmeier had a huge sign painted and attached to his building saying the same thing, and of course Wordelman's Furniture Store's main window said, "Fulda, Home of Mrs. Minnesota, Mrs. Rex Wordelman. The city of Wells, Minnesota, even set up a day to honor Connie on August 20, 1965, but unfortunately, they didn't realize she was on her way to the Mrs. America pageant in San Diego, California!

Another list was started as Connie studied the requirements for the Mrs. America Pageant in San Diego. It stated that she was required to pass a driving test, complete a flower arrangement, complete a laundry event, bake a cake, compete in a grocery shopping event, and perform a creative routine, along with another cooking competition. Plus, she had to write an essay on "How the Role of the Homemaker has Changed Over the Past Ten Years in the World, in the Community and in the Home"! Connie's head was spinning as she got busy writing the essay on the airplane from Minneapolis back to Worthington! She had only a week to prepare and she knew she needed every minute!

Remembering how her children reacted when they walked into their Grandma's kitchen and saw a deer hanging from the center of the ceiling, made Connie wonder if she was truly doing the right thing. Somehow, the vision of a pig hanging in the old farmhouse came rushing back to her, and she knew that shooting a deer, skinning the animal and gutting and butchering the animal for subsequent meals was a family affair. She was engaging her children in a lifelong learning process, just as her father had done for her. So, here she was, preparing for the Mrs. America pageant. She knew it would be a great learning experience for her as well as her daughters, but she only had a week to prepare for the upcoming pageant! Now she needed a creative expression routine and a cake recipe, plus she needed to type up her essay! Why in the world was she thinking about a pig hanging from the ceiling, or the deer hanging in Grandma Wordelman's house?

Years earlier, Rex had introduced Connie to the sport of archery. Together they would go out deer hunting, and as soon as either one of them shot a deer, it would be tagged under Connie's name. That pleased Connie, as she didn't have to go along after the first deer was shot. Then the deer would be hung up in Grandma's kitchen to be skinned and butchered. She liked being able to say she was helping put meat on the table for her family, but Connie's archery prowess didn't stop with deer hunting. Rex noticed her accuracy with the bow and arrow and began to help her hone her skills. He introduced her to several archers in the area and taught her to shoot targets. Doc Schwartz had an archery range right behind the furniture store, so it was convenient for them to go to target practice after work. Connie became so adept at shooting targets, her accuracy won her the title of 1964 Iowa Women's Freestyle Champion. She also placed in the top tier of the Minnesota state archery competition as well. She and Rex designed an archery presentation to show the students in local schools just how lethal and useful archery could be. They visited many area schools and demonstrated their archery skills, showing the students different types of arrows and bows and how to respect these as true weapons.

One arrow Connie liked to share with the students was called a "Snarro". It was an arrow with a circular spiral instead of the usual sharp tip. It could stun a rabbit and knock it out, but it could also burrow its way through a bale of hay. Although it looked innocuous, she taught the students the bows and arrows she was using were deadly weapons. Then to demonstrate her accuracy, Rex would throw a paper plate up in the air and Connie would shoot it mid-air. Next Rex would toss a balloon into the air and as it dropped, Connie would pop it with an arrow. The finale of their presentation always had the wow factor as Rex swung a ping pong ball back and forth in front of his face, and Connie would shoot the ping pong ball out of his hands, usually making the ping pong ball fall from the swinging string! She truly was a talented individual when it came to archery!

She continued to read over the application for the Mrs. Minnesota pageant and wondered, "What should I do for my talent? I can sing, play the piano and even play the violin, but everyone knows how to do those things!" she thought. "What can I do that no one else can do?" she asked herself. "How can I stand out to the judges?" And then it came to her, "Archery!" she thought. "I'll share my archery program at the Mrs. America pageant!" She immediately contacted the pageant officials and obtained permission to wear shorts, use her bow and arrow, and allow Rex to assist her during the competition.

On August 20, sixty vehicles, carrying approximately 150 people from Fulda, joined a caravan to escort the Wordelman family to the Worthington Municipal Airport. It was quite the celebration as everyone lined the fences of the airport waving their goodbyes and shouting their well wishes to Connie as she and Rex boarded the little prop jet to Minneapolis. Once in the Twin Cities, they would change to a larger airplane that would take them to San Diego.

Upon arrival in San Diego, the contestants were greeted at the

MRS. MINNESOTA AND BEYOND!

airport by Jacques Cosse, Director of Community Relations and Military Affairs, from the Chamber of Commerce. They each were assigned a San Diego Policeman to drive them around San Diego for the entire week. Next, they were all whisked off to the El Cortez Hotel where they were greeted by Mr. Baron Von Hilton himself!

Saturday found the contestants enjoying a picnic lunch in Balboa Park with a photography session in the park's beautiful surroundings, and Sunday, August twenty-second, was Connie's thirty-second birthday and after a wonderful breakfast, she and Rex walked with Mrs. Colorado and her husband to the oldest Presbyterian church in San Diego. That afternoon they met their local sponsors who were from Tyler, Minnesota. Judges interviews went on throughout the afternoon and evening, with Connie meeting with the judges at 8:00PM.

Monday, August 23, after a welcome ceremony by San Diego's mayor, Frank Curran, and Mrs. America, 1963, the contestants were introduced to the judges. Here the judges stressed "This is not a beauty pageant. You will be judged on your talents, achievements, community activities and how you present yourself in public. There will also be an interview with your husband! They are an important part of the title for Mrs. America." The participants were then presented with flowers and asked to compete in a floral arranging event! Mrs. Utah won that competition. All the contestants then met business owners for lunch. They each had an individual sponsor who had their pictures displayed in their businesses with their floral arrangements. Connie was amazed to be given a tour of the May department store; a seven-story shopping extravaganza owned by her sponsor. She had never seen anything quite like it in Minnesota! In the afternoon, the contestants were introduced to Officer George Heckenkamp from the California Highway Patrol who was there to assist with the driving competition. Not only did the contestants have to take a written test, but they had to take a driving test. Connie confidently headed to the staging area where she was offered a sedan or a limo for her driving test. Having plenty of experience driving the hearse for the funeral home, she confidently chose the limo and did an excellent job.

Tuesday, the participants were taken on a tour of the Salk Institute in LaJolla, California. For lunch they attended the Kiwanis club luncheon, and after lunch they went back to their hotel where they competed in the laundry event. They had to iron and fold a white shirt in ten minutes! Tuesday evening found all the contestants attending a champagne reception for the Carnation Festival and then attending the Shakespearean play called "Merry Wives of Windsor" at the Old Globe Theater in Balboa Park. Connie wrote in her letter to her girls that her feet hurt and there wasn't a free minute in her day.

The cake baking event on Wednesday was quite a spectacle watching fifty women all baking cakes at the same time in a very large kitchen. It started with a mixing event, followed by a money management quiz while the cakes baked and cooled. Then all the contestants decorated their cakes and the cakes were tasted and judged. Sadly, Connie's decadent chocolate cake didn't win any prizes. Everyone participated in a packing event where the contestants were judged on how well they packed their suitcases. Once the suitcases were packed, everyone was instructed to leave their suitcases in their room while they were all taken on a tour of the University of California in LaJolla. "More walking in heels," thought Connie! Heading back to their hotels, they were surprised to learn their suitcases had been transferred for them to the Hotel Del Coronado on Coronado Island.

Thursday proved to be a very interesting day. All the contestants participated in the creative talents event. As Connie imagined, many of the other women displayed their musical abilities, but she was the only one who did an archery presentation! Connie, assisted by Rex, awed the crowd with her accuracy with the bow and arrow. When Rex tossed the paper plate into the air and Connie nailed it with her first arrow, the crowd cheered. When she shot the balloon before it hit the floor, the crowd again was impressed, and they let out a gasp when she shot the ping pong ball off from the swinging string. But when she shot an arrow into the middle of the bull's eye on the target, and then put the second arrow directly down the middle of the first arrow, Robin-hooding the first arrow, the crowd roared! Performing flawlessly, her debut on national television didn't seem to faze her amazing archery skills. She was an amazingly impressive archer, and she had the most unique talent of any one in the competition! The feeling of pride Connie felt at that moment was overwhelming! She took a risk with the archery presentation, and it paid off!

During the entire week the husbands were escorted to various activities, one of which was a deep-sea fishing adventure. Sadly, Rex got terribly seasick on the fishing trip and wasn't good company. The husbands were also taken to Tijuana to see the race tract and watch a horserace. They also played several rounds of golf at various golf courses around the city, but unfortunately Rex wasn't a golfer, though he did try. Connie later found out Rex had avoided being interviewed by the judges, although they finally tracked him down. The fact that he didn't change his clothes the entire week was also seen as a negative aspect. Rex didn't appear to be what the Mrs. America judges were looking for in a husband.

That afternoon, Connie enjoyed the luncheon and the tour of Sea World at Mission Bay, thankful that her archery presentation was complete. Friday morning was the grocery shopping event. Then the contestants were divided into four different groups where they served their dinners to their local host and hostess. Saturday, the group was to have a day to themselves, getting ready for the final coronation of Mrs. America in the Hotel Del Coronado Ballroom. Connie was thrilled to learn she had placed 2nd in the Creative Talent Competition for her archery presentation, 3rd in the Driving Competition and was selected to be Mrs. Savings Bond USA, 1965. This was quite an honor as it required a tremendous amount of time speaking at engagements around the country. However, Connie declined this title due to the extensive amount of time she would have to be away from home. She felt it was more important to be home with her daughters, not wanting to leave them home alone with Rex.

Elated with her experience, Connie returned home with many cards and letters full of accolades from friends in Wells and Fulda. The surrounding area newspapers had many articles printed about her, and she began to put everything into a large photo album, called her "Mrs. Minnesota Book". It contained newspaper articles, professional photographs and memorabilia from her time at the Mrs. America pageant in San Diego. She also had a plethora of speaking engagements to attend from Red Owl engagements in Mankato and Minneapolis to the Turkey Day parade with Hubert Humphrey in Worthington, Minnesota! All told, she participated in over two events every month during her reign as Mrs. Minnesota for 1965-66.

The prize for winning the title of Mrs. Minnesota, 1965-66, was a brand new red Karmann Ghia Volkswagen sports car! This car was to take her to her many speaking engagements she was required to attend as the reigning Mrs. Minnesota. She also received a crown, a fancy wig and a beautiful woolen cape from Great Six, Inc. one of the sponsors of the Pageant, made by Fairbault Woolen Mills. During her reign, Connie was the emcee for many various fashion shows put on by the Woolen Mills and she spoke about her life as a new mother without ever having a mother of her own and how important family was. She also spoke about the foster care system and more importantly she shared her thoughts, hopes and dreams as a young active mother, encouraging others to strive to do their very best.

As one local newspaper stated, "Most everyone in and near the small town of Fulda, in Southwestern Minnesota, is familiar with the flashing, radiant smile of auburn-haired Connie Wordelman. Busy with home activities, helping out now and then in her husband's business, on call for many church and community events and organizations, Mrs. Rex Wordelman exhibits vitality and vivacity that helped to put her in that most enviable position as this year's 'Mrs. Minnesota.' This, of course, is no surprise to all her friends and acquaintances who see her daily in her role as housewife and homemaker.

Mrs. Wordelman is a former 4-H member and is still a booster for the 4-H projects. Though she says her cooking is 'simplified country style,' her family attests to her skill in the culinary arts. She sews most of the clothing for herself as well as her three daughters, Caryn 13, Cathy 12, and Lisa, 6. Whenever the occasion requires, she may be found assisting her husband, Rex, furniture retailer and funeral director. She is an accomplished violinist and along with Rex, shares the interesting hobby of archery.

Both Rex and Connie Wordelman are graduates of Wells, Minnesota, high school. Rex attended the University of Minnesota where he graduated in 1950 from the Department of Mortuary Science with an honor citation. Rex joined his father in the mortuary they operated at the time at Wells, moving in 1956 to Fulda where they purchased the Reusse furniture store, and later the Reusse Funeral Home where he and his father are now partners.

Fulda is a small town with a population of just around 1,200. There is no large Metropolitan center nearer than the Twin Cities - Minneapolis and St. Paul, for recreational and cultural opportunities. The Wordelman family therefore prove to be living examples of alert, progressive and popular individuals who make things move in these junior size communities. And Connie Wordelman is a most attractive ambassador who will help put her hometown and the state of Minnesota on the map!"

Connie, Mrs. Minnesota, 1965-66
Turkey Day Parade in Worthington, Minnesota.

CHAPTER **25**

WAR ON THE HOMEFRONT

LIVING BEHIND CLOSED doors was Connie's biggest challenge, not to mention how tremendously painful it was to keep secrets from her friends. Constant tension had invaded the home and Connie's life of kudos and praises had turned into criticism and condemnation. Several times friends would stop in to visit, and by all pretenses Connie would cheerfully greet them, acting as if everything was wonderful. The Wordelman household was your typical, happy Christian family, attending church on Sundays and participating in local activities. But eventually her friends started to see changes when Connie could no longer hide the tension mounting on the home front.

Once Connie was giving a home permanent to her friend Dolores, the two ladies chatting with each other and laughing about the antics of their children when Rex came raging through the door. He picked up a dining room chair and smashed it to smithereens, cursing and swearing as he destroyed not one but two pieces of furniture. Dolores stood, and tried to stop him. "Rex is this really necessary?" she said, trying to stop him.

"Run! Dolores, Run! You don't know what he'll do next!" cried Connie. Seeing the sheer terror in Connie's eye, Dolores ran from the house, curlers in her hair with the towel flapping around her shoulders. Luckily, Dolores lived just two doors down from the Wordelman home. She ran to the safety of her home and waited for Connie to appear. The two-year-old temper tantrum and violent rage Rex displayed stemmed from the fact that a prominent community member had passed away, and Rex had not been called to do the funeral. He had taken the gentleman to the hospital in his ambulance and had not been paid for his services but was anticipating he would receive money for the older gentleman's funeral when he passed away. Unfortunately, Hustad Funeral Home had instead been called to take the funeral and Rex did not receive the business!

Rex's immature rage reminded Connie of the bull on her father's farm. Her brain flashed to the bull exploding without warning, and that in turn triggered her brain. "Run, Connie," she said to herself as she remembered the raging bull. She, too, needed to run! She also knew she needed help! In a split second she followed Dolores out the door, running to get her father-in-law, Al Wordelman. Rex's father seemed to be the only one who could calm him down, and luckily, they lived right next door. Al, being retired, was home and able to come to her rescue. It had been necessary for him to intercede many times over the years, calmly helping Rex cool down, and then waiting with him until he could get his temper under control. No one wanted to be around Rex when he had these explosive moments, especially Connie.

After these explosions, the tension in the home increased tenfold. It was tremendous. No one knew what would set off the beast that raged inside of Rex. Connie knew he had problems, but she didn't know how to address it other than walking on eggshells most of her married life. "What in the world could make him the most generous individual one minute and turn into a raging maniac the next?" wondered Connie.

There was a tremendous amount of camaraderie amongst the small business owners in the little town of Fulda. Each one belonged to the Fulda Chamber of Commerce and each one supported the other. The motto "Shop Local" was highly recommended and everyone tried to abide by this motto. If business was slow throughout the day, the proprietors would often visit with each other, either chatting out on Main Street, or taking a morning or afternoon coffee break at the local cafe. It was common for these men and women to leave their business unattended and walk down the street. Some left their business in their wife's capable hands while they took turns taking breaks. If a patron happened to go into a business when the owner was not there, he or she would look around, call out the owner's name and if no one answered, they would know to check the coffee shop to find the owner! Everyone in Fulda was very trusting!

Rumors of Rex's temper had spread and many of the local businessmen were looking out for Connie's welfare. On one such occasion, one of the city councilmembers entered the furniture store through a back door, his usual entrance, only to find Rex holding Connie up against the wall in a choke hold. Rex was cursing and yelling at her and both were caught by surprise. After all, Rex was a Deacon at the First Presbyterian Church and was involved with the youth group. He was a volunteer Fireman and a highly respected member of the Civic Chamber of Commerce in the small town of Fulda.

The council member, in total shock, yelled at Rex, "What are you doing? Take your hands off her!" Rex quickly released Connie and she ran to stand behind the council member near the back door, eyes wide open in fear of what would happen next. The Council man, standing six foot, five inches tall, clearly eight inches taller than Rex, then grabbed Rex with both hands and shoved him up against the wall in the same fashion Rex had held Connie. Intimidating him with his size and deep voice, he bellowed, "How do you like it? Is this the way you want to be treated?" As he released Rex, he glared down at him and snarled, "Don't ever let me catch you treating your wife this way again, or I'll be back to show you more of the same!"

He turned to Connie and asked if she was okay, and she modestly replied, "Yes, thank you!" embarrassed to need his help. The Councilmember left the store through the door he had entered, and from that point on Rex made sure his abusive attacks were done in private. He knew he could not be seen like this again. But that didn't mean the abuse stopped. Quite the contrary! He continued to berate Connie and treat her poorly in front of their three daughters. Many times, over the next few years Connie wondered, who knows what is going on behind these closed doors?

During one exceptionally hot summer day, Connie decided to help mow the lawn and trim the bushes. She had already spent hours weeding the flower gardens during the week and she thought, "I'll mow the lawn, so Rex doesn't have to do it tonight after work. Plus, it's a great way to work on my tan!" She got the large riding lawn mower out of the garage, checked to see it had enough gasoline and oil, and then proceeded to mow their large lawn. When she finished the lawn, she carefully put the lawn mower away and got out the trimmer. She diligently edged the lawn and put all those tools away. She truly wanted to help Rex, and she was hoping when he got home, he would be pleased to see how much work she had done. She was still yearning for his praise and the kudos she so missed from her father. Thinking that helping Rex would help keep him on an even keel, she went to clean up, thinking, "It's also good to have the girls see me helping him." Then she mused, "With me doing the lawn and the bushes, he'll have time to work on some other little project he has around the house." She spent a long hot morning, driving the lawn mower over their one-acre yard, making sure she'd cut every blade of grass and trimmed every bush. As she looked around, she felt pride in how well manicured the yard and bushes all looked.

But when Rex came home, he became enraged and started ranting and raving, yelling, "You mowed the grass in the wrong direction!" He screamed, "Can't you do anything right?"

Connie was in shock! She silently walked away, not wanting to confront Rex's temper. "What difference does it make?" she thought to herself. She wanted to scream at him, "I was just trying to help?" But then she got angry. She was livid, "How dare he yell at me. All I wanted to do was help him! From now on I will never mow the lawn again!" She knew she couldn't confront him. She knew she couldn't scream at him. She knew what would happen if she did! It seemed to be the little things that threw him into these rages. When he wasn't in control, he went off into a tirade. "Why? Oh, why had I thought I could help this poor man? she asked herself. "Nothing seems to satisfy him!" she said as she left him alone to carry on his rage.

Rex was always busy trying to build things. He had a million schemes, and he would often stay up all night long working on his schemes or projects. Once when the girls were only one and two years old, he had a very clever idea. He would collect tractor seats and weld them onto an even larger commercial tractor tire rim and make a merry-go-round for the girls. There he was, night after night, designing and welding, making a merry-go-round for the girls. "It was a clever idea," Connie thought, but the girls were much too young to enjoy it on their own. He welded them a beautiful swing set and was often tinkering in the barn, coming up with unique ideas. He, too, was looking for kudos and praise and this seemed to be the way he earned it. He wanted everyone to notice what he had done, and how well he had done it.

Everyone in Fulda remembers his pink papier Mache rocking elephant which he made to sit on the second floor of the furniture store. It was a real draw for the furniture store. People would come in to browse at the furniture in order to let their children rock on the pink elephant. He loved designing ideas for the annual Water Festival and many people remember with fondness his giant recliner made for a parade float advertising Wordelman's Furniture Store. Still others remember how he carpeted the walls of his bedroom or stitched carpet samples together to make a unique carpet for his daughter's playhouse. Rex was a very creative individual and he was always dreaming and scheming.

His mind was always busy. As a very intelligent man, scoring the highest on his mortuary science exam, as well as any other tests he'd taken, he had a quest for knowledge! He wanted to impart this quest on his daughters and loved sitting down with them in the evening to read the Encyclopedia!

Out of the clear blue, when the girls were much older, he decided to purchase a building on the edge of town. He loved remodeling and building things. He had already remodeled their home and had added a three-car garage onto it. He had added a bathroom and a utility room to one side, and he had added a laundry room and large closet to the other side. He had built the girls an elaborate playhouse in the backyard, equipped with electricity and folding bunk beds. It was truly a tiny house before tiny houses were in vogue. The new building, he purchased, would be used as a backup storage area for the furniture store. He could order extra furniture and house it in this building. Not a bad idea, or so everyone thought. But mulling this over in his head, his plans changed.

Rex got to thinking, "Connie has a female poodle named Fifi, and Lisa has a male poodle named, Onassis." Out of the clear blue sky he announced, "We should breed poodles!" There was no amount of rationalization that would stop him. He began building kennels in the back of the building originally purchased for furniture storage. He painted the concrete block walls in a sage green. Next, he researched the kind of whelping cages he needed and proceeded to build those. Then he started looking for poodles for sale through the Minneapolis Tribune. Lo and behold, he found a place with over thirty dogs for sale. The breeder wanted to go out of business, so off he went to purchase a bunch of old dogs someone wanted to get rid of. He hadn't done any research on what it takes to be a breeder or how to care for new puppies, but he had his mind set on bringing these dogs back to his new business called, "Pets Galore!"

Off he drove to northern Minnesota, in the family's gold 1963 Vista Cruiser Oldsmobile station wagon. He returned the next evening with thirty-seven poodles of assorted sizes, males and females, miniatures and standards, all piled into the family car! They were the ugliest dogs Connie had ever seen. None of them had been bathed or cleaned for months, maybe even years, and the mess they made in the family station wagon was horrendous! He immediately called his dad to come and help, and together the three of them, Connie, Rex and Alvin, worked all night long shearing and shampooing all those dogs! Rex had no idea most of these dogs were coming from an abusive situation and were not domesticated. They had all lived on wire mesh floors and many of them were crippled and vicious.

As they worked through the night to clean the dogs and put them in appropriate kennels, Rex hadn't realized his building was not soundproof. The building had been a local creamery and was made of solid cement blocks, and located in the middle of a residential neighborhood, not zoned for livestock. He never anticipated how loud thirty-seven angry barking dogs could be inside concrete block walls! The neighbors immediately started to complain about the noise, but Rex trudged on with his endeavor, thinking if they fed the dogs, they would calm down.

Rex also discovered some greyhounds who were for sale from a different breeder, so off he went to purchase greyhounds to add to the menagerie. These poor dogs were the ugliest, most pitiful looking dogs Connie had ever seen in her life, and Rex never lifted a finger to help her with their care after that initial evening. He never really was a dog person but thought this was something Connie would love to do!

Initially, Rex placed ground up corn cobs in the larger dog runs to absorb the urine, which required constant maintenance. Much to their displeasure, Caryn and Cathy were enlisted to shovel the urine-soaked corn cobs into a wheelbarrow every Saturday morning, and then shovel them from the wheelbarrow into a garbage receptacle outside the building. Once this task was complete, they went back inside and shoveled dusty corn cobs back into the dog runs for the next week. Rex brought in stacks of newspapers which were to go into the whelping cages, with the expectation that Connie would care for the smaller dogs and puppies if, and when they arrived.

Several of the dogs arrived pregnant, so Connie had to oversee their care as the bitches began to whelp puppies. But at one point, Fifi, Connie's own female, climbed into the whelping cages, and scared the mothers into eating their own babies to protect them. This case of cannibalism was more than Connie could endure. She immediately contacted the local veterinarian, Dr. William Mears, and asked him to come and help her! "I don't know where to start!" she exclaimed as Dr. Mears walked into the kennel area, Rex's business is failing before it's even begun.

Dr. Mears looked around and explained, "Many of these dogs are probably going to need to be put down."

"I know," said Connie forlornly, "but I don't know if we should start with the bitches here in the cages or with the big ones in the back."

"You mean there's more?" asked Dr. Mears, stunned by what he was seeing.

"Yes!" replied Connie, "Let me show you!" Together they walked to the back-kennel area, a large room with cinder block walls. The first thing to hit them was the putrid stench of wet corn cobs soaked in dog urine, combined with fresh paint. The noise was deafening as all twenty-four dogs in the back kennels began viciously barking, defending their territory. The old standard-sized poodles, placing their paws on the top of the metal kennels made them look adult height. Standing as tall as the old emaciated greyhounds, all the dogs were ferociously barking, expressing their fear of the new intruders. Dr. Mears noticed the curled toes and exceptionally long toenails of the large animals, crippled from living on wire cage floors, their legs wobbling from not having had the ability to fully stand in months, or maybe years! The cement block walls seemed to amplify the barking as they moved along to each dog run looking at the animals. Each dog was so emaciated from malnutrition, it was difficult to imagine they were ever viable pets or sleek racing animals, let alone capable of breeding. All the dogs looked as if they hadn't been fed in weeks, their rib cages clearly showing lack of nutrition. It was obvious they were coming from an abusive situation, and in desperate need of medical attention.

"Well, I guess Rex has rescued these critters. Let's look at them, one at a time," said Doc Mears in his calm methodical voice.

"How in the world will these dogs ever be able to be breeders?"

she asked Dr. Mears. "It's an awful mess Rex has gotten us into!"

"Well, you're right about that!" said Dr. Mears. "This certainly is a mess! Let's see what we can do." he said as he looked around. He'd been a veterinarian covering Murray County for almost fifteen years and had set up a satellite office in Fulda. "We need to go through each dog and look at them individually," he commented. "Which dogs do you think need attention first?" he asked Connie, as they headed back to the whelping cages.

"I think we better start with the bitches in here," she said. "They are the ones who are eating their own puppies!" Together she and Dr. Mears looked at each individual dog in the whelping cages. They had to decide which dogs could be breeders, and which ones needed to be euthanized. After looking at the bitches in the whelping cages, they went back to the larger cages and began working with the larger dogs. Dr. Mears was amazed at Connie's confidence as she helped hold the dogs while he diligently vaccinated each of the dogs deemed viable. And he was amazed at the kindness she showed to the dogs that needed to be euthanized. The work seemed overwhelming, but with Dr. Mears helping her, the two of them finished checking on each of the forty some dogs, working all night long!

"Well, that about does it," said Dr. Mears, as he packed up his bag.

"I don't know how I can ever thank you, Doc," said Connie, using the nickname he had received over the years as a veterinarian. "This was not my choice!" she added. And sadly, it was not a job Connie had asked for, but instead was one of Rex's hair brained schemes. She was content to have Fifi and Onassis, her pets at home. She had not signed up for this ridiculous number of dogs!

"You'll get my bill!" laughed Dr. Mears as he headed toward the door, "But I'll be back in a day or two to check on how the puppies and their mothers are doing. Just make sure you keep your own dogs out of here!" and he turned and headed for his truck.

"This is a bigger job than dealing with the cows on the farm!" Connie thought. "I have to be down here every morning and every night taking care of these dogs. Rex has no idea what he's gotten us into!"

At this point in time, Rex was moving on to other projects. He had his wife occupied with the dogs, and he was now able to move on to something new. Connie felt he never followed through with any of his projects. He always left something undone, and it was the same with Pet's Galore. This time, he dropped all the dogs into Connie's lap, expecting her to make money for the family. Maybe his interests had shifted as soon as he had dropped the dogs off, Connie didn't know, but he became totally engrossed in archery, attending competitions in Minneapolis, or leaving on hunting trips for weeks at a time.

Connie's little red Volkswagen Karmann Ghia, which she had won as a prize for being Mrs. Minnesota, was an adorable little sports car. Rex was tremendously jealous. He hated having his wife running around town in this sporty looking little car. He hated seeing her chat with other merchants. Seeing her in that little red car only added fuel to his jealous fire. The Karmann Ghia enabled Connie to travel to her various speaking engagements throughout the state during her 1965-1966 reign as Mrs. Minnesota, and that reign was over, her speaking engagements were finished. Caryn was soon going to be sixteen and of driving age, and Rex felt the Volkswagen was not a safe vehicle for her to drive. Rex deemed it his very own hunting vehicle. He set to painting it a battleship gray using a paint brush and a can of paint he'd gotten from the store. It was no longer Connie's adorable little red sports car, and in his mind, it was his. He then proceeded to take the ugly little grey Karmann Ghia to his various hunting or archery outings. Connie was terribly upset. She vehemently protested, but as usual he won, using the fact that he didn't want his girls driving such an unsafe car. Connie's adorable little red sports car had been destroyed and turned into an ugly gray hunting vehicle.

When Rex was out of the home for his archery competitions or his hunting trips, Connie noticed how the tension in the home was lifted. The girls were more relaxed and felt comfortable laughing and talking after meals, feeling free to share their daily activities without his scornful criticism. It was as if a veil had been lifted from the entire household. Connie, too, felt freer to be herself. She could laugh and not be criticized for having a laugh which was too loud. She could relax and enjoy her children, so she welcomed Rex's hunting trips and archery competitions.

It was on one of these trips Rex unknowingly started unraveling his marriage. He had taken Connie's very expensive archery equipment along with him to a competition in Minneapolis. The equipment had been manufactured by Bear Archery and given to Connie when she won first place at the Women's Iowa state Target competition. Now, at the competition in Minneapolis, Rex gave Connie's equipment to another woman. No one knew Rex was now involved in an affair with another woman. But, when this woman showed up at a competition using Connie's equipment, it became evident something was amiss. Connie's equipment had been used in the Mrs. Minnesota tournament, so she and her equipment were well known. Rex hadn't realized just how well known her archery equipment had become. The day of the competition, the head of the Minnesota State Long Distance Archery Association, Bob Rhodes, contacted Connie. "Where are you?" he asked. "Your husband's here with another woman, and she's using your equipment! Why aren't you here?"

Connie wasn't shocked at all. A few days earlier she had found a note from the other woman in her car, thanking Rex for the beautiful archery equipment! Evidently, he had told the other woman his wife was no longer interested in archery. Connie also wasn't shocked when her daughter, Caryn, a new teenage driver, had discovered a box of pearls underneath the driver's seat of the Vista Cruiser when she was cleaning it out. The note in the box of pearls was also addressed to the other woman. Not only had Rex given this woman Connie's very expensive archery equipment, but he had also spent hard earned family money purchasing a gift for her. With the notes, the pearls and the long-distance phone call from Bob Rhodes, Connie now had proof of Rex's infidelity. In her mind, she finally had witnesses to substantiate her accusations of abuse, and she had evidence of his infidelity. She promptly filed for divorce in the state of Minnesota on irreconcilable differences. It was June of 1970, and she had endured twenty years of abuse; physically, mentally and emotionally. It was time to stand up for herself.

People often wonder why women stay in abusive relationships, but what they don't realize is that these young women often feel they have nowhere to run. Connie had tried to run, even leaving her precious girls when they were just two and three years old, but Rex had found her and convinced her to come back with him because he would change. Sometimes leaving an abusive spouse is a matter of pride. Sometimes it's a matter of finances, and sometimes it's a matter of safety. For Connie, it was a matter of pride. She was a proud woman. The first time she had run away, Rex had said he would change. She knew she needed to return to protect her children, and she felt she needed to protect the family name. She remembered her father's words, "Remember who you are and who you represent." She also remembered her father's divorce and how miserable it had been for her as a child going through a divorce. It certainly wasn't something she wanted to do, but she realized it was a necessity for her daughters and for herself. She didn't want her daughters growing up believing this was the way husbands treated their wives. So, in 1970, in a small town in southwestern Minnesota, Connie finally had the strength to fight back in the best way she knew how. Divorce was the only way to deal with her situation.

Of course, Al and Alice Wordelman pleaded with Connie not to go through with the divorce, but she finally had the evidence she needed to escape her marriage to Rex. Connie's brave act of filing for divorce made the war on the home front rear its ugly head once again. When Rex was served separation papers by the sheriff, he came storming into the house. He discovered Connie had locks installed on every door, and began to go into a huge rage, screaming and shouting, "We've never had locks on this house before and there is no way this house is going to have locks now!" He got his tools and furiously went from door to door removing each of the locks, cursing and swearing the entire time. Once all the locks were removed, he stormed out of the house! Later, seemingly calmed down, he returned, and calmly put all the locks back onto all the doors. When he finished, he yelled at Connie, "If you think locks are going to keep me out, you've got another thing coming! I'll be back and I'll have a gun and I'll shoot you and your precious daughters!" and he stormed out of the house! Connie immediately contacted the Sheriff to let him know what was happening, and she requested a restraining order be placed against Rex. The sheriff immediately came to the house and installed a red telephone. Connie and the girls were instructed to use the red telephone if Rex were to return to the house.

Going to court was not easy, but Connie stood up and told her side of the story. She had several witnesses testify on her behalf as to the abuse she suffered mentally and physically. She did not want her daughters involved in choosing between her or their dad, so she did not allow her daughters to attend the divorce proceedings. The divorce was finalized in the state of Minnesota after one year, under irreconcilable differences. Connie received custody of the three girls and the house, and Rex was ordered to pay $150 in child support. For Connie, the chains of control and abuse had been released. She felt free to be herself. Her daily walk on eggshells was over, and the war on the home front seemed to finally be over. Connie was ready to move on.

CHAPTER **26**

WHERE TO GO FROM HERE

WITHIN THE NEXT year, Connie began working at Rune's furniture store in Worthington, Minnesota. She knew she needed to earn money to support her girls. Unfortunately working in a furniture store wasn't what she wanted to do! Dusting and vacuuming around furniture left a bad taste in her mouth after having done it for so many years. Rex was supposed to pay the minimum child support demanded by the state which was $50 per child/month. However, Connie knew he wouldn't pay her any money, so she started working where she could find an income and Rune's offered her a job. Even if Rex did pay the $150 a month, she knew that amount wasn't going to go very far. With Caryn turning eighteen years of age, Connie knew college debts would be looming soon, along with Cathy following right behind. Connie not only needed a job for finances, but she needed something she could enjoy, and something to fit her daughter's schedules.

Always enjoying journalism and writing book reports, Connie learned that the Fulda Free Press was up for sale. With her father's support, Connie was able to purchase the local newspaper and she became the only woman editor in Minnesota, in 1971. She learned, with the help of Jim Frick, one of the employees, how to put together and print a weekly newspaper. The year she owned the paper just happened to be the 100th Century celebration for the little town of Fulda, so the newspaper office was inundated with historical pictures and articles. She loved putting the issues together and enjoyed keeping a log of the ads she sold and the dates of local events. She even enjoyed learning about visiting the court to collect "legals". She had a major learning curve with the newspaper but was proud to have received many accolades for her job as editor. She truly felt like she was in her element!

With the kennel situation behind her, Connie thought how beneficial it had been! "What a blessing." she thought as she reminisced about all those filthy, motley-looking dogs. As much as she hated that horrible situation, she knew it was the best thing that could have ever happened to her. Through this mess with Pets Galore, Connie had met Dr. William Mears.

Bill, as she called him, stood almost a full foot over her 5'2" frame, with his 1960's crew cut adding a little extra height! His nose appeared too long and crooked, having been broken during his football playing days as a young boy in Canada. But he was the kindest man she had ever met, next to her father, of course!

Growing up in Canada, Bill had faced a life very similar to Connie's. His father had passed away when he was around three years old. His mother proceeded to marry another man who had two older daughters. Sadly, his new stepfather, Mr. Leech, did not want Bill and his brother, Jack, to live with them. In fact, Mr. Leech wanted nothing to do with the two little Mears boys. Both Bill and Jack were sent to live with their grandmother, who lived around the country road from their mother's house. Over and over these two little boys, just four and five years old, continually walked back up the road to be with their mother. And sadly, they were immediately taken back to their grandmother's house, forbidden to stay with their own mother. When Jack passed away a few years later at the age of nine, Bill was left to be raised with his Grandma and Grandpa. His life of losing a mother was something he could easily relate with Connie's childhood separations from her mother and various caregivers.

When Bill had turned sixteen, he had joined the Royal Canadian Air Force and received training as a radar technician. He was sent overseas to England and was assigned to a group that maintained the Royal Canadian Air Force Bombers. After he returned from service, he obtained his high school diploma through the Canadian GI Bill, and then went on to attend the University of Ontario at Guelph. He married Dorothy Pushinsky, and with her support, he eventually obtained his Doctorate in Veterinary Medicine. As a young veterinarian, he and Dorothy moved to Worthington, Minnesota, where he practiced for a short time. In 1954, a veterinary clinic became available in Slayton, Minnesota, and Bill and Dorothy moved their small family to take over that business. Slayton and Fulda were just twelve miles apart, which was the small town in which Connie had been living. Being a large animal veterinarian, Dr. Mears covered the entire Murray County area and often took care of local pets on an as needed basis. Wanting to replace the carpet in their older home in Slayton, Bill Mears had gone to Wordelman's Furniture store to purchase new carpeting. The two Fulda business owners hit it off and would sometimes have coffee together when Bill was doing veterinary work in Fulda.

And so, it was that Dr. Bill Mears was in Fulda to help Connie with the dogs at Pets Galore. She reminisced about that day when she was immediately drawn to his kind spirit as they worked alongside each other, deciding what each dog needed. He praised her ability to calm the animals and the skill with which she tended to their needs. Enamored with his kindness and his gentle demeanor, they each began to look forward to their morning visits, mainly as friends in the beginning. The chemistry between them was incredible as they worked side by side to help the dogs at Pets Galore. Connie had never believed in "Love at first sight", but even with all the dogs barking in the background, she had developed quite a crush on Dr. Mears. "Am I feeling this way because he was my knight in shining armor?" Connie wondered. "Are these feelings coming on because he eased my miserable situation?" She kept her thoughts to herself as she dealt with her miserable homelife. "Does he feel the chemistry that I'm feeling?" she asked herself. Her mind and her heart were in a tizzy. She'd never felt this way before. "I wonder if he can tell I'm falling for him?" she wondered.

One morning, Bill sensed something was amiss and said, "Connie, what's wrong?" She obviously had been crying, and she told him she had just served Rex with divorce papers and all hell had broken loose. She had come to the kennels to escape what was happening at home. They chatted and he assured her she had done the right thing.

"Escaping the abuse is paramount for you and your daughters," he said. Connie nodded, tears welling up in her eyes. "You know, I too, have wanted to get a divorce." he told her, "The love is gone between my wife and me. We're just going through the motions. Plus, with six kids and a large veterinary practice, life has just gotten in the way. I seem to be just going through the routine. How can I walk away from it all?" he asked, not really wanting an answer. And then as he looked at Connie he said, "I wish I had the guts to do what you've done! I know it wasn't easy." He told her how proud he was of her decision, knowing full well that many people continue to tolerate the hand they've been dealt, and he told her he would help her in any way he could. He sounded just like her father when she talked to him on Wednesday evenings.

Each day Bill came to help at Pets Galore, the two of them would chat, more about life than about dogs, and their friendship began to grow into a mutual respect and admiration for each other, eventually leading to more than either of them ever intended!

During those spring months, Dr. Mears had taken his truck into the local gas station to have the snow tires removed and the regular tires put back on. Unfortunately, the lug nuts of his large veterinarian truck were not tightened properly, and as he was driving in high winds, one of the lug nuts worked its way off, allowing one of the tires to come off from the axle. As the tire broke away from the axle, it caused the truck to careen into the ditch. Dr. Mears was knocked unconscious, losing control of the vehicle as the cab separated itself from the frame of the truck. The cab then continued to roll up over the fence, rolling over and over approximately six or seven times, until it finally came to rest in a farmer's field. With the cab completely detached from the chassis, Dr. Mears was securely held inside by his seatbelt. But when he came to, he could still hear the engine running. He reached over to turn the key off only to discover the engine was across the field still sitting in the ditch!

Since he had been collecting payments from clients that morning, he realized the glove compartment had broken open and the checks he had just collected were blowing across the field. Somehow, he managed to extricate himself from the cab and chased after the blowing checks! Once he had secured all the checks, he then walked to a nearby farmhouse, explained his situation and asked for a ride into town. Since Connie's house was close, he immediately went there to tell her what had happened. She took him to the Slayton hospital where they took an x-ray. They put him in a neck brace and arranged for him to visit a specialist in Sioux Falls, South Dakota. After visiting a specialist in Sioux Falls, Dr. Mears was told he had suffered a broken neck, but luckily, he had not severed his spinal cord. The specialist prescribed a four-poster neck brace and told Dr. Mears to avoid any jarring to his spinal column or he could sever his spinal cord permanently. He was advised not to practice on any large animals, so Dr. Mears decided to make some changes in his life.

"This break is a perfect time for me to make a break from my marriage," he admitted sadly. Within a very short time he acquired a small trailer and moved out of his Slayton home which he had shared with his wife for 25 years.

JUST KNOW I LOVE YOU

I only want to share, every minute, every day and
every night of your life.
And, I want you to know that whatever you do, wherever you go,
forever, I will be your wife.
Always remember that this one loves only you.
No matter what comes, I'm always your girl.
Just remember, I love you more than anything in this whole wide world.
I'm so happy that I'm the one that you come home to.
That's what love is for, a shoulder, when you're blue.
Let me help weather the storm.
Yet, I truly need your support and lifting strength.
Most of all, give me security, keep me warm, humble,
proud with dignity.
May this be the best of what's to come.
Forever, together and sharing. Ours, yours, nine, and "give some"
Hold our heads high, realize our together goals,
Hold each other, cling to life, surge ahead.
I accepted you, Trusted and tears, I've cried.
Now, let's smile - - - instead!

Bill and Connie, photo taken by Bill's daughter, Ann Grimes.

CHAPTER **27**

OFF TO LAS VEGAS

WHEN DR. BILL Mears decided to break away from his own family and his own practice, he headed to Las Vegas to gain residency so he could obtain a divorce. On his way, he stopped in Loveland, Colorado, to meet Alfred Bates, Connie's father. Alfred was tremendously impressed with this young doctor. "He's exactly who I would want you to marry!" he shared with Connie over the phone during one of their weekly Wednesday chats. Connie was thrilled to know that her father approved of Dr. Bill Mears!

Once in Las Vegas, Dr. Mears attended the Western States Veterinary Conference, and there he met Dr. Lilly, a local Las Vegas veterinarian who just happened to be looking for another veterinarian for his practice. Bill jumped at the chance to work with Dr. Lilly. After spending six weeks obtaining his Nevada residency, Bill called Connie. "I know what we are going to do", he excitedly exclaimed, "We are going to throw our snow shovels away and move to Vegas! You'll have to sell the newspaper and your house and move out here so we can be together!" Connie immediately completed that week's newspaper and flew to Vegas to be with Bill. When she arrived, she was thrilled to be able to go with him on one of his house calls. There, she was amazed to see him treat one of the "Circus Circus" elephants for diarrhea!

Connie spent the day at Paradise Pet clinic where Dr. Lilly told

Bill, 'If you don't marry this little gal, I will!" Bill and Connie enjoyed a dinner show with Dr. Lilly and his wife, and then they drove down the Las Vegas strip, at which point Bill pulled the car over and proposed! Since Las Vegas was open 24 hours a day, they then drove to the courthouse downtown and obtained a marriage license. Connie went back to Fulda and started proceedings to sell her house and the newspaper. Luckily, Jim Frick, who had been working for Connie, said he would love to purchase the paper! Someone came forward and purchased the house with all its furniture, and Connie flew back to Las Vegas within just a few weeks. It all happened so quickly; Connie knew it was meant to be! She and Bill went to a dinner show with Dr. Lilly and his wife again, and then Connie and Bill took another drive down the strip. This time they stopped at the Church of the West and there, on June 30, 1972, Connie and Bill were married. The next day she called her dad to tell him she and Bill had gotten married, and he was ecstatic to know Connie was finally happy!

Due to his injuries, Dr. Mears took the Sioux Falls specialist's words of advice and decided not to work on large animals any longer. In order to increase his viability as a small animal doctor, he decided to go back to school to obtain his small animal certification. Together, he and Connie packed their few belongings and headed to Columbia, Missouri, where Bill attended the Veterinary School of Medicine at the University of Missouri. He obtained his orthopedic certification there, enabling him to efficiently work on broken bones for smaller animals. He then flew to Carson City, Nevada, to take the state boards and obtain his Nevada Veterinary license. When they returned to Las Vegas to make it their home, Dr. Mears again worked for Dr. Lilly at the Paradise Pet Clinic.

Having owned his own practice for over twenty years and having three other partners working with him, Dr. Mears soon wanted his own clinic. He wasn't one to work for someone else, so in 1974, he and Connie decided to build their own veterinarian clinic. In 1975, Chaparral Pet Clinic came to fruition. Together they had accomplished their dream. Chaparral Pet Clinic stood on the property at Desert Inn and Sandhill Avenue in Las Vegas, Nevada, for twenty-five years.

Being low on funds in those days, and not afraid of work, Connie decided to use her talent to bring in some extra income. She became a "relief" violinist for major hotel show rooms in Las Vegas, eventually being hired full time with the Sands Hotel orchestra, playing for Wayne Newton. Connie prided herself on being listed as one of the violinists on one of Wayne's albums. Her dad was so proud of her! She was finally using her musical talents, but in the back of her mind she wondered, "What is my mother doing right now? Would she be proud of my accomplishments?" And of course, up to the forefront came the question that had been plaguing her for years, "Do I look like her?" Not one to sit idle, Connie's mind was always going.

It was a grueling schedule, playing two shows a night, one at 8:00 PM and one at midnight. Forcing herself to go to bed by 3:00 AM, after she had quieted her mind from the loud hectic evening performances. She wanted to be a good wife and mother, so she was back up at 6:30 to get Bill up for work and her younger daughter, Lisa, who was fourteen, off to school. One of Bill's sons, Bruce, also lived with them and attended the University of Nevada. With two extra mouths to feed, Connie was determined to bring in more money while they built the new clinic. Once everyone was off to school and jobs, Connie would try to get more sleep. But she was a morning person and sleep was difficult in those days. Somehow, she managed to trudge through her days, happy just to be in a home where there was no tension!

When the clinic was finished, Connie dug in to help Bill. Between the two of them, they hired vet techs to be assistants in Bill's surgery and Connie became the office manager and bookkeeper. She ended up taking over the hiring and firing of employees so Bill could focus on his medical expertise. Some days he would call her "Cricket" as she jumped from the back office helping clients to the front office to do bookwork. Other days he would call her the "Energizer Bunny!" as she was always on the go! Together they accomplished whatever they put their minds to. They hired two special employees, Sonja and

Kelly, who spent fourteen years working as assistants to Dr. Mears. This stability told anyone walking into the clinic that Dr. Mears was a wonderful man to work with. They were a well-oiled team, attending to patients on Las Vegas' 24-hour schedule. Many nights, after working all day, Dr. Mears and his team would be called to the clinic to tend to an animal who wasn't feeling well, when its owners had arrived home after their 2:00 AM shift. Las Vegas proved to be an interesting town.

It was in those wee hours, Connie would wonder, "What would my mother think of my life? Would she be as impressed with my accomplishments?" It was about this time that her daughters, Caryn and Cathy, were starting to encourage her to begin a search for her birth mother.

"What if your mother has some major genetic problems you should know about?" they asked. "Is there something she has faced that could help us with our medical situations?" Connie knew she had to do something, but was it the right time to start searching? And how do you search for someone who has abandoned you?

"I promised myself that I wouldn't search while my dad is still alive," she told the girls.

"That's fine," said Cathy, "But you know it could take a while. She was eager to start looking for Viola Lundberg, her grandma.

"I just can't right now," said Connie, delaying the search and surrounding herself with other activities. She immersed herself into her rose garden and writing poetry, and then along came the grandchildren.

FIRST OF MANY

Flounces, dainty ruffles, pigtails, midnight snuffles.

Little pink bows. Ten perfect toes. June seventeenth arrival,

Cathy's motherly survival. Father Charlie's ecstasy,

Now a family of three. Gurgling coos, a sigh –

You cannot deny, Carissa is all girl, with a little blonde curl.

Precious heavenly bundle, accepting love and fondle.

Our family of nine, (Some not mine.)

With individual personalities, striving for their realities.

Seeking education and careers, facing earthly fears.

Some eager to "produce", others proving worldly "use".

I truly feel unending love and zeal, warmth and tenderness,
I must confess,

The "first of many" I'm truly a "Granny"!

Connie and first granddaughter, Carissa Hopkins-Hoel

HER AGE OF INNOCENCE

My arrival at Boston was filled with anxiety,
As I searched the jostling crowd for David, Caryn and ollie.
All were waiting with their familiar grins and looking for me.
A proud Papa, an expectant Mama and an adorable little Mollie.
Luggage arrives in great shape, David finds the van and takes it all,
as I gape!
It's home to Newport, after a Chinese meal.
Mollie is tired, but happy.
Oh boy! Do I feel the next two weeks will be a real challenge!
For there's bottles and diapers, that always need a quick change.
The days pass slowly as we all anxiously wait.
For a new baby's arrival that's passed the due date.
But little Mollie is so eager to learn, and the time goes quickly as my
keep, I earn!
We dance a few steps, some forward and a few back.
A cuddle, a kiss, and a "No-No", and then "hit the sack!"
She's so innocent as she watches our each and every move.
"Please." "Thank you," Mama," and "Daddy," somehow prove
That Mollie is exceptional at learning new things.
As "dances", "sits down" and is always piling her "rings".
She knows only love, warmth and that smiles are great.
No knowledge that the world is filled with war and hate.
Only duplicating everyone's actions and antics,
Unaware of nuclear warfare, demonstrations or politics!
Wouldn't it be magnificent if we could capture
That spirit and enfold the world with its rapture?
To feel faith, love, still have the good sense
To live happily, lovingly in the Babe's realm of innocence.

SOME DAY
By Connie Mears, March 1981

These are endless days of enduring length.
It takes stamina, patience, and all my inner strength.

To meet the demands of a hurried and busy schedule,
Scurrying here and there and still being careful.

Quick trips for items and our necessities,
Keeps me planning ahead, with lots of anxieties.

No time to read a recommended book,
Window shopping is extinct; no time to cook!

A speedy trip, with deposits to the bank,
Postage to buy, quarterly reports and then fill the "tank".

Each number on the calendar has a great significance –
Rents to pick up, "seconds" to make, there's little time for neglected romance.

Nights are restfully spent with relaxing and hushed quiet –
Just waiting for tomorrow's demands, who needs a diet!

Grass to mow, weeds to pull, hedges need a sculptured clip,
Groceries, new glasses a needed haircut – all make me zip.

When all the flurry of traffic ceases,
will I really relish the quiet that increases?
Read that neglected book, take more time at my daily work.

OFF TO LAS VEGAS

Feel relaxed and tackle duties with a whimsical smirk?
I'm slowly growing older, on the threshold of tranquility.

It only makes me realize I physically don't have ability.
Yet, I live and love each day, to the fullest and enfold every busy
minute,

Helping others, Listening, Smiling, Growing and Doing.
I Love it!

ODE TO ALL GRACES

Immovable elements in our daily living
With more thought, we should be giving.

Cupboard corners, wooden or glass door,
Objects loom from the floor,

Obstacles waiting for "Cranium Crashes",
Jolting abruptly, plummet me into "Facial Smashes".

Entering in my graceful, lady-like fashion,
Never expecting an onset of battin' or gashin'.

Only wanting to make a grand entry,
I'm met with a rigid immoveable sentry.

Should I go around, over or under?
Is there another way in or out, I wonder?

For it seems "Damn things appear",
Catch me off guard, "Oops, too late, I fear"!

Table legs, corners, zoom in, attack with hate,
Snag my passing body, "Damn" it's fate!

Striking blows, tripping to a screeching halt,
Landing spread-eagle, "Another Damn default"!

Bruises of purple, yellow, green and blood red.
Thighs, elbows, constantly skinned, knots somewhere on my head.

OFF TO LAS VEGAS

Walking tall, attempting some pose and grace,
Carefully, making more time trying to save face,

Forever, surging ahead, forget idleness, no desire to atrophy
A Klutz is what I really am,
Stumbling, bumbling, slipping, sliding, Catastrophe!

NEW ARRIVAL
Written for Mimi, Caryn and David's 2nd baby, born in Newport, Rhode Island.

A long-awaited birth produced from Caryn's girth!
Brought happiness, tears and joy, everyone knew,
this one would be a boy!
But God made his own decision, lovingly created a girl in His vision.
June ninth was the arrival day, telephone rings with David to say,
"It's a girl, 7 pounds, 9 ounces," so it's more pink ruffles and flounces.
A sister for Mollie will be great, also cheaper for the "First Mate"!
They named her Merrie Lee! Grandparents anxiously wait to see,
The newest bundle of love sent from God above!

Connie with Caryn's first granddaughter,
Legend Jeannotte, Mimi's daughter.

BOOKWORK

Bookwork is a grudge, a drudge, an Obligation!
I mumble, and fumble with great frustration!

The rows of numbers seem unending,
Totals somehow appear for taxes pending.

Ledgers, postings, and quarterly reports,
Category numbers, check writing and meetings with cohorts,

Produces a final tabulation.
I reach a conquering realization better and neater bookwork,

With concentrated efforts for filing, will keep the CPA smiling.
Taxes, insurance, interest and principal,

That are compiled for yearend results,
Show laborious, endless hours and a hope for no defaults.
Sit on it, IRS!

ANOTHER BOTTLE ON THE SHELF

I have a typical woman's pharmacy
That boasts rare and magic potions.
There are wrinkle creams, astringents and age disguising lotions.

All sizes of bottles and jars galore,
to the point of saturation.
All filled with empty promises to starve off maturation.

As long as we have a shred of hope
Us "gals" are willing patrons
To avoid being labeled as unattractive "matrons".

Cosmetic maker's claims are absurd
But for "Beauty's Sake" we'll take them!
But somehow the only benefit guaranteed is to the "Ones" that make 'em!

TOGETHER ALWAYS

MATING MALLARDS

Mallard ducks upon the pool water,
Sitting in morning sunlight, doing what they "oughter".
Spring arrives early, with a red, glowing sunrise.
Each year, at this time, it's really no surprise,
To see a mated couple swim close together.
Two beautiful creatures with elegant feather,
Cavorting, preening each other in bird-like fashion.
Soft guttural quacks echo early morning passion.
Teal and purple crest the lustful male's head.
Mother's muted browns a camouflage for her bed.
She seems almost oblivious of the aggressive lust.
Sedate and aloof, she calmly does what she must.
Soon proud Mama will parade a flock in a row,
Our pool is a sunlit haven for ducklings to grow.
Their sudden appearance and awakening of spring.
It's Mother Nature, fulfilling her marvelous "thing"!

A SALE

Little colored tags spinning and reeling,
Hang from shirt sleeves and look so appealing!
Propaganda of a sale's hours, for day and night,
Bring shoppers, squealing with exuberant delight!
They paw and shove to look at racks,
While paying for merchandise, the owners, their lips smack!
For what they thought was a bargainer's treat
Is the shop owner's taxes he has to meet!
Prices are doubled and then slashed in half,
To buy at cost is really a laugh!

THIS GRANNY

A rocking chair for me? Forget it!
It's off to the office or shopping.
This Granny goes every minute.
No shelf to sit! This Granny's hopping!

This Granny is aggressive, outspoken, yet versatile.

No pies in the oven baking,
Bookwork, errands, for all people, a smile.
For this Granny is earth-shaking!

Up early, busy hours before bed.
Meeting schedules, no time to cook,
Poems created, gush from the redhead,
This Granny is writing a book!

Aches and pains quickly disappear,
As Granny life is romancing.
No hours for "Granny-time, "I fear.
This Granny has taken up dancing!

TOGETHER ALWAYS

SPOTLIGHT ON SPIRIT

Just when I thought I had a step under control
Undone it was. Start over, forget a muscle pull.
No stopping to rest, the music must go on!
Everyone will be involved; dates are picked for fun.

Foot stomping, legs swinging from hips,
Eagerness produces only happiness from our lips!
Stand tall, a little to the left. Is my head, right?
Tummy's tucked in, buns aligned, we are ready to fight!

In Universal, you learn properly, forget not!
"Valzes", Swing, Latin Rhythms,
and the ever lovin' Fox trot."
Alone, no one is allowed to sit, together we dance.
Let us join the Regals and Stylists and give a hand to Dance.

Shake a leg, feel a rosy inner glow,
Put effort forth and make it your show.
Instead of sitting back, Give it a whirl.
Reach for winning, watch flags unfurl.

Involvement means inviting guests,
A costume be a sponsor.
Total the points, join in the festival fun!
Set a goal, Let's score!

RECIPE FOR GOURMET COMPETITION

Take a familiar song, add four dancing feet,
Listen to rhythms, clearly count the beat.
Stir in two dancers,
Warm slowly over moderate heat.
Sift lessons gradually, one hour at a time,
Only efforts will make your creation sublime.
Follow recipe directions, ingredients need gentle stir
No exchanges, use firm support, Build confidence for him or her.

A pinch of styling, be it Tango, Waltz, Fox Trot,
Blend ever so slowly, Simmer in a bubbling pot.
Spice the routine, Fold in Steps of Left and Right
Sweetened with "Lifts and Drops", molded perfectly, be not uptight.
Ladle mixture gently so bubbles won't burst.
End results blended will produce only a First!

Bake in a low oven, wait for doneness test
Cool gradually, rise or fall. It means doing your best.
Sprinkle attitude, perseverance, smiles, perhaps a dimple,
Spread frosting with glide, try not hard, keep it simple.
Rondes, Twinkles, and Checks require excellent lead.
Pile high with trust and confidence, my partner, I do need.

To Hacienda Competition, Dance your creation,
Enter Bronze, Silver or Gold.
Swing, Sway with jubilation, Togetherness - - -
Hearts happy, Heads up for fun competition.
Here we come United at Dance Institute,
I know we've won!

CHAPTER **28**

DADDY'S GONE

CONNIE CONTINUED WITH her many activities, playing the piano, dancing and writing poetry. Over the years, she and Bill became involved with Opportunity Village, a not-for-profit organization for intellectually disabled men and women in Las Vegas. Together they helped raise money for the organization's annual Magical Forest. Connie, relying on her days of selling ads for the newspaper, went from business to business obtaining donations through ticket sales. Their goal was to get donors to purchase seats at the large gala. Since Dr. Mears was Liberace's veterinarian, caring for all twenty-two of his dogs, Connie was able to ask Lee if he would donate. To her astonishment, his $5,000 donation put her over the top as a fundraiser! She and Bill were honored at the annual banquet for helping obtain such a high amount of money.

She became involved in Dance competitions and often sewed her own dresses, many times hand sewing on the beads and feathers to create just the right look. Her Tweety Bird costume accompanied by Sylvester was quite the hit. No one could figure out who she and Bill were when they walked into the competition that night. But her favorite costume was the dress that weighed twelve pounds from all the beads she had sewn onto it!

On the weekends, she and Bill scoured the town of Las Vegas to see the sights and enjoyed playing tourist. They went to the various buffets and often Bill's work would take them to the Mirage or "Circus Circus" to check on the animals at those destinations. They also had the opportunity to see many of the local lounge acts as well as the big shows. On one of their sightseeing trips they came over the rise to see the London Bridge at Lake Havasu, and right in front of them was a magnificent double rainbow. Together they decided a rainbow would be their symbol of togetherness and love! "No more birds or butterflies for me," said Connie, "when I'm dead and gone, look for rainbows. I'll be somewhere over the rainbow! In fact, you can play that at my funeral!" she joked!

It was during her time in Las Vegas when she became engrossed in collecting clowns. Bill bought her the most beautiful Emmitt Kelly clowns and her daughters and granddaughters always gave her clowns for every occasion, whether it was her birthday or Christmas, she would get several clowns of every size. She loved the song, "Send in the Clowns" and had several musical clowns that would play this song, along with, "I'd Like to teach the World to Sing." She also had a bell collection, remembering how important a bell had been for Mary Lee. And along with the clowns, the girls would also bestow Connie with bells as well as clowns for every occasion. Anything musical was adored by Connie, and it didn't take long for each of these collections to have their own enormous glass display case. If her collections were any indication of how much she was loved, one would say, "To the moon and back!"

But times weren't always easy. Together Connie and Bill purchased nine different homes as rental properties, with the intention of being able to leave each one of their adult children a rental property of some value when the two of them passed. They were from the era where parents left their money to their children. Along with the houses, they also purchased an apartment building, hoping it would be a good financial investment. Bill, and his son, Bruce, learned to do many kinds of maintenance on each of these properties, while Connie maintained the bookwork. She would collect rent, pay mortgages and taxes, along with meticulously maintaining receipts and bookwork pertaining to these properties. Some days there were a lot of headaches! People moved out without giving notice, others left a putrid mess behind, or someone's toilet overflowed. Somedays the pool wasn't working, or an apartment needed to be repainted or new carpet installed. Together, along with Bruce's help they managed to survive.

Connie thrived on her routine. She tended to her roses early in the morning, doing her crossword puzzles, playing the piano for a relaxing break or cleaning the house or pool mid-mornings and then managing the clinic during her afternoons. She was always busy and liked it that way. On weekends she continued to follow almost the same schedule, minus working at the clinic. She loved rising early, having a cup of coffee and reading the morning paper while she watched the sun rise against Sunrise Mountain. She loved their view looking over the neatly manicured ninth hole of the National Golf Course, which was directly on the other side of the fence from her pool in the backyard. The pristinely manicured lawn of the golf course provided a perfect backdrop for reading in the mornings, and she loved doing the crossword puzzles or writing poetry out on her beautiful patio. More than anything she enjoyed chatting with her daughters on the phone or having her grandchildren visit. But in the back of her mind, Connie still had that one nagging question; who do I look like?

Looking at her daughter's pictures on the wall, Connie now began to wonder, who do **they** look like? They certainly weren't built like she was. She was small and petite, wearing a size 2 or 4, while her daughters were much larger boned and heavier. "Who do they resemble?" Connie would ask herself. "Do they look like other relatives? Maybe the grandchildren even look like someone else, and I don't even know it!" Connie's questions were starting to drive her crazy! All the questions that had stuck with her from her childhood often came rushing back. She kept these questions hidden, but her brain was constantly questioning.

She thought back to her fifteenth birthday. She had always been told she was adopted. She'd been told she was special. Her dad had instilled in her the fact she had been chosen. "Out of all of the boys and girls at the orphanage, we picked you," her dad had told her. He made her feel more special than any other little girl in the world! And now she remembered her fifteenth birthday when her father had given her the special envelope. He had told her, "It's time you know your birth history. It will tell you about your birth mother and your birth father. But always remember, you're my true daughter, Connie, and you will always be mine, but I think you are mature enough to understand this information." It was as if it was just yesterday. She could hear his deep voice reassuring her of his love.

Connie had always wondered what her mother had looked like. "Do I look like my mother?" she wondered. When she saw people on the street, she would wonder, "Could this woman be my real mother? Do they look like me? Could they be related to me?" She held this curiosity deep within her heart because her dad had been the best dad in the whole wide world. She never wanted to hurt her daddy's feelings, so she never voiced these questions out loud, but instead had held them deep in her heart. Again, she got out her birth information, and opened the special envelope. It was well worn with age. "This envelope is almost fifty years old!" she told Bill one morning as she decided to share the information with him. As she again read the information about her mother, she said to him, "I wonder who I look like! Will any of this information help me if I started a search for my mother?"

"Well, you don't really have much to go on. You probably need more information," said Bill. "And women marry and change their names, so you're probably not even looking for Viola Lundberg anymore!" he told her.

"I can't do anything anyway." she said, and put the papers back into the envelope, and gently placed the manilla envelope back into her silver metal box for safe keeping.

As often as Connie had wondered about her birth mother, she kept telling herself, "I don't want to hurt my dad's feelings. I have a father and mother." She didn't want him to think he wasn't enough, but her daughters were again encouraging her to do a birth search for medical answers.

And then it happened. The week of March 7, 1980, Connie was called and informed that Alfred was in the hospital. She and Bill immediately flew to Loveland, Colorado, to be with her dad. It was a long week where she spent time at the hospital, and time in his home sorting through his garage and various papers. Only a week later, on March 14, 1980, Alfred passed away while Connie and Bill had gone out to dinner. Her daughters flew in from California and Minnesota, respectively, and sang at their grandfather's funeral. Full Masonic Rites were conducted at the graveside service that cold March day, and then Connie and Bill flew back home to Las Vegas. She knew it was time to search for her birth mother.

Alfred Bates, Connie's father in Loveland, Colorado.

DEAR OLE DAD

Whimsical looks, a furrowed frown,
Laughing eyes, somedays a real clown!
He's always been called "Daddy" to me.
A guiding hand to set talents free.
Singing my heart out long hours of practice,
Violin etudes, piano recitals, some not so nice.
Learning to dance, get the rhythms just right.
Solving math problems that kept us up all night.
A jolly, robust, honest, hardworking soul was he,
He's gone now, but he'll always be, "Daddy" to me!

Alfred E. Bates
March 18, 1891 - March 14, 1980

"DADDY'S" GONE

Death is God's way of having us say "Good-bye".
It's not easy to remind us that someday, we too, must die.
Our chosen paths of life are set for a single course.
Each steppingstone of failure and success, we must endorse.

It's hard to accept the deep impact of losing one so dear.
Years of learning, inner strength will always hold him near.
For he gave me courage, patience and the ability to hold,
Precious moments, joys and sorrows, as my life does unfold.

Being picked up and held by one so bold and tall,
Left me speechless, "O, Daddy, don't let me fall!"
Hands so big with powerful wrench-like strength,
For him, I'd pursue my utmost to any length.

He always listened and smiled, as my worries I would tell.
Just a knowing nod, a word of assurance, and all was well.
An open heart, a loving way, and a clever wink,
Kept me on my toes, let me know that he'd never let me sink.

Memories of growing through the teenage years,
His powerful presence nearby when I shed useless tears.
"Stand straight and tall! Hold your head up high!"
Don't shirk your duties, work needs doing," and I'd sigh.

A constant push for achievement. Some days I couldn't do enough.
Failures and successes were conquered along a road so rough.
He knew me better than I knew myself.
Shaped and molded talents, never letting them sit on the shelf.

"Look at me when I speak and quit kicking the rug!"
All this parental discipline understanding of true life.
Reminds me daily, to be a good mother
And yet, a better wife.

Daddy's gone now. He only said a quiet "Goodbye".
I'll forever miss our closeness, and silently cry.
Daddy's gone, but for Him I'll strive to always do,
The best that I can do!

CHAPTER **29**

WHO DO I LOOK LIKE?

CONNIE HAD ALWAYS wanted to find her birth mother. She often found herself wondering what had happened to her real mother and father. She wondered if there were other relatives out there who might know what had happened to her mother and father. She had no idea where to start, so with encouragement from Bill and her three daughters, Connie finally started to pursue the search. Once Alfred Bates, her adopted father had passed, she was able to feel she wouldn't hurt his feelings. "He was my real father," she told her daughters. "Without him I would not be who I am today, but you're right, I need medical answers. I need to find out if some of the things I'm facing medically were things faced by my own birth mother or other relatives."

So, on February 24, 1982, Connie entered a search agreement with the Children's Home Society of Minnesota, agreeing to pay $100 deposit to cover worker's time and long-distance telephone costs. A year later, in 1983, Connie received a letter from Meg Bale, the case worker from the Children's Home Society who was assigned to her case. The letter stated that more forms must be completed for Connie to get her birth certificate! Minnesota adoptions were originally closed adoptions and were not to be opened for one hundred years! Luckily the law changed before Connie began her search, but she was flabbergasted when they wanted more paperwork! "What more could they want?" she said to Bill, not realizing this was only the beginning!

Luckily for Connie, Minnesota opened the records across the state, but there were still more forms to be signed. In March of that year, she received a more formal letter from the Children's Home Society stating she should stay in touch with Meg Bale, who was her case worker. She would be her best option for obtaining any birth information! So that is exactly what Connie did! She and Meg became best friends, talking frequently with Meg constantly reassuring Connie that "these things take time."

During May of 1983, Meg Bale sent Connie a copy of her father's name and address in Peoria, Arizona. Connie immediately called Meg and asked, "Did you give Howard my name and address?"

"Yes, I did!" said Meg excitedly from Minneapolis. "He has been informed that if he wishes to receive more information, he needs to complete the papers I enclosed for him. He has to have them notarized and signed and return to me at the Children's Home Society before he can get in touch with you."

"How long will that take?" asked Connie, anxious to move the process along. Fifty years after her birth, Connie had her birth father's name. Was it possible she was finally going to meet her birth father? What a surprise she was given! She didn't want to wait a minute longer!

On the other end of the line Meg was telling her, "We'll have to wait and see how long it takes Howard to get the paperwork notarized and returned to our office in Minneapolis." Meg Bale was reassuring as she calmly said, "You know, Connie," she said hesitantly, "You have to be prepared yourself. Not everyone wants to be found!"

"I understand." said Connie as she laid down the receiver and ended her call with Meg.

"Imagine that!" she excitedly told Bill that evening. "Instead of finding my birth mother, after fifty years, I've found my birth father!"

"It certainly is a slow process, but you're doing it!" commented Bill enthusiastically.

"All these years I've been wondering what my mother looks like and now I might get to meet my birth father! This is crazy!" she mused as she turned on the tv to take her mind off from the excitement.

It was a very hot June day in 1983, when Connie and Bill boarded a Southwest airplane for Phoenix, Arizona, with Howard's name and address tucked neatly inside her purse. When the plane landed in Phoenix, they collected their bags and rented a car. It was only a thirty-minute drive from the airport to Howard's home in Peoria, Arizona, but for Connie it seemed like a lifetime. She heard every tick of the clock! She was so nervous. Her heart felt like a huge bass drum beating inside her chest. She wondered if Bill could hear it, it was so loud!

Connie had always wondered about her birth mother. When she was in school, all the other girls would have people comment, "Oh you look just like your mother." But Connie was always aware that no one had ever said those words to her. She had always wondered who she looked like, but she hadn't really thought about looking like her birth father! He hadn't even crossed her mind! It was such a shock to think she was truly meeting someone from the papers she'd gotten at the age of fifteen! Those papers were well worn by now, but never in her wildest dreams had she thought about meeting her father.

"I have a father," she said to herself. "He was the best father in the world. It's a mother I'm missing." But here she was going to meet her birth father.

As Connie and Bill slowly walked up to the small little house and tentatively rang the doorbell, it seemed as if Howard had been waiting for them. He immediately swung opened the door, and there stood Howard and Connie, face to face, staring into each other's eyes. They stood on the threshold of the door, nose to nose and toes to toes, each mesmerized by the sight they saw across the threshold. It was as if they were staring into a mirror! Their eyes were identical. Connie couldn't believe her own eyes. The person across the threshold looked like her. She had found the person she looked like! "Maybe God wanted me to find Howard first," she thought. "Maybe

I'm supposed to find Howard because Howard is the one who I look like!" Her thoughts were reeling as if she were on a ride at the amusement park. "Don't throw up," she kept saying to herself. "Don't throw up!" as she tried to calm her racing heart!

When Howard seemed to regain his composure, he invited them inside. "Come in, come in!" he said excitedly. Connie introduced Bill and Howard said, "This is my wife, Riggie." But, before Connie and Bill had even been invited to sit down, Howard said, "Let's head to the restaurant for lunch!" Once they were all nestled inside the rental car, Connie sitting in front, while Bill drove, Howard look at Connie and said, "I've always known about you."

And Riggie added, "I could never understand why they wouldn't let him take you home when he went to the orphanage to see you."

This was news to Connie! "Oh my!" she exclaimed. "You wanted to adopt me when I was little? I didn't know you had seen me! Where was I?" she asked.

"Oh yes!" said Howard excitedly. "When I found out Viola had signed papers releasing you for adoption, the orphanage sent me a letter. I hurried over to the orphanage to see you. I wanted to adopt you.

"Oh my gosh!" said Connie. "No one ever told me."

"You know, I had been making child support payments to the state for almost two years when I went over to see you at the orphanage."

Riggie nodded in agreement. "We wanted so badly to have a little girl, and you were just adorable!" This was news to Connie. She had no idea Howard had tried to adopt her.

"I remember remarking to the social worker how much you looked like your mother! The resemblance was uncanny!" commented Howard. "I never had any children of my own, but I would always tell my friends, 'I have a beautiful little girl named Sally somewhere in Minnesota.'" He beamed with pride as he looked at Connie.

"This is amazing," said Connie as she couldn't take her eyes off from Howard.

"Riggie and I just have one son. He's from Riggie's first marriage.

He's much older than you, and we never had any other children." Howard explained.

"Tell me about my mother," said Connie. "What do you remember about her?"

"Your mother loved to dance," he said quite matter of fact. "I had a little dance band back in Thief River Falls, Minnesota, and she was always there ready to dance. In fact, she would dance with anyone who was willing to dance with her. That's how we met; you know. I even danced with her!" said Howard. "She always wore a red dress at the dances!"

"I love to dance, too!" said Connie, "And I've won lots of dance competitions and have lots of awards."

"Viola and I were both very musical. Are you musical?" he asked.

Connie excitedly explained she had learned to play the violin when she was a little girl, telling Howard how she had won several competitions and had even played with Gustavus Adolphus Orchestra and the Minnesota All State Orchestra. "I used to play in the Sands Hotel Orchestra with Wayne Newton," she blurted out.

"Oh my, I'd love to hear you play." Remarked Howard.

"I also took piano lessons from the nuns in Wells, and I took voice lessons, too," she said. "My daddy had an orchestra near Wells, Minnesota, where he played the fiddle. My adopted mother was a music teacher at Wells High School until they had me. Then she gave lessons in our home," she offered. "I also played the organ for church and sang in the choir, too, in Fulda, Minnesota where we raised our girls. I guess you could say I'm musical," she laughed. "And so are my daughters!" Connie added excitedly.

"Oh, how I wish I could have adopted you." said Howard. "It made me sad to learn that you ended up in the foster care system. I just couldn't understand why they wouldn't let me take you right then, and there!"

As lunch went on, Connie learned more about Howard and Riggie. It appeared to Connie they were living on Social Security and maybe a pension from the police department, but they seemed rather poor. Connie didn't realize just how poor they were until the bill arrived. No one fought with Dr. Mears to help pick up the tab!

The visit flew by with lots of laughter and tears. They took pictures of their first meeting fifty years after Connie had been born, and then Connie and Bill headed back to the airport! They had made a whirlwind trip to Phoenix, flying in and out the same day, but plans were made for Howard and Riggie to travel to Las Vegas to visit Connie and Bill in their home.

Connie wanted to get to know her father better, and she wanted him to meet her daughters, so it was arranged for Howard and Riggie to visit Connie in Las Vegas on the July 4 weekend of 1984. Connie invited her daughters, and their families to visit that same weekend. Excited to meet their new Grandpa, the girls arrived in Las Vegas from their respective homes. Caryn and her husband, David, arrived from San Diego with their two children, Mollie and Mimi, while Cathy came from Minnesota with her two daughters, Carissa and Amber. Lisa, who lived in San Francisco, was unable to make the trip, but waited eagerly to hear how the meeting went! Connie was so proud of her daughters and loved to share her talented children with anyone who would listen, but to share them with Howard, her biological father, the band leader, was the epitome of pride for her! But to share them with Howard, her biological father, the band leader, was the epitome of pride for her!

Caryn and Cathy had been performing together for years, first in church when they were in elementary school, often singing duets or trios with Connie, and then at school together when they were in college where they put on performances for the elementary school children at the Campus Laboratory Elementary School. As they began their infamous song called, "Joy is Like the Rain," tears began rolling down Howard's cheeks. Song after song, he was amazed by their talent as they put on a mini concert for Howard and Riggie in Connie's den. It was then that Howard realized fifty years had passed him by. Fifty years of schools, meetings, dances and being a father and a grandfather. He realized he had missed out on all the events that had taken place during those fifty years.

How excited he was to learn his oldest granddaughter, Caryn, had played guitar as well as the string bass in a folk band during college, as he, too, played the string bass. And he was thrilled to learn that his second granddaughter, Cathy, was also a singer and loved to dance, just like Viola. And when he saw a picture of Lann, he said, "That's the one who looks the most like Viola. She had the softest milky smooth skin just like Lann!" It was a moment Connie will never forget. Her youngest daughter, Lann, looked like her mother!

The mini reunion of father and daughter certainly entertained the idea of nature versus nurture. Connie and her daughters learned they had inherited these musical traits from Howard and Viola, but Connie's adoptive parents, Alfred and Mary Lee Bates, who were musicians nurtured those talents. Connie felt so blessed her heart wanted to burst. To think the people who chose her, were people who nurtured all of these God given talents, and helped her become the woman she was meant to be!

Howard was truly amazed! Looking at Connie and her girls, he was awestruck. He was learning as much as he could about his newly found daughter and his granddaughters, and then it hit him, "Oh my goodness," he announced, "Your daughters all have Viola's beautiful smile!"

"And we all have your beautiful deep brown eyes!" exclaimed Connie, and everyone laughed!

Again, the time flew by during this hot humid July fourth weekend in Las Vegas, and Howard was amazed with his newly found daughter, granddaughters and even a few great granddaughters! In fact, he was so enamored with everyone, he wanted to move in with Connie and Bill, or at least move into one of their rental homes in the area! "I need to make up for fifty lost years," he said with tears in his eyes. But Connie knew this relationship was moving far too fast.

"Howard," said Connie, "we need to take this one step at a time! There's plenty of time to get to know each other."

Sadly, Howard passed away in 1985, just a year after they had met. He had been on the operating table and suffered a stroke during the operation. Connie was able to attend his funeral, and there she met Howard's sisters, Blanche and Pearl, and Howard's cousin, Edna. It was there that Blanche and Pearl confirmed how much Howard had wanted to adopt her. But more importantly, Connie was meeting her aunts!

Connie and Howard Oberg, her biological father.

I LOVE...

<u>Life!</u>
Bill, and all our family members!
<u>Sun!</u>
Warmth and red glowing embers!

To laugh,
To make love,
Open presents,
and the stars above.

Children's antics,
Romping puppies,
Ice Cream cones,
and Chocolate sundaes!

Grand children,
Good friends,
Soft music and new trends.

Shoes,
Boots and hats,
The colors green, orange and brown,
And Bill when he makes his silly frown!

All things beautiful
Birds, Music, collecting clowns,
Clocks that tick,
And thoughts that "stick".

There's so much to love and enjoy,
So much to see and do,
But loving everyone for who and what they are
Is really a lifetime ploy!

CHAPTER 30

WHO'S LOOKING FOR WHOM?

NOW CONNIE WAS on a mission. She contacted Meg Bale at the Children's Home Society and flew to Minneapolis to meet her. Meg had information to pass along to Connie! "Viola's relatives are looking you. Would it be alright for me to give them your address and phone number in Las Vegas?" Meg asked.

"Absolutely!" cried Connie, "I've been searching for relatives for years, and I've been wondering about them even longer! Please! Please! Please share as much information as you can! I can't wait to meet them!"

What Connie didn't realize in her excitement to find new relatives was the fact the new relatives were looking for her. Meg Bale had said "Viola's relatives are looking for you!" Connie was so engrossed in her own search for Viola, she didn't realize Viola's relatives weren't looking for Viola Lundberg. Viola wasn't lost. They were looking for Connie.

Connie had flown to Minneapolis to be the Emcee for her high school reunion in Wells Minnesota, but while she was there, she used the opportunity to meet with Mega Bale at the Children's Home Society. Saturday had been reserved for the class reunion and Connie had contacted her Aunt Minnie for a Sunday afternoon get together after church.

WHO'S LOOKING FOR WHOM?

Minnie was Cora's sister, and had been Connie's aunt for the five years Cora had been married to Connie father. But more importantly, Minnie was Dr. Barr's receptionist, and she had known Connie since she was a little girl. She had seen Connie when Alfred and Mary Lee had adopted her and would bring her into Dr. Barr's office for her wellness checks. And Minnie had seen Connie whenever she made a visit to the dentist, because his office was just down the hall from Dr. Barr's office. They would often stop in and say hello to Minnie. Connie had also stayed with Dr. Barr and his family when Mary Lee had been so sick with throat cancer, and Connie had gotten to know Minnie even better, long before Alfred had ever married Cora. Connie loved Aunt Minnie and Minnie adored Connie. It was no surprise that the two of them wanted to see each other when Connie came to Wells for her class reunion.

When Connie and Bill pulled into the little town of Wells, Connie was thrilled to show Bill around. "Here's the hospital where I worked," she said, acting as the tour guide, showing Bill the paces near and dear to her heart "And this is the high school and here is the park where I used to ride my bike."

Sunday after church, Connie and Bill drove over to visit Aunt Minnie. She had never married, and for the five years she had been Connie's adopted aunt, the two had frown very fond of each other. Minnie loved to take Connie to do fun things. In fact, Connie had cherished Aunt Minnie and had spent many days with her during those middle school years, escaping the wrath of Cora!

By now, Minnie was well into her eighties and as they parked their car in front of her house, she excitedly came out to greet them. Once introductions were made, she quickly invited them in. Her house was exactly as Connie had remembered it with the floral couch ad lacey curtains framing the windows. As she and Bill sat down, Minnie breathlessly chortled, "I'm so glad you're here. I have something special for you!" She could barely contain her excitement as she produced a small black velvet pouch from her pocket and handed it to Connie. "This is something I've wanted to give you for a very long time!" she said, and she placed the pouch in Connie's hand. As Connie meticulously pulled open the strings of the pouch, she dumped six small pebbles into the palm of her hand!

"Diamonds!" Connie gasped. "Why on earth are you giving me these beautiful diamonds, Minnie?"

"Some of those diamonds are from Cora's wedding ring and some are from my diamond earrings, and I want you to have them," said Minnie beaming proudly.

"Why, they're beautiful," said Connie. "But why do you want me to have them?"

"Well, you're the only family I have left for one thing, and Cora took so much from you through the divorce, I just thought you're the one that should have them!" she said smiling sweetly at Connie.

"Oh, my goodness!" said Connie. "That is so thoughtful of you, Minnie. Thank you so much! You certainly didn't have to do that!"

"Oh! It's my pleasure," said Minnie beaming. "You deserve them! After all, you're my favorite niece!" she said as she gave Connie her special wink.

Connie and Bill stayed to have some coffee and cake with Minnie and left her house treasuring the diamonds. When they returned to Las Vegas, Bill took the diamonds to a jeweler and had all seven of them made into a lovely ring. Connie always wore her beautiful new ring for her performances at the Sands Hotel and thought of Minnie every time she put it on.

Later that year, Connie and Bill again headed to Minneapolis, Minnesota. This time they were on a mission to meet those relatives! They flew to Minneapolis and then took a small little prop jet to Detroit Lakes where Great Aunt Effie Ritsche met them and gave them a ride to the armory. The Detroit Lakes Armory was a huge brick building and Effie escorted them into the large double doors and down the hall to a large meeting room where four or five tables were set up, each table seating approximately eight people. The room was buzzing as people intermingled, but as Effie, Connie and Bill entered the room everyone stopped to see Connie, the former Mrs. Minnesota and long-lost niece of Ella Ranum.

Great Aunt Effie took Connie around the room, introducing her to various relatives, starting with Ella, Viola's younger sister, who was Connie's aunt, Ella had been just nine years old when Connie had been born, Ella then introduced Connie to her own children, Gregory and Elodee, who were Connie's first cousins. Next, Connie met Viola's half-sister, Joann Henry, who was also an aunt, but only a year older than Connie. There were so many relatives in attendance it made Connie's head spin. Everyone wanted to talk with her, but after meeting the immediate relatives, Connie and Bill were ushered to the food table. There, they found every kind of hot dish, salad and dessert a true Minnesota potluck could contain. It was a wonderful smorgasbord, but Connie could barely eat. She was flabbergasted by the number of relatives who had come to meet her.

First of all, her nerves were getting the best of her, but secondly, the relatives kept coming over to her table, wanting to talk with her. There was no way she could eat. Eventually, once Connie appeared to be finished, they invited her to stand up and speak. After all, she was the former Mrs. Minnesota! In their minds, she was a celebrity from Las Vegas. At this point, she was very thankful for the speaking experiences she had done in the past, because this was truly a new type of speaking engagement for her. As they opened the question and answer segment, Connie started to feel a sense of calm come over her. She was at ease telling them her life story. But she was still astounded t how many relatives were there. She had grown up as an only child and now she was meeting aunts, uncles and cousins galore. She learned her Grandpa, Phillip Lundberg, had ten brothers and sister in his family, and her Grandma, Clara Chapman, had eight brothers and sisters. This meant there were dozens of relatives in Minnesota for her to meet! She figured there were over thirty people in the armory, all wanting to get to know her!

Her first reaction upon meeting her Aunt Ella and Great Aunt Effie was, "Now I know who my daughter is built like!" Connie was very petite and small boned while Caryn, her oldest daughter, had much wider shoulders and hips. Connie learned she was built exactly like her father, Howard, and now she was learning her daughters were built more like the Lundberg and Jensen families, just like Aunt Ella and great Aunt Effie!

Effie was forthcoming with information and told Connie, "We have always known about you, Connie! Viola paid for two years of child support for you when you were little, but we didn't know how to find you after you were adopted."

Great Aunt Esther from Shakopee added, "Did you know I tried to adopt you when you were about two years old?" Connie was astonished. This was news to her. Not only had she learned her father, Howard Lundberg, had tried to adopt her, but now she was learning one of her great aunts from Shakopee had also tried to adopt her. They had even come to see her in the orphanage!

"No, I had no idea! Why in the world would the state demy one of Viola's aunts from adopting me?" wondered Connie out loud, "Wouldn't they want me to be with family?"

"Well," explained Great Aunt Effie, Viola's aunt, "Esther didn't have enough money in her bank account to satisfy the state. Back in those days, you had to have enough money to adopt. Remember, it was the 1930's and almost everyone was poor. In those days you had to prove to the state that you had enough money in the bank to take care of a child."

Connie again was astonished, and then it dawned on her, "Oh my gosh!" she sputtered, "Alfred and Mary Lee Bates, my adoptive parents, must have been considered very wealthy. They owned three farms and a private business! That's why they could adopt me and not my own family!" she said, amazed at what she was learning. "My own relatives were considered too poor to be good parents!"

"You've got it!" said Ella. "We were all too poor to adopt a child in those days!" she said and then she added, "Of course, I was too young!" and everyone laughed. Ella had only been nine years old when Connie was born. She would have been no more than eleven years old when Connie was put up for adoption. They would have been more like sisters than aunt and niece.

After everyone had said their goodbyes, Great Aunt Effie said, "Connie I have some pictures for you. You can look at them while we drive out to the old homestead. Your Great Uncle Carl still lives on the property.

"Oh my!" said Connie, "I've wondered for over fifty years what my mother looked like! If you have any pictures of her, I'd love to see them!" Ella had driven off, along with all the other relatives to get to the farm to set up for an afternoon of chatting and then the evening meal when Effie produced a packet of pictures. One was a picture of Viola in second grade and two were pictures of Viola from her high school years sitting with her sister, Ella, and their father, Phillip Lundberg. Connie's brain was spinning! "I'm actually holding pictures of my mother!" she thought" and then she said it out loud, "I'm holding pictures of my mother!" and Great Aunt Effie laughed. She couldn't believe this was the little great niece she had heard about for the past fifty years!

Looking at the pictures, Connie thought, "The picture of little seven-year-old Viola. Do I look like her?" And she had to ask, "Do you think I look like Viola?"

"Oh my, yes! You look just like her!" replied Effie, and with that she and Bill piled into Effie's car.

"And this man in the picture, is that Viola's dad?"

"It sure is!" said Effie nonchalantly as she headed the car up over the grassy lawn and out onto the street. Connie and Bill looked at each other apprehensively thinking they should have ridden with someone else out to the old family farmstead, but they were captives in Great Aunt Effie's car!

Then Connie said, "He'd be my grandpa. What's his name again?" asked Connie.

"His name was Phillip Lundberg and he was married to Clara Jensen, Viola's mother, but they were divorced when she caught him in bed with the nanny! There's a picture of her when she was older! She was quite the worker. She would get up at 4:00 in the morning to bake bread and pies and serve the railroad workers all day at the railroad café. Oh, and there's a picture of Ella in there, too. I thought you might like that since we don't have any pictures of Viola when she was older."

Connie was learning about the relatives in quick fashion as Effie drove them out to the old farmstead near Thief River Falls. Carl Jensen, Clara's brother, and his wife, who was also named Viola, were now the owners of the original farmstead. All of Clara's eight brothers and sisters had grown up here with Great Grandma, Synneva Jensen, and Great Grandpa, Anton Jensen. As Effie parked the car, Connie put the pictures away in her bag, but her mind was still thinking about the picture of fifteen-year-old Viola in her beaded necklace and fancy dress. Connie wondered if her fifteen-year-old picture showed any similarities. "I'll have to check," she thought as she joined Bill and the others. They were all heading out to the grove to visit the original cemetery still on the property where several family members were buried.

Great Aunt Effie explained to Connie, "Many of your mother's relatives were very creative writers. I've published several books, too. One of them is a poetry book."

Again, Connie was amazed as she, too, loved to write poetry and had even written many different poems. She had even won a poetry contest and was hoping to publish her own poetry book someday! It was one of her favorite hobbies, along with music and tending her roses. She was pleased to learn that those creative juices ran on both sides of her family and Alfred and Mary Lee Bates, her adoptive parents, had nurtured those talents.

Learning her birth father was a musician and her birth mother loved to dance, made her realize that she was truly blessed. There were musicians and writers on both sides of the family, and she was benefiting from the union which happened after a dance near Lake Sallee! This was truly nature versus nurture or was its nature being nurtured! Whichever way she looked at it, Connie knew she had been blessed. And to think all these people were here for her was unfathomable. She had grown up an only child with no other relatives but her grandmas and grandpas!

Connie meeting Viola's relatives, Viola Jensen, married to Connie's Great Uncle, Carl Jensen, Bill and Connie Mears, Center, Aunt Ella Ranum, and Great Aunt Effie Ritsche.

CHAPTER **31**

ODE TO A BROTHER

THE TRIP WAS mentally and emotionally exhausting, but Connie knew she had to continue the journey she had started. She truly enjoyed meeting with Meg Bale and putting a face to a name. She and Meg had become great friends, chatting often over the telephone. Connie couldn't believe she had met her Aunt Ella and some cousins as well as her Great Aunt Effie, who seem to be a plethora of information. She had met people who knew her mother and knew about her!

Eventually, after much research, Meg Bale was able to tell Connie she had a brother. She learned that Viola had given birth to a baby boy on Sept. 3, 1936, at the same Home School for Girls in Sauk Center, Minnesota, just as she had done with Connie. She learned that Viola, their birth mother, had nursed him for two months, just as she had with Connie, and then she put him up for adoption, just five months after she signed the paperwork to put Connie up for adoption. Connie's brother, Anthony Peter, had lived in the same nursery she had lived in at the Children's Home Society in St. Paul. They had missed being together in the nursery by just five months. Connie left the orphanage on June 14, 1936 and was placed in the home of Alfred and Mary Lee Bates, while Anthony had been placed in the Nursery at the Children's Home Society in St. Paul on November 14, 1936, at just two months old!

Lydia and Harold Kester took Anthony Peter into their home on

ODE TO A BROTHER

August 5, 1937, when he was just eleven months old. They changed his name to Earl Harrison Kester. He was never told he was adopted, and was raised as a very special, only child. He had infantile arthritis, requiring many doctor visits and subsequent surgery on his hands. He also had amblyopia or "lazy eye", requiring him to wear a patch over his stronger eye hoping to help uncross his left eye. His adoptive parents said they would have surgery performed on the lazy eye, but instead let it go and later tried to correct it with glasses. His mother's constant reminder of how difficult his birth was, stating, "I suffered so much having you. You were such a big baby!" Earl never had an inkling that he was adopted.

At the age of eighteen, Earl's parents were out of town for a weekend trip, and he had met with the local military recruiter. Wanting to sign up immediately for the military, he headed home to look for his birth certificate. He went rummaging through some boxes in the attic, where much to his surprise, he found his original birth certificate stating his name as Anthony Peter Lundberg with his birthdate as September 3, 1936. He discovered he had been adopted! His mother and father had lied to him his entire life. She had never endured a painful natural birth to have him! His emotions were spinning like a tilt a-whirl.

He immediately confronted his parents and his mother continued to deny he was adopted. She continued with her story of how difficult his birth was for her! Earl was so upset when his mother denied his adoption papers, he immediately got in his car and drove through the night to get to St. Paul and waited for the Children's Home Society to open. There he met with Meg continued to deny his adoption! After several phone calls, Earl was finally able to get his father to admit they had adopted him. He finally admitted that there were papers in the attic verifying his adoption. His mother had been in denial for 18 years.

Now, years later, Meg Bale was able to confirm Earl's adoption with Connie and was able to put the two of them in touch with each other. It was fifty years after earl had been born! Their initial telephone conversations were full of laughter and tears as they related their growing up years, often realizing they had many similarities. They both discovered their contagious laughs as they talked over the telephone.

When they met for the first time, Connie felt as if she were looking into a mirror, but this mirror showed mannerisms! They learned each of them enjoyed getting up early in the morning and sitting outside watching the sunrise. They also learned while watching the sunrise, they both enjoyed smoking a cigarette. Another similarity to starting their day was to have a cup of coffee while reading the morning newspaper, and even more unique was the fact that they each had a second cup of coffee to leisurely do the morning crossword puzzle. The more they talked, the more they marveled at the similarities that filled their day. The only evening drink either of them ever ordered in a restaurant was an Old Fashioned. Both Connie and Earl had been raised as only children, and both had been taught they were special, just for different reasons!

When Connie learned that Earl was coming to Las Vegas to meet her in person, she contacted the Las Vegas Sun, the local newspaper, and a reporter came out to interview them. It was 1986, and Earl was fifty years old, while Connie was fifty- three. The article appeared in the paper with the headline reading <u>Siblings Find each Other After 50-year Separation.</u> Catching up after 50 years, both Connie and Earl had a lot to learn about each other. Connie had grown up being told she was adopted, while Earl found out he was adopted when he turned eighteen years old, and even then, his adoptive mother denied it. Luckily, they were raised with similar values during the 30's and 40's.

At that first meeting Earl produced a gift for Connie. He had purchased two beautiful champagne wine goblets to celebrate their initial meeting. Together they shared their toast, "To life, friendship and having a sister!" said Earl. As they talked, they discovered that Earl's adoptive father, Howard Kester, had a sister in Minnesota, a woman whom Connie had taken voice lessons from in 1949! They remember possibly playing together at her house when they were early teenagers!

Connie remarked, "You know, someone once told me that you'll never know the love of a brother until you have one! This is a whole new experience!"

"Yeah, but we'll see how much love there is when I try to borrow a few dollars!" Earl joked.

Connie and Earl became two peas in a pod after those initial phone calls and that first meeting, calling each other every week to chat. Earl visited Las Vegas several times, always enjoying the company of that new word in his vocabulary; sister! For Connie, Earl filled the void her father had left.

The years went by and as the search continued, both Earl and Connie were involved in finding Viola Lundberg, their birth mother. This is when Connie's daughter, Cathy Peterson, became involved in the genealogy of the family. With her passion for Ancestry.com and her computer expertise, Cathy took on the search. Would Connie, and now Earl, ever find their mother? The story continued. Connie shared her pictures with Earl and encouraged him to obtain his birth information from the Children's Home Society in Minnesota, but she had a secret that she hadn't shared with Earl. Could she share it with him, or would it hurt his feelings?

Earl and Connie meeting after 50 years apart.

ODE OF LOVE TO BROTHER EARL - HE AND SHE

A gentle, loving man, walked into my life
Acceptance acknowledged by my husband and his wife.
Tall, distinguished is he. Petite, verbal and redheaded is she.
Both eagerly sharing their past, two siblings together at last.

Same expressive eyes and dominant chin,
Beguiling smiles, each keeps sensitivity within.
Obviously aggressive, yet more than direct, loving all other, still demanding respect.
Early morning "Crosswords" bring challenges each day. Surging toward goals before we play.

Organizational lists compiled, with date and fact, two "Sammies", left us with an impact.
Doodlers exactly to a "tee", boxes and circles, draw he and she.
Anger kept subdued, and muffled at length, yet our "pointed arrows" depict our strength!
Smokers, inspired with gallons of coffee, loving sunrises, seeking adventure, he and she.

A joy for sharing, speed reading a book, mental retention for memory, both can cook.
That same pensive frown, a similar grimace, seeing yourself, true likenesses of each face.
New burst of energy, when inspiring thoughts "stick", faces glow at the sound of a clock tick.
Hands creative, whether left or right, originality, mechanical design and ability to write.

No tempers flare voices we never raise. Clean, neat, appearance perfect, yet, we need praise.

TOGETHER ALWAYS

Knobby feet, arthritic hands and knees, our pain forgotten, while others we please.
True love for all others, encircling a new family, now a wider circle encompasses he and she.
A future lies straight forward and beyond, together, we'll share above, dearly and so fond

Silver, inscribed champagne glass to be exchanged, when he and she pass.
Date to long be remembered, together. Memories touch our inner souls, forever and ever.
We are grateful for our common Mother, friendship, now bonded, between sister and brother,
Instant love, felt only, by he and she. Questions answered, our hearts set fee.

No one, not any other, will realize memories we keep,
The love for each other, Precious and deep.

                              Fondly written by your sister, Connie,
                              February 11, 1984

ODE TO A BROTHER

SIBLINGS TWO

Mother's rejection, for two,
Brought acceptance, to renew,
Two, having same Mother,
Siblings - a sister and brother.
Each having a different dad,
Acknowledgement was sad.
Pursuing search for sibling,
Earl, a name, no quibbling.
Face to face, yet to be,
Is there likeness, a similarity?
Anxiety, for meeting together,
"Two birds of the same feather"
Tears of happiness flow, He and she onward will go!

Connie and Earl

CHAPTER **32**

SEARCHING FOR VIOLA

CATHY WAS ABLE to obtain Viola's birthdate from relatives and retrieved Viola's Social Security number from governmental forms, but it still proved to be a very difficult process. Even when she thought she had found the correct match, it appeared there were two different women with the same birthdate and Social Security number! "Surely," thought Cathy, "having the right birthday and social security number should make this an easy search." Unfortunately, she and Connie felt like the search was unending. It seemed Viola didn't want to be found.

Connie learned from Elodee, Aunt Ella's daughter, that Ella had disposed of a red address book before she died. Relatives now believe because Ella and Viola had been so close as young sisters, Ella had maintained contact with Viola over the years. In fact, when Bill had met Ella at the family reunion in Minnesota, he left the reunion with a bad taste in his mouth for Ella. "She's lying!" he told Connie. "She knows where your mother is, and she is not talking. Instead of the family searching for Viola, they were searching for you. They knew where Viola was all the time!"

"Well, that puts an entirely different light on the search," said Connie, "But it's not getting us any closer to finding Viola." She was frustrated! The little red address book, which contained all the addresses and information about where Viola had lived, was gone. Ella,

253

knowing she was dying, had taken the address book and thrown it into the garbage before driving herself to the hospital. "You're right," said Connie. "She knew she was dying, and she didn't want anyone to know she knew where Viola had been all along!" Ella was saddened to think her Aunt Ella had been lying to her.

When Aunt Ella passed, her daughter, Elodee searched high and low for her mother's little red address book. How in the world was she going to inform her mother's friends about her mother's passing? Elodee was unable to locate the book, and all the names and addresses seemed to be gone. Elodee felt sure her mother had kept track of Viola and her husbands and their addresses, as well as any information she could obtain about Viola's children and where they lived. But Ella had never let anyone look at her address book. A lifetime of information was purposely tossed away, unbeknownst to other family members.

Luckily, while Elodee was cleaning out her mother's house, she found a shoebox in her mother's closet. In the box she found a piece of paper with Connie's address written on it. Elodee immediately contacted Connie and explained the situation. Having met Connie at the family reunion, she wanted to contact her and explain what had happened. "Connie, this is Elodee, your aunt Ella's daughter. I just wanted to let you know my mother has passed away. But I've also discovered something else."

"Oh my! I'm so sorry Elodee. What have you found?" quired Connie sadly.

"Well, evidently Viola didn't want to be found." she told Connie. "My mother would never let me see her address book, and now that she has passed, I've been looking high and low for it and haven't been able to find it. I think my mother threw it away before she drove herself to the hospital to die!"

"That's devastating," said Connie.

"Well, luckily I found your name and address on a slip of paper in my mother's closet. I think she and Viola stayed in touch and kept their communications a secret for the past fifty years. Sadly, my mother took any information about Viola to her grave! I'm so sorry, Connie."

Bill had been right. Ella had been lying. When they had met years earlier, the family wasn't looking for Viola, like Connie was. They were looking for Connie because Ella had lost track of her when she had been adopted. They never realized Connie Wordelman, Mrs. Minnesota, 1965-66 was their long-lost niece, Sally Constance Lundberg! This all gave Cathy more impetus to push forward and continue the search to find Viola. She and Connie had no idea if they were looking for someone who was still alive or not, as Viola was nine years older than Ella, who had just passed away.

Cathy painstakingly looked through public records trying to find evidence of a Viola who lived in Joliet, Illinois, the last known address anyone had for her. This is where relatives were able to tell Connie Viola had gone after giving her up for adoption, and they believed she had back to Joliet after having her second baby, Earl. They even said they thought there was another son named Greg, but no one could confirm any of that information. Everything was hearsay. No one remembered Greg's last name.

Cathy searched census records and was able to do a search on the history of the family. Knowing she had the names of Viola's parents, Phillip Lundberg and Clara Jensen, she began to work her way forwards. Records show that Phillip and Clara Lundberg had a son, Lloyd, born in 1913, two years prior to a daughter, named Viola, who was born in 1915. She also discovered the older brother had sadly passed away from an accidental gunshot wound at the age of twenty-two in 1935, a few months before Viola had signed paperwork for her daughter, Sally to be adopted. Cathy found Phillip and Clara had a baby boy who died at only three days old of pneumonia, named Clifford, and she found Viola's sister, Ella. She tracked them through census records, only to discover Clara and Phillip Lundberg had divorced in 1927. She also found Clara's subsequent marriage to Joe Pim Henry and the birth of their daughter, Joann Louise Henry, in 1932, just a year before Sally was born. Knowing that Sally was born

255

in 1933, led Cathy to another dead end. After that date, Viola no longer showed up on the Minnesota census records.

Cathy assumed Viola had obviously changed her last name through marriage, as most women do when they marry. All the secrecy about her name and address reealed by Elodee made Cathy think Viola didn't want to be found. Although Connie and Earl both had obtained their Family history from the Children's Home Society, the slight differences in the father's description indicated they had different fathers. Earl never had a father's name listed on his birth certificate, while Connie's father's name was listed. Viola had refused to identify the father of her second baby, and probably for good reason.

Connie had learned from Great Aunt Effie the key to Earl's identity. The secret she felt she needed to keep from Earl. Aunt Effie had told Connie the story while driving from the armory in Thief River Falls out to the old homestead. After having signed papers to give Sally up for adoption, Viola had gone to Chicago. She and a friend were sneaking around in the hotel rooms looking for money to steal from the railroad workers on payday when she was almost caught. In order to escape, she and a friend jumped out a second story window. Viola had broken both her ankles. Needing a place to recuperate, she went home to stay with her mother, Clara Henry. Clara and her husband, Joe Pim Henry allowed Viola to recuperate in their home. Viola was a cute little twenty-year-old girl who had been in Chicago during the World's fair, but she was completely bed ridden. Rumor has it that Joe Pim Henry raped Viola. When Viola learned she was pregnant, she told Joe Henry. He then withdrew $400 from his savings account and gave it to Viola, telling her to run away. Not knowing where else to turn, Viola went to the Home School for Girls in St. Paul, where she gave birth to a little boy on Sept. 3, 1936. She named him Anthony Peter, who would later become known as Earl Kester Harrison.

Connie felt so bad for Earl. Here he was, not only an illegitimate baby, but a product of rape. She didn't have the heart to tell Earl who his real father was! Consequently, Earl went through life never knowing his father was Joe Pim Henry, a tall slender handsome man whom

Earl resembled in height and looks.

Finding Viola became like looking for a needle in a haystack. Cathy traced every possible lead, even once going to Washington state on advice from a psychic. She continued searching whatever documents she could find and sent out many, many letters trying to get leads on the elusive Viola Lundberg. They had met Howard Oberg and his family and pieced together any information they had from him. And Connie and Bill, along with Cathy, had met all the Lundberg family in Minnesota. They had pieced together information from them, but they weren't getting any closer to finding Viola.

CHAPTER **33**

HOW CAN I GO ON?

CONNIE AND EARL continued to fund the search, while Cathy kept combing through documents, writing letters and making phone calls. But in 1992, Bill started having bone pain in his pelvis and legs. Connie became more involved with helping her husband. When he finally went into the hospital, he said, "I'm not leaving here until you tell me what's wrong." Sadly, his diagnosis was prostate cancer. Various bone scans and MRI's showed that the cancer had already metastasized to many bones in his body, and his cancer had already developed to Stage four. The pain in his legs was excruciating, making it difficult to stand in his veterinary practice.

Wanting to sell the Chaparral Pet Clinic and retire, Bill announced to Dr. Sam Lynch, who had become his partner, he would like to retire and sell his shares of the clinic. Fortunately, Dr. Leech felt it was perfect timing for him, and he willingly stepped up to purchase the clinic.

There were times when Dr. Mears was angry about the cancer, and he and Connie would talk every morning about what was going to happen. When anyone asked how he was doing he would eagerly reply, "I'm getting better every day," trying to psyche himself up and keep a positive attitude. He managed to survive two more years after undergoing an orchiectomy to stop the spread of the cancer. He also had progesterone hormone treatments and chemotherapy. But when the radiation treatments started, Bill said, "No more! I want quality of life over quantity of life!"

Bill passed away, June 26, 1994, at the age of seventy years old, leaving Connie a widow at 61 years of age. She was devastated at the loss of her best friend. They had shared every day of their twenty-two years of marriage together.

Connie immersed herself into her routines. She still got up early, had her coffee, worked in her garden and cleaned her own pool. She still mowed her lawn, trimmed the bushes, and meticulously worked on bookkeeping for the trust fund Bill had left her. She started attending church on Sunday mornings and choir practice on Wednesday evenings. She walked every morning, completed crossword puzzles from two newspapers and read novels every afternoon. She prided herself in taking care of her castle, painting the exterior and interior of the house five different times as well as having the kitchen and den remodeled.

Her therapy became creating doll houses. In fact, she built twelve doll houses from kits. She built a schoolhouse and a country store; she built a fishing cabin and the "Rich Bitch's House" to name a few! Each day would find her shopping for miniature furniture or sewing minute little curtains or bedspreads. She cut carpet, and glued miniscule board together, building stairs and walls, creating a miniature world of her own. Once her office was filled with doll houses, she felt she was ready to move on! The doll houses had provided her grief therapy, as she cocooned herself into her own little kingdom.

TOGETHER ALWAYS

WHY?

Pain appeared so suddenly, from nowhere.
Bill became quite ill and slumped in his chair.
A trip to the hospital seemed quite evident.
Needles, x-rays and tests of great extent,
Soon produced a picture of the real cause.
Time was of the essence, no time to pause.
Anesthetics, more IV's and loads of antibiotics,
were our only promise for he was so sick.
I wonder why God gives us the challenge to cope,
for we worry and so desperately hope.
Can we earnestly handle the daily stress?
Face each day with prayers and a serene calmness.
Why, oh why does it hurt so much,
seeing a loved one suddenly out of touch?
God grants me an inner peace to face with strength,
Conquering each day regardless of its length.

HOW CAN I GO ON?

MY BILL

He met GOD on wing of dove
Memories, photos, and children to love
Gone from Earth, but not to end
Husband, Lover, My best Friend.
Kind, Compassionate man, my Bill
Filled life with wit, devotion, a thrill
I'll keep "Heart Treasurer" tucked away
Remembering a loving man,
Always,
Every Day.

Your loving wife,
Connie

MISSIN' YOU

Mornin' talks, Holdin' hands!
Ramblin' walks, Meetin' demands.

Dinin' out, Expressing' delight
Rightin' my pout, callin' me "Dinah-myte"!

Watchin' birds, Lovin' my flowers
Pickin' right words, Buildin' dream towers!

Sharin' a thought, Creatin' goals and ideals,
Real Estate bought, Watchin' dance reels.

Sharin' your bed, Hearin' you shave,
Rubbin' you neck and head. So naughty, behave!

Your humor, wit and pun, Waitin' for you to come home,
Strivin' for time for our fun! Seein' your head become a dome!

Pickin' up your sox, Ironin' your shirt,
Bein' an "Old Fox" kissin' my hurt!

Cryin' together, Easin' you pain,
Bein' Best Friends forever, Travelin' lover's lane.

Sayin' "Good Night", pattin' my rump,
Holdin' me tight, Icin' a bump.

Ploddin' a mile, Cherishin' your smile.
Noddin' in agreement, Givin' a card of sentiment.

Why did it have to end? My husband! My Friend?
No one to tag along. My memories will keep me strong!

I love you, Bill!
June 26, 1994

SOLACE
By Connie Mears, July 1994

Memories in my heart and soul,
Veterinary profession took its toll.
Mastering strength to live a new life
No looking back, no more being a wife.

I remember only the good years, sharing fun,
Working towards a goal, Bill's wit and pun.
A driving force, to achieve and excel,
Building a clinic, we did it quite well.

Not seeking fame or a fortune
Making each moment so opportune
Caring for all others, forgetting himself,
Holidays, vacations, left on the back shelf.

Becoming a victim of disease, interrupted our life
New transition for husband and wife,
Taking each day, one at a time,
Sharing the tears, another mountain to climb.

Facing our Destiny, plans were made
Leaving a legacy, hopes for future, firmly laid.
A role model for family, supportive to wife
He met his God, accepting heavenly life.

There's Peace and Sorrow,
Another day, another tomorrow.
Accolades for triumph's won,
In God's words, "Well Done".

Written for the family book she gave to Bill's daughter, Anne Grimes.

Connie and Bill after he secretly took dance lessons so he could be her partner on the dance floor.

CHAPTER **34**

A BREAK IN THE SEARCH

FINDING PHILLIP LUNDBERG'S obituary was a small gold mine, and it finally provided the break Cathy needed in the search for Viola. Phillip's 1958 obituary listed two surviving daughters: Mrs. Frank Bambic, Jr. ad Mrs. Stanley Ranum. Having met Ella Ranum in Minnesota, she ascertained Mrs. Frank Bambic Jr. had to be Viola Lundberg. She then found court documents showing Marlene Kramer as Frank Bambic in 1947.

Women often change their last names through marriage, but Viola had changed her first name when she married Joseph Kramer. Marlene and Joseph lived in Joliet, Illinois, and they had a son named Gregory Joseph Kramer, born in 1943.

Records indicated Viola gave birth to Connie August 22, 1933 in Sauk Centre, Minnesota, and the birth father, Howard Oberg was named. The evidence leading to Anthony Peter's birth in 1936, named no father, although speculation leads to Viola's stepfather, Joe Pim Henry. According to the family, as told by Aunt Effie, Viola's stepfather, Joe Pim Henry raped Viola and when he found out she was pregnant, gave her $400 to disappear.

When Marlene married Frank Bambic, Jr., in 1947, her son, Greg Kramer, was only four years old. Frank adopted Greg, giving him the name Gregory Joseph Bambic. There truly was a Greg and the rumors had been correct. Marlene stayed married to Frank Bambic until 1953, when Gregory was ten years of age. One night after work she ran off, leaving Greg behind with his adoptive father and grandmother.

"Where's mom?" asked Greg one morning when he woke up.

"She's gone." Greg's stepfather, Frank Bambic, calmly replied.

"When's she coming back?" asked Greg. There was obviously no love lost between the stepfather and stepson.

"She's gone and she's never coming back." said Greg's stepfather rather stoically.

"Never!" asked Greg.

"Never." replied his stepfather quite calmly, offering the little boy no comfort.

"How could she do this to me?" thought Greg. "How could she leave me?" He was totally thrown for a loop! How could his mother leave him with the evil stepfather? Greg was angry! Here he was only 10 years old and his mother had left him with a grumpy old man who didn't even want him, and a grandmother who wasn't even really his grandmother.

Greg was never able to gain closure over his mother abandoning him, and he grew into a very angry teenager. He held very bitter feelings towards his mother for the abandonment. Later, he received a letter from his other with a check for his birthday, but when he went to cash the check, it bounced. After a few years, Greg received a letter from his mother, whom he knew as Marlene Bambic, stating she had married another man and Greg now had a new baby sister. He didn't care. She had left him, and he was angry. His mother never returned.

Over the years, Greg remained very bitter towards his mother, so when Connie contacted him in 2010, saying they had the same mother, he wanted nothing to do with anyone related to his mother! Poor Connie had no idea why he so vehemently despised his mother and displayed such anger towards her and their mother. It took two years, and a long letter from Cathy, for Greg to realize he had relatives who cared about him, even if they were related to his mother.

Finally, after many phone calls, and Cathy's letter, Greg met Connie and her two daughters, Caryn and Cathy, at a restaurant in

Las Vegas. They had a wonderful time getting to know each other, and it was then Greg admitted his mother had sent him a letter telling him he had a little sister. Unfortunately, he didn't remember the girl's name or when the letter had arrived.

The search takes a huge leap when Connie is contacted by a woman researching unclaimed bank accounts in California. The woman telephoned Connie stating she found her name listed as the oldest surviving child in Marlene McEwan's obituary! This was news to Connie, and she immediately had the woman contact Cathy, who was now in charge of the search! This was when Cathy discovered Marlene McEwan was the name of the other woman who had the same birth date and social security number as Viola Lundberg! There were two names attached to the same birthdate and social security number, but there was only one person, not two! Cathy was starting to put the pieces of the puzzle together.

The woman researching unclaimed bank accounts explained, "Marlene McEwan has several bank accounts in Torrance, California. There hasn't been any activity on them for the past ten years, so I'm researching to see if I can find the relatives for Marlene McEwan who is the owner of the accounts." Connie was listed in Marlene McEwan's obituary, along with Earl Harrison Kester, Gregory Joseph Bambic, and a daughter, Patricia McEwan. Imagine the family's surprise, to learn Viola had lived in Torrance, CA with her daughter, Patricia, until she passed on June 2, 1998. More importantly, and possibly more shocking was the fact the names of her biological children were all included in her obituary; the children she had given up for adoption some sixty-five years earlier!

Somehow, Viola had followed the lives of her children, and where they had been living. Putting the pieces of the puzzle together, it became evident the only one with this information was Viola's sister, Ella! She had indeed helped Viola keep track of her biological children. Thus, Ella's little red address book had held the family secrets. Ella had known every address Viola had occupied, and she had tracked each child. When Ella passed away in 2002, she took those secrets and Viola's whereabouts with her when she tossed the red address book into the trash bin. She had been the one who was able to help Viola follow her biological children for sixty-five years.

And, Bill had been right! Ella had been lying and keeping an enormous family secret. It became very clear Ella had not been looking for Viola. She had been trying to find out what happened to Viola's first-born daughter, Connie. After Connie had been adopted, Ella had lost track of her. Once the adoption records were opened in the state of Minnesota, and Connie began her search, it was perfect timing for Ella to look for Connie. It was only fate that the two parties were able to find each other through the Little Red Stocking Adoption Agency in St. Paul. With the adoption records open, Connie was able to share with the Minnesota relatives about Earl, which enabled Ella to share this information with Viola. Greg had been easy to keep track of because he maintained his adopted name.

Through Greg, the family learned Viola had left Frank Bambic, his adopted father, when Greg was just ten years old. Court documents show Marlene Bambic marrying Charles James McEwan. Viola didn't appear to be pregnant at that time, although she gave birth to Patricia five years later. It's interesting to note all of Viola's husbands were from the Joliet, Illinois area, which is where she went after giving her first two babies up for adoption. When her last husband, Charles McEwan, passed away in 1983, she and Patricia remained in the apartment complex in Torrance where Charles had been the caretaker.

As a woman, changing not only her last name through marriage, but legally changing her first name by choice, made it difficult to find Viola. Cathy had searched documents in Joliet, Illinois. She had searched social security numbers, birth certificates, marriage certificates and death certificates, and she and Caryn had even traveled to Washington state on words from a psychic! When Cathy put all the information together, finding Marlene McEwan instead of Viola Lundberg, had taken thirty-three years. Finding out Viola had been living in Torrance, California, was quite a surprise for the family, as

Caryn and her family had been living in the area while David was stationed at the Long Beach Naval Shipyard. Connie had even visited them in 1987.

The research in Torrance provided a death certificate for Viola under the name of Marlene McEwan. Sadly no one had claimed the body and she was buried in a pauper's grave in Los Angeles. Patricia was found living in a state run. She had been institutionalized due to her mental instability. The summer of 2015, Caryn and Cathy were able to take Connie to Los Angeles to meet Patricia. All totaled, Viola had four children from four different fathers, and had been married three different times, Connie discovered she was no longer an only child, but the oldest of four!

While meeting Patricia, Connie received pictures of Viola. One picture was uncanny. It was a picture of Viola/Marlene floating in a pool. Connie had similar pictures of herself floating on her pool in Las Vegas. The faces in the pictures could be the same person they are so similar! Another picture shows Viola sitting in a chair smoking a cigarette. Connie also has a picture of herself sitting in a chair, but instead she is holding her violin.

Connie was very grateful to Patricia for sharing photographs of her mother. At one point, Connie was so flustered realizing she was meeting someone who had lived with her mother, she asked Patricia, "What did you call your mother?"

"I called her mom!" said Patricia, rather befuddled.

Realizing just how flustered Connie was, Caryn stepped in and said, "I think mom wants to know what your mother's name was."

"Marlene," replied Patricia, still bewildered by all the questions. Patricia explained, "My mom had a stroke and they came and took her away. The last time I saw her, she was in the ambulance and they were taking her to the hospital."

"That must have been scary. What did you do then?" asked Caryn.

"I started screaming and screaming. I sort of freaked out," replied Patricia. "A neighbor called the police and they came and brought me here. I never saw my mother again. I didn't have any way to get to the hospital to see her. She died a few months later in the hospital." It was a very sad story. All Patricia had left of her mother were some picture albums which she shared with Connie.

At that point, Connie felt bad for Viola. Life had dealt her some hard blows and she had done her best as a mother, which meant giving her first two children up for adoption so they could have better lives. What a monumentally difficult task that must have been! She and Earl felt extremely grateful to Viola for giving them the opportunity to live a better life. Connie felt bad for Viola leaving Gregory behind in order to escape an abusive relationship herself, not knowing what life had in store for him, but knowing life there was too difficult for her to face. Connie had lived that life! And finally, Connie felt sad for her mother, who died alone. She ended up staying with Patricia, her last child, possibly because she finally found a man she truly loved, or possibly because Patricia had a mental disability. In the end, Connie felt sorry for the life her biological mother must have had. It was another loss Connie had to bear.

The three women learned that Viola passed away from a stroke in 1998, before Connie's search had been completed. Although Connie felt sad, she couldn't meet Viola in person, she looked at the positives from her birth search journey. She was able to see pictures of her mother, presented to her by a newly found half-sister, Patricia. She met Greg Bambic, her half-brother, living in Las Vegas near her. And Connie found her birth father whom she looked like, as well as many maternal relatives in Minnesota. But her favorite part of her search was locating her half-brother, Earl, who remained her best friend and confidante until his passing in 2017. He truly gave her someone who understood where she had been on this miraculous journey!

With Cathy's continued search, more family details have arisen, and Connie has learned of many cousins, nieces and nephews. She now has a family tree which has many branches, but the most important figure in Connie life remains her adoptive father, Alfred Emery Bates. Although he passed away many years ago, they remain "Together Always".

Earl Kester, Connie Mears and Greg Bambic.

Connie meeting her half-sister, Patricia McEwan.

Connie and Alfred Bates, 1940.

EPILOGUE

AS I SIT by the window in my mother's assisted living facility, I'm surrounded by her things; a few clowns, a few bells, pictures of my sisters and our children and grandchildren, and a bookshelf to hold all of the keepsakes dear to mom's heart. She is now helplessly glued to her recliner, unable to move of her own accord, frozen from Akinetic Rigid Parkinson's. It was 2017, when I noticed mom was unsteady and doing "the eighty-year old shuffle", as we called it. I even secretly videotaped her to show my husband. She fell several times over the past year, one time stating she had fallen asleep on the toilet and another time tripping on a cord from the window blinds. We joked about how difficult it was to keep mom from climbing the ladder. She prided herself on painting her castle inside and out five different times. "I'm just doing a little touch up," she said. But her new unsteady gait baffled me.

"We need to get you into the doctor," I had told her that October, "Something's wrong, but I'm not sure what," seeing how unsteady she had become. Living in Washington state, I tried to visit mom a few times a year, but the small changes had escaped me. Sadly, we couldn't get in to see the doctor until December, so I went back to Washington, convinced that mom seemed to be handling everything in stride, getting her morning newspaper, fixing her breakfast, making her lunch and shuffling over for her evening meal.

Returning in December to take her to her doctor's appointment, I noticed more unsteadiness. And my husband, David, who'd not seen

EPILOGUE

her for a few years noticed a major change. The doctor's visit with her primary care physician went quickly enough. She basically watched mom walk across the room and said, "I'm going to send you to a neurologist in Henderson, but the earliest appointment I can get for you is in January. Dr. German, the neurologist, is out in Henderson. Can you get there?"

"Yes," I replied, "I can come back in January and take her to that appointment." So, after Christmas, Dave and I returned home, only for me to fly back to Las Vegas two weeks later to take mom to the neurologist's appointment. "In the meantime, please don't drive anywhere." I told mom. "You have enough of everything to last until I get back." With her uncertain gait, I was afraid she could never stop in an emergency.

It was at the Neurologist's office in January, where Dr. German watched her walk the length of the six-foot-long room, freezing halfway through her journey. It was obvious to me she was desperately concentrating to keep her feet moving in a left-right walking motion as she slowly turned around and headed back to her chair. The concentration was evident on her face, eyes focused on her destination with her mouth pursed in determination. Shaking with anticipatory tremors, she literally crashed into the hardback chair next to the doctor. He gently reached for her hand and said, "It's Parkinson's my dear. It's Akinetic Rigid Parkinson's, and there is no medication that will help you. I'm very sorry." Mom was frozen! Stunned, really! It was as if someone had just knocked the wind out of her. We sat there in the room for a moment, gathering our wits as the doctor and nurse quietly said their goodbyes.

Shuffling out of the tiny exam room, down the hall to the appointment window, I now knew that mom's "eighty-year-old shuffle" was not normal. We made more appointments for more testing later in January. I was destined to spend the month of January helping mom deal with her new diagnosis.

As I helped her get into the car, I could tell mom was exhausted. Just walking into the doctor's office was more than she could physically handle, and the mental anguish was taking its toll. "Parkinson's," she said with a voice so soft I had to listen intently. "No medication will help. I kind of thought it would be something like this." she whispered. And then she was angry. "At 84 years of age! Why do I get Parkinson's at eighty-four?" she asked.

"Well, it's certainly better than getting it at sixty-four!" I quipped, trying to lighten the mood. We made the return trip home in silence, both of us deep in thought.

Realizing mom was incapable of staying alone, I arranged to spend the entire month of January in Las Vegas with her. But eventually, I needed to get home. She had been living alone, and she had so proudly chosen this place on her own. However, she hadn't realized in order to get to her evening meal, she would have to walk over a mile to the dining hall and a mile back, quite a feat for a healthy eighty-year old, let alone someone with a disability. I knew this was a monumental challenge with her gait continually freezing, and her susceptibility to falling. We obtained a walker to assist her, but sadly, her instability made her fall even more quickly. Little did we know Parkinson's patients need walkers with tennis balls on the back, so they don't fall backwards. Crashing with the walker falling on top of her gave her PTSD and she was literally afraid to use it. Later we found that the walker was much too large for her five-foot frame.

Next, we tried a scooter. Setting the speed to "turtle" off, mom drove with no training, refusing to practice in the parking lot. After crashing into the front desk and another wall in the lobby, mom was embarrassed. She hated drawing attention to her lack of physical ability. Once we returned to her apartment, she said with tears in her eyes, "Get rid of that beast! I don't want it!"

Mom was having anticipatory tremors reaching for objects or finally reaching her destination. She would literally fall into a chair when she felt she was close enough to sit, but she truly wasn't. Looking at her sitting in her recliner, one would not suspect there was anything wrong. She shows no signs of tremors and looks like a perfectly normal lady in her eighties. The shaking only appears when

EPILOGUE

she wants to reach something, such as her fork or toothbrush.

January was filled with more visits to the neurologist's office for more tests. We spent our days together cleaning and organizing. Everything seemed to be in order from her previous move five months earlier. She had moved from her three thousand square foot house, downsizing with an estate sale. But cleaning was what mom did. She cleaned!

Those days spent with mom provided the two of us many hours to reminisce about days gone by. She had started her story, an interesting synopsis of her beginning years with Grandpa Bates. Over the years we laughed and cried together at different stories and I'd say to her, "That sounds like a perfect chapter for your book!" and she would diligently write it down. But now, she couldn't write at all. In true Parkinson fashion, her writing had shrunk to illegible scribbles. That, in and of itself, should have been a sign something was wrong with her brain, if only we had known the symptoms for Parkinson's. We weren't watching for Parkinson's; we were watching for Alzheimer's. This disease had attacked one of Howard's sisters and his mother, but mom seemed to be very cognizant of life going on around her.

In February, my sister, Cathy, traveled to Las Vegas and stayed with mom, taking her to several more doctor's appointments and escorting her to a stint in the hospital. At the end of February when mom was admitted to the hospital, I again went to Las Vegas. On March 1, the hospital transferred her to the Life Care Facility near her home. It enabled Cathy and I to stay in her retirement apartment while we visited her daily. Sadly, mom became very depressed and lethargic. She hated the food. She hated being confined to a bed, unable to transfer herself to the bathroom. She hated the physical therapists. She hated what had happened to her. She hated her life. Her care there was not what we had expected or wanted, and she was slowly going downhill. She'd lost ten pounds on her already thin one-hundred-pound frame. Cathy and I fighting with her Medicare management company, decided mom needed to be moved into an assisted living facility. We carefully selected the place we felt she would like the best. We chose a facility that was light and bright with a room filled with morning sunlight. It seemed like a very cheery atmosphere.

While she lay in bed at the skilled nursing facility, we carefully downsized her retirement home, putting most of her things into storage, and choosing the most precious items to be displayed in her new assisted living home. On April 3, 2017, she moved into The Bridge at Paradise. The staff there helped to get her up and dressed every morning. They took her to the dining hall for three meals a day and hospice workers came to bathe her and provide more comfort. She was finally returning to the feisty eighty-four-year-old we knew!

I stayed with her for the month of March and then returned home. Cathy also visited as often as she could, both of us flying in from Washington state, or Minnesota, respectively. We each tried to do our part to make this aspect of her journey more comfortable.

Fortunately, mom allowed me to finish her story! As I type, I'm blessed to know mom is still cognizant and able to talk. When I have questions about events in her book, I've called her and she's answered my questions, often adding more tidbits to her stories. I consider myself very fortunate to know she still has the mental capabilities to answer, although her body is rapidly failing her. Her voice, once a strong soprano soloist, has lost its volume and timbre. Her legs and lower back are frozen, as are her shoulders. The disease continues to wreak havoc with her body, and I realize she may not be able to answer my questions much longer.

As she shakily pulls her favorite blue blanket up over her frigid hands, she snuggles down into the cocoon formed by her recliner. There is no coffee cup or cigarette sitting on the table, for she stopped smoking years ago. There's no crossword puzzle sitting next to her now, for her handwriting is indistinguishable, but she can still amazingly tell me the answers when I read her the clues.

She turns to me and says, "You know I want to run away," and I nod, not knowing what to say. "Well, at least you can go for a walk if you want to," she says, "I'm stuck here. I'm so tired of looking at these four walls."

EPILOGUE

"Well, let's go!" I say, but mom says,

"Not so fast. I have to call the caregiver to take me to the bathroom first. The aide arrives after a five-minute wait and lifts mom from the recliner and sets her into the wheelchair with great effort. She's dead weight, unable to help in the transfer. They head to the bathroom and once she is ready, we head out into the hall. Mom can no longer participate in any of the activities, other than concerts. Her hands can't hold the cards and her voice is so soft, none of the other elderly, hard of hearing residents are able to hear or understand her.

We walk around the building, reading the name plates of the residents who share The Bridge of Paradise with her. She knows tidbits about each resident she's gathered in the dining hall or from caregivers. Her mind is still curious and very active, remembering their names and what they did for a living. As we walk past each door, I read the nameplate, and mom relays what she knows about that resident. I know she desperately misses her morning walks around her old neighborhood and tending her rose garden. I know she misses reading outside on her patio, or in her own recliner. I know she misses looking out the window on the swimming pool where the ninth hole provides a beautiful lush green backdrop to her beautifully manicured yard. I know she misses the golfers who cheerfully greeted her every morning from the ninth hole. They were her friends.

Mom's lived quite a magnificent life with God by her side, and I know she prays every night to join Him in heaven. She's had the love of a kind wonderful man, Bill, and his children. She's known the affection and pride of three loving daughters, and seven successful grandchildren as well as nine rambunctious great grandchildren! Thankfully her brain is still capable of understanding what is going on around her, and although her voice is starting to fail, she is still able to communicate with others.

Now, just past her eighty-sixth birthday, she faces Parkinson's with a stalwart heart though her body is failing her miserably. "I've always had to look out for number one," she said with her soft voice, and I'm reminded of her story as an orphan, when she was adopted by a wonderful man.

Life is not always easy, and it certainly isn't fair, and we're learning that God isn't finished with her just yet, but one thing has made Connie's life incredible. This one last testament is to her father, the man who rescued her at the orphanage; the man who virtually made her the woman she is today. Many parts of her story may have long been forgotten, but the most important part is recognizing Alfred Emery Bates, the man who taught her who she is and who she represents. The man that I called Grandpa Bates. May they be Together Always.

EPILOGUE

DAUGHTERS THREE

Memories of precious moments linger in cop-webs of my mind,
Struggles of each achievement - only rewards are what I find.

Developing individually, each year
suddenly, growing away - I shed a tear.

God grants each birth so lovingly testing my "Motherly" ability.
Teaching with love and discipline daily asking for help within.

Characteristics emerged - each with her family resemblance.
I faced each "awaking stage" hoping to keep some semblance.

Guiding, always, with constant love, searching, with my own struggles.
Asking for strength, from God above.

Each has left the "feathered nest".
How I cherish memories in my breast!
Did I do well, with his divine gift to me and teach independence,
faith and reality,
For my daughters three.

Celebrating Connie's life August 22, 1933- February 14, 2020
Daughters: Caryn Mears, Cathy Peterson and Lann Wilder

Sally Constance Mears
August 22, 1933 - February 14, 2020

"a Rose"

Written by Connie Mears as a tribute to a dear woman from Wells, MN who passed away from cancer. This poem was published in the Wells Mirror. Connie described Leora Rathal as a beautiful, compassionate happy person who lived and loved with grace and poise.

"a Rose"
In Memory of Leora Rathal

Regal names of beauty, Glory and Radiant elegance are heaped upon her head, as one's garden she does enhance.

Accolades are laid upon her feet, Truly one of God's Beauties.

Groping for existance, fulfilling God's marvelous duties.

Warmed and Nurtured deep within a Ripe Mother Earth

A precious seedling, coddled and dependent upon Her girth.

"Budding" upward slowly, somewhat afraid to gloriously erupt.

Facing a cruel world makes her birth, almost seem too abrupt.

Maintaining a faithful stronghold upon her Mother Stem.

Nestled secure, as she wrestles with the ageless "Growing" problem.

The earth's incubator of warmth and golden sunlite eagerly produces a budding head of wondrous exuberant delight.

Days of warm winds and gentle falling showers

Givers her an acceptance, among the bed of "select flowers."

Inward struggles of growth and virginity, as she calmly sways,

Flirting with temptation, coping with resistance, fills her days.

Small piercing thorns begin to pain-stakingly emerge

Growth continues, a new stage comes with a surge.

Brisk winds of ice and chill, shudder her new-awakened heart.

"Adolescence" is upon her, as she leaps with a start

Her petals open ever so slowly - uncurling each precious fold

Suddenly she's a beauty, for a world to have and behold

Her long slender stem holds her erect and tall

A regal head ablaze with fire - No worry of a Fall.

A glorious transformation from bud to regal flower

Delights an aggressor, as he selectes from the "Towering bower"

"Pollination" is a Loving caress, she savors only it's tenderness.

Yearning, yielding, enjoying the Lust and revelling in its "fullness."

New buds have arisen on her young and tender stalk

Amazement and wonder of it all - an event, she only treasures the bulk.

Her full glory has reached the newest stage of decision

Regalness bursts forth, a miraculous flower of purest vision.

She Lowers her head as she meets the next command.

Following the endless cycle that God can demand.

The dew is so Luxurious and fresh upon her tired brow.

A majestic struggle before her Last wordily bow

The world must slowly turn without a pause

She exhibited her Heritage and served a "just cause".

Petals slip slowly, a blush erased from her tender face

Sadly she succumbs her role, unable to keep the rapid pace

A forlorn and wilted flower drops upon the warm earth

Life is over now, her seeds will produce a "new birth."

A Lifeless flower, no Longer able to retain her dignity.

A stature of glory - She must relinquish her security.

One of God's mysteries of Life and it's fateful destiny

To Bud, to flower, with bloom and the acceptance of her Reality.

She Is Woman

by Connie Bates Mears

Spa
Mears